Transitions in social democracy

Manchester University Press

Transitions in social democracy

CULTURAL AND IDEOLOGICAL PROBLEMS
OF THE GOLDEN AGE

edited by John Callaghan and
Ilaria Favretto

Manchester University Press
Manchester and New York

distributed exclusively in the USA by Palgrave

Published by Manchester University Press
Oxford Road, Manchester M13 9NR, UK
and Room 400, 175 Fifth Avenue, New York, NY 10010, USA
www.manchesteruniversitypress.co.uk

Distributed exclusively in the USA by
Palgrave, 175 Fifth Avenue, New York,
NY 10010, USA

Distributed exclusively in Canada by
UBC Press, University of British Columbia, 2029 West Mall,
Vancouver, BC, Canada V6T 1Z2

British Library Cataloguing-in-Publication Data
A catalogue record for this book is available from the British Library

Library of Congress Cataloging-in-Publication Data applied for

ISBN   0 7190 7467 3   *hardback*
EAN   978 0 7190 7467 7

First published 2006

15 14 13 12 11 10 09 08 07 06   10 9 8 7 6 5 4 3 2 1

Typeset in 10/12pt Sabon
by Graphicraft Limited Hong Kong
Printed in Great Britain
by Biddles, King's Lynn

Contents

Contributors

Jenny Andersson is Postdoctoral Fellow at the Department of Economic History, Uppsala University, and is the author of *Between growth and security: Swedish social democracy from a strong society to a third way* (Manchester, Manchester University Press, 2006). She is currently working on a book comparing discourses of the Knowledge society in Swedish social democracy and British New Labour.

Stefan Berger is Professor of Modern German and Comparative European History at the University of Manchester. Recent relevant publications include: *Inventing the Nation: Germany* (London, Hodder Arnold, 2004); *Writing History: Theory and Practice* (edited with Heiko Feldner and Kevin Passmore) (London, Hodder Arnold H&S, 2003); *Nationalism, Labour and Ethnicity, 1870–1939* (edited with Angel Smith) (Manchester, Manchester University Press, 1999); *Social Democracy and the Working Class in Nineteenth and Twentieth-century Germany* (London, Longman, 2000); *The Search for Normality: National Identity and Historical Consciousness in Germany since 1800* (New York and Oxford, Berghahn, 1997); *The British Labour Party and the German Social Democrats, 1900–1931: A Comparison* (Oxford, Oxford University Press, 1994).

Norman Birnbaum is University Professor Emeritus at the Georgetown University Law Centre, Washington, DC. Recent publications include *After Progress: American Social Reform and European Socialism in the Twentieth Century* (Oxford, Oxford University Press, 2001).

Lawrence Black is Lecturer in Modern British History at Durham University. The author of *The Political Culture of the Left in Affluent Britain, 1951–64: Old Labour, New Britain?* (Basingstoke, Palgrave, 2003) and co-editor of *An Affluent Society?* (Aldershot, Ashgate, 2004), he is working on a thematic (consumerism, communication, culture) survey of post-war British political culture and a study of Arnold Wesker.

John Callaghan is Professor of Politics at the University of Wolver-hampton. Recent publications include *The Retreat of Social Democracy* (Manchester, Manchester University Press, 2000); *Interpreting the Labour Party: Approaches to Labour Politics and History* (Manchester, Manchester University Press, 2003) and *Cold War, Crisis and Conflict: The History of the CPGB 1951–68* (London, Lawrence and Wishart, 2003).

Ilaria Favretto is Professor of Contemporary European History at the Faculty of Arts and Social Sciences of Kingston University (London). She is author of *The Long Search for a Third Way: The British Labour Party and the Italian Left since 1945* (Basingstoke, Palgrave Macmillan, 2003); *Alle radici della svolta autonomista: Labour Party e PSI, due vicende parallele (1956–1970)* (Rome: Carocci, 2004) and *Storia d'Europa nel XX secolo: Gran Bretagna* (Milan, Unicopli, 2004). She also serves as review editor of the *Journal of Southern Europe and the Balkans* (Abingdon, Taylor & Francis).

Steven Fielding is Professor of Contemporary Political History at the University of Salford. He is author of *Labour and Cultural Change*, Vol. 1: *The Labour Governments 1964–70* (Manchester, Manchester University Press, 2003); *The Labour Party: Continuity and Change in the Making of New Labour* (Basingstoke, Palgrave Macmillan, 2003); (ed.), *The Labour Party: 'Socialism' and Society since 1951* (Manchester, Manchester University Press, 1997); (edited with Peter Thompson and Nick Tiratsoo), *'England arise!': The Labour Party and Popular Politics in 1940s Britain* (Manchester, Manchester University Press, 1995).

Nina Fishman is Professor in Industrial and Labour History at the University of Westminster and author of (edited with Geoff Andrews and Kevin Morgan), *Opening the Books: Essays on the Social and Cultural History of British Communism* (London, Pluto Press, 1995); *The British Communist Party and the Trade Unions, 1933–45* (Aldershot, Scolar Press, 1994); (edited with John McIlroy and Alan Campbell), *British Trade Unions and Industrial Politics*, 2 vols (Aldershot, Ashgate, 1999).

Holger Nehring is Lecturer in Contemporary European History at the University of Sheffield. His Oxford D.Phil. thesis is a connective history of the protests against nuclear weapons in Britain and West Germany in the late 1950s and early 1960s. He has written widely on the transnational history of social movements, for example, recently, 'Westernisation: A New Paradigm for Interpreting West European History in a Cold War Context', *Cold War History*, 4:2 (2003/04), 175–90; 'The British and West German Protests against Nuclear Weapons and the Cultures of the Cold War, 1957–64', *Contemporary British History*, 19:2 (2005), 223–41; 'The Growth of Social Movements', in Paul Addison and Harriet Jones (eds), *A Companion to Contemporary Britain, 1939–2000* (Oxford, Blackwell, 2005); 'Politics, Symbols and the Public Sphere: The Protests against Nuclear

Weapons in Britain and West Germany, 1958–1963', *Zeithistorische Forschungen/Studies in Contemporary History*, 2:2 (2005).

Paolo Pombeni holds the Chair of Comparative History of European Political Systems at the Faculty of Political Sciences of the University of Bologna and is editor of the academic journal *Ricerche di Storia Politica*. Pombeni has published extensively on the political history of Italy, France, Germany and Great Britain in the nineteenth and twentieth centuries. Main publications include: *Crisi, legittimazione e consenso* (Bologna, Il Mulino, 2003); 'The Roots of the Italian Political Crisis: A View from History, 1918–1945–1989', in Carl Levy and Mark Roseman (eds), *Three Post-war Eras in Comparison: Western Europe, 1918–1945, 1989* (London, Palgrave, 2002) and *Partiti e Sistemi Politici nella storia contemporanea* (Bologna, Il Mulino, 1994).

Gareth Pritchard is Lecturer in German History and Politics at the University of Canterbury (New Zealand) and author of *The Making of the GDR 1945–53: From Anti-fascism to Stalinism* (Manchester, Manchester University Press, 2000).

Donald Sassoon is Professor of Comparative European History at Queen Mary College (University of London) and author of several books and articles on the European Left. His *One Hundred Years of Socialism* (London, I. B. Tauris, 1996) won the Deutscher Prize 1997 and has been translated into Italian, Spanish, Greek, Swedish and Portuguese.

Marcel van der Linden is Research Director of the International Institute of Social History in Amsterdam and Professor in Social Movement History. Recent publications include: *Transnational Labour History: Explorations* (Aldershot, Ashgate, 2003); (edited with Lex Heerma van Voss), *Class and Other Identities. Gender, Religion and Ethnicity in the Writing of European Labour History* (New York and Oxford, Berghahn, 2002).

Introduction

John Callaghan and Ilaria Favretto

Much of the recent resurgence of academic interest in social democracy has been inspired by four inter-related developments: globalisation; the end of Communism; the decline of class and the rise of a post-class politics based, variously, on identity, libertarian values, or a new individualism; and finally claims that a 'Third Way' has been found to modernise social democracy in response to the first three developments.

In the first place, if only for the frequency with which the word has been used since the mid-1990s, is 'globalisation'. Globalisation has been associated with the resurgent neo-liberalism of the 1980s and the related claim that American capitalism represents a sort of 'gold standard' which must spread if a successful adaptation to internationally mobile capital is to be made by the more regulated and egalitarian capitalist political economies of continental Europe (Albert, 1993). Globalisation allegedly undermines the management of national economies on which Keynesian social democracy was able to base its post-war 'strategies for equality'. In so doing it renders social democracy impotent and irrelevant; by nullifying state planning and regional policy; by forcing the reform (marketisation) of welfare systems; by generating inequality of income and wealth and opportunities for capital exit and tax avoidance; by generating flexible labour markets and undermining collective bargaining and job security (Gray, 1996).

Second is the collapse of the Communist regimes in Eastern Europe and the Soviet Union. The events of 1989–91 which ended the one-party dictatorships and command economies of socialist Europe were greeted in some quarters as signalling the end of socialism in any of its variants (Dahrendorf, 1990: 38). There was dismay on the left at the manner of this collapse which initially appeared as a headlong rush to market economies devoid of the collectivist provisions which many had seen as positive features, if not the saving grace, of the Communist experience. The peoples of Eastern Europe had left all that behind them, or so it seemed. But with the demise of the Communist system it was also argued that the left was unburdened of its association with a tradition that the social democrats had always rejected. The Cold War was finally over and that could only clarify the domestic and international, political and socio-economic issues which it functioned to distort and obfuscate in its heyday. The way was also now clear for the revival of social democracy in Eastern Europe and a new beginning in the former colonial and semi-colonial world in which the Cold War was often fought out to the detriment of the people. Thus the collapse of Communism could be annexed as empirical evidence of the globalisation argument, or simply perceived as evidence of the spread and strengthening of global capitalism; but it could also inspire the argument that a false road, a wrong turn had finally been corrected, freeing the left from a divisive and damaging legacy. Social democracy had been vindicated and was now free to take advantage of its rival's demise.

Third is the perception that secular socio-economic change has transformed the occupational and class structures and value systems of the advanced capitalist world in which social democracy once flourished. The blue-collar working class, together with the heavy industries and manufacturing plants in which it was based has shrunk and continues to shrink. Worlds of labour, working-class communities and the collectivist values they sustained have been destroyed. Tertiary-sector workers predominate throughout the advanced capitalist world. Much of this workforce is feminised, subject to divisions arising from immigration and prone to internal differentiations arising from the growth of inequalities of pay between a relatively secure minority at one end of the continuum and a mass of unskilled, semi-skilled, part-time, casualised and unemployed workers at the other extreme. The division between public-sector workers and those in the 'exposed', hyper-competitive industries subject to international competition overlaps with and sometimes reinforces these divisions. Trade union organisation and collective bargaining are placed under strain and subject to decay, particularly in the private sector. Membership in trade unions has fallen across Western Europe in the 1990s, following a fall in the incidence of industrial disputes in the 1980s by comparison with the previous decade. The reorganisation of labour markets, the erosion of class as an organising principle and the reduced fortunes of social democratic parties have been invoked to explain this retreat of the unions and their shrinking capacity to speak for the working class (Western, 1995). Voting trends provide another indicator that a profound shift is underway. What was observed in the USA in the 1960s – declining voter turnout, increased voter volatility, falling levels of partisan identification, the reduced salience of political parties in the everyday lives of voters – were said to be 'familiar phenomena to observers throughout the world' by the late 1970s (Wolfe, 1978: 113–14). Though these changes affected all the established political parties, social democracy was said to have particular cause for concern because of the more rapid decomposition of the working-class and collectivist values, bringing to an end social democratic attempts to build parties of social integration linking diverse aspects of society to the political process.

Fourth is the alleged modernisation of the social democratic programme to meet the needs of multi-ethnic, multi-cultural, affluent societies in an age of globalisation. The electoral successes of 'New Labour' in Britain since 1997, following on from the success of Bill Clinton's 'New Democrats' in the US presidential elections of 1992 and 1996, focused attention on the idea of the 'Third Way', the retrospective rationale for New Labour fashioned, above all, by Anthony Giddens (1998). Tony Blair's proselytising zeal for welfare state reform, market economics, flexible labour markets, and globalisation, together with his successful detachment of British Labour from 'old social democratic values' – above all his electoral successes at a time of relative economic strength in post-Thatcher Britain – ensured that the Third Way would attract the critical scrutiny of his beleaguered counterparts in continental Europe, as well as a host of academics.

The work on social democracy stimulated by the four developments mentioned above has also necessarily involved attempts to reconsider the history of social democracy. Generally this has been motivated by a concern to better understand the problems facing social democracy today, to locate the roots of recent thinking, to identify change and continuities in social democratic history, to test the novelty or otherwise of apparently modern problems such as globalisation. In this volume Donald Sassoon (chapter 1), one of the principal contributors to this debate, discusses socialism as a regulator of capitalist society, tracing the historical causes of its abandonment of system-change and the rise of the revisionist position, which increasingly identified the state as the vehicle for political, economic and social reforms accruing to individual citizens. In the 1930s this programme was gradually taken up by other political forces, at a time when social democracy augmented its interest in public ownership and macro-economic management, the latter becoming a tool for the maintenance of affluence by the 1950s. Marcel van der Linden (chapter 2) considers the 'organisational explosion' which has seen membership of the Socialist International grow by 147 per cent in the period since the mid-1970s, years in which the number of parties belonging to the International has grown even faster. He explains this growth of affiliations in terms of the diminishing specificity of the social democratic identity, which he links to socio-cultural and psychological changes in the period of post-war affluence. Norman Birnbaum (chapter 3) situates the problems of the contemporary Democratic Party in the USA by tracing the rise and fall of the New Deal coalition and the shifting social landscape of contemporary America in which a 'kaleidoscope of ethnic, generational, regional, racial and religious perspectives' have flourished at the expense of a strong centre-left sense of the nation itself. Stefan Berger (chapter 4) examines the historiography of social democracy in historical context with reference to Britain and Germany, arguing that the major task is to move the comparative history of social democracy from its traditional focus on organisations, ideologies and institutionalised politics to a cultural history of social democracy which asks specific questions about the making and unmaking of social democratic subjectivities and identities and the place of religion, class and gender in the make-up of these identities. He leaves open the possibility that such an approach will emphasise the heavily contingent and local bases of social democratic success and failure and perhaps displace the explanatory role of universal processes such as industrialisation and modernisation.

Collectivist principles permeated many aspects of life in the 1950s and 1960s in all the countries where the centre-left was strong. State expenditures on social policy, public housing, and health, for example, tended to grow throughout Western Europe. Standardisation and uniformity characterised many of these provisions. Public-sector enterprise represented a larger share of employment than anything seen pre-war in countries such as Italy, Austria, France and Britain. Trade union membership was expanding. Politicians talked of planning, regional policy, macro-economic management on Keynesian principles, and steering the economy for faster economic growth. It was an era of confidence in technological, scientific and material advance – indeed progress was measured by indicators such as these. Even the Soviet economy was regarded as a success, certainly a threat and sometimes a model to be copied. This was the era of the 'social democratic consensus', when the model of the Keynesian, national, welfare state held sway in Western Europe. It was the 'golden age' of social democracy, though social democratic government was unusual if not entirely absent in many of the countries of Western Europe and socialism seemed to be stifled by both affluence and the Cold War (Anderson, 1965). Nina Fishman (chapter 5) compares the gains and reversals of the labour movements of West Germany, Italy, France and Britain in class struggles since the inter-war years to explain the emergence of this more congenial balance of power between employers and organised labour which arguably underpinned the post-war 'social democratic settlement', even in countries lacking social democratic governments.

The beginning of the golden age came soon after the opening of the Cold War. Outside Europe colonialism was restored in the face of nationalist opposition in countries such as Vietnam and Indonesia. The European left was suppressed in Greece, Spain and Portugal, with the support of anti-Communist elites from the western democracies. In Italy and France the largest left parties, the Communists, were confined to opposition after May 1947. The German left was divided by the partition of the country. Gareth Pritchard (chapter 6) considers the ill-fated merger of the social democrats with the Communists in the Soviet zone of occupied Germany – a former stronghold of Weimar social democracy – identifying the motives and decisions on both sides of the divided left in the immediate aftermath of the

Second World War. In doing so he explains how the unfolding Cold War accelerated authoritarian processes, already at work, which led to the suppression of social democracy for more than a generation, an experience repeated, with local variations, across Eastern Europe. The experience of Eastern Europe before the war – with the exception of Czechoslovakia, economically underdeveloped, predominantly rural, and politically authoritarian – had never been congenial for a reformist social democracy. The war made matters worse and Soviet intervention eliminated any potential there might have been for democratic politics by preventing national self-determination and destroying all opposition to Communist rule. The Communist Parties themselves were transformed in the process by a combination of Soviet-inspired purges in the years 1948–53 and their fusion with the state. Even in countries where there had been mass support for the Communists, such as Czechoslovakia, the legitimacy and political vitality of the Communist parties was massively weakened by the Cold War division of the continent, while social democratic elements were completely stifled.

If social democracy was weakened in Germany by the Cold War division of the continent, left-reformism was stranded in many other Western European countries. In France and Italy, Finland and Iceland, large Communist parties held the allegiance of sections of the working class. The upshot was the enfeeblement of a divided left in all these countries, with the reformist left at best a minor governmental player. In the long-lived authoritarian systems of Greece, Portugal and Spain – now found to have their uses in fighting Communism – social democracy was a non-starter. Nationalist Ireland was not much more congenial. But none of the social democratic parties of Western Europe ever commanded the support of 50 per cent of the electorate and only the Swedish and Austrian parties obtained over 50 per cent of the votes cast (in 1968 and 1971 respectively). Between 1945 and 1973, when the golden age came to an end, only the parties of Austria, Norway, Sweden and Britain averaged between 40 and 50 per cent of the vote. With the exception of the Scandinavian countries and neutral Austria (where near-continuous coalition governments prevailed), majority social democratic governments were either rarities in Western Europe, as in Britain, or conspicuous by their absence, as in Italy.

The Cold War placed severe limits on social democratic parties of the west by tying them to a foreign policy of support for reactionary anti-communist regimes around the world and ruinously high defence budgets, as British left-wingers realised as early as 1947 (Crossman *et al.*, 1947). In the British case this development followed smoothly on the assumption, which all Labour leaders shared, that Britain was a Great Power and should remain so on the historic basis of the Empire-Commonwealth. Post-war British foreign policy was punctuated by wars and military interventions which derived from this assumption in Greece, Malaysia, Kenya, British Guiana, Egypt, Cyprus, Aden and elsewhere. The 'special relationship' with the USA enabled Britain to extend the life of its Great Power role, according to its critics, at the cost of uncritical support for US foreign policy and a chronic balance of payments problem consequent upon its inflated global commitments (including maintenance of sterling as a reserve currency). Defence of the national interest, as conservatively defined, was not confined to British Labour. Socialists in France rallied to the same standard when they justified and helped to implement the military suppression of the Algerian revolt of 1954–62. Belgian and Dutch socialists belonged to governments doing similar things in their own colonies.

Social democratic identification with the nation was exposed in all its vulnerabilities as early as 1914, with the outbreak of the First World War. As it approached mid-century social democracy had very little experience of government and very few tangible achievements to its name. The radicalisation promoted by the Second World War provided new opportunities, especially during the post-war economic boom. But the post-war world was also one of rapid change in Western Europe, containing more dangers to social democracy than the description of a golden age might suggest. In Britain, for example, the Conservative Party was returned to power as early as 1951 using the slogan 'Set the People Free', firmly associating the outgoing Labour Government with rationing, shortages, restrictions and bureaucracy. When they succeeded in winning a third consecutive general election in 1959, the Labour opposition was widely supposed to be disadvantaged by affluence and the transformation of capitalism, which the left had helped to set in train when it introduced the welfare state in the 1940s. Labour's core constituency of the manual working class was said to be in decline; poverty was almost abolished, along with unemployment; people were acquiring more aspirations and learning to regard capitalism as a system of expanding opportunities for individuals and their families. Some of these changes were not new of course. Eduard Bernstein had spoken of the need for the left to find support beyond the ranks of the working class in the 1890s; Evan Durbin had warned the Labour Party of the embourgeoisement of the better-off working class as early as 1940 (Durbin, 1940); a little later George Orwell was describing the decay of class cleavages in Britain and speculating that a classless society might be within sight (Orwell, 1948). But by the end of the 1950s such arguments had special salience for Labour in the context of repeated electoral defeats and the strong conviction that the dysfunctional features of capitalism had either been abolished or suppressed by effective macro-economic management of the mixed economy. Paolo Pombeni (chapter 7) identifies similar problems elsewhere and argues that the affluent 1960s was a turning point for the left in West Germany, Italy, France and Britain and the beginning of a dilemma that is still with us. The age of affluence had been delivered in all these countries under conservative auspices. The question it posed for the left – could social justice be harmonised with the goal of maintaining and enhancing private affluence in a capitalist society – was no less complex than the problem it posed for conservatives anxious about the corrosive effects of the new individualism on the preservation of the social hierarchy.

In what, then, did the 'golden age' consist? The answer is that the radicalism generated by the Second World War promoted constitutional changes in some countries (such as the women's vote in France, democratic settlements in West Germany and Italy) combined with social reforms that led to the emergence of welfare states throughout Western Europe in the years 1945–55. These gains were sustained by two further developments, one real, the other ideological. Talk of 'social citizenship' and the rights that go along with it (in health, housing, social insurance and so on); the commitment to full employment; the integration of organised labour into economic and social decision-making; the need for economic planning and the abolition of the dysfunctional features of market capitalism such as poverty – all these familiar aspirations of social democracy were embraced by centre-right parties in Western Europe in the immediate aftermath of the war. But it was the fact of sustained economic growth in the 1950s, leading to full employment in many countries, which enabled these ambitions to remain on the practical political agenda, to generate something akin to a consensus within the political class. In the circumstances of rising incomes and tax revenues welfare states became the vehicles of a strategy of equality on the social democratic left, while fulfilling a strategy of economic growth, political legitimacy and containment on the right. The belief that Keynesianism had provided the analytical tools for successfully managing 'mixed economies' for the achievement of both sets of political goals flourished under these circumstances (and just as easily fell into disrepute when 'stagflation' took over in some countries in the 1970s).

It was commonly assumed when these welfare systems emerged – whether in Catholic Italy and France or increasingly secular Britain – that men remained the active 'breadwinners' and heads of families, while women would resume their place in the family as unpaid carers and homemakers. But economic growth soon led to tight labour markets and the need for additional workers drawn from the female population as well as from immigration. Ideological, programmatic and organisational change within social democracy reflected aspects of the prevailing experience as the affluent society became a realisable prospect. Steering the economy was now deemed possible and the old demand for the abolition of capitalism had either been fulfilled (Crosland, 1952) or had become otiose. The growth of ownership of televisions, cars, refrigerators and washing machines was taken as an indicator of a social revolution as well as signs of material affluence. There was talk of the 'end of ideology' and the advent of technocratic management in political economy. But social democracy was more impressed by some aspects of social and political change than others. It struggled to understand 'teenagers', often operated within the prevailing stereotypes when it came to the 'woman question', and was slow to react to racism, which infected its own ranks. In Scandinavia, particularly Sweden, steps to gender equality were unusually advanced thanks to the combination of social democratic governmental hegemony and tight labour markets. But everywhere in Western Europe an expanding political agenda began to emerge in the early 1960s that was alien to the social democratic and Communist parties.

Jenny Andersson (chapter 8) takes up the theme of affluence raised in previous chapters to examine the relationship between economic growth and security in the thinking of the Swedish social democrats. Initially articulated as coherent and mutually supportive ideological objectives, apparently reconciling the dilemma Pombeni alludes to in chapter 7 between equality and efficiency, this linkage was thrown into doubt by radical critics of the SAP programme in the late 1960s who identified systemic connections between economic growth and social exclusion. This leftist critique of growth was displaced in the course of the 1970s as a growing preoccupation with cost-efficiency promoted the perception of the diminishing marginal utility of welfare expenditures in the face of obdurate social problems. Both left and right critiques of the welfare status quo were taken up within Swedish social democracy, as they were in other social democratic parties elsewhere in Western Europe.

Lawrence Black (chapter 9) raises the issue of social democracy's failure to permeate civil society, examining the British context where its failure, according to radical critics, allegedly stemmed from a narrow reduction of the struggle for power to electoral contests, leaving its opponents free to dominate the agencies of cultural reproduction. His examination of the Labour governments of the 1960s presents a more complex picture showing that the party attempted a variety of interventions in such fields as education, sexuality, and the arts, some of which aimed self-consciously at a politicisation of culture. Steven Fielding (chapter 10) looks at the British Labour Party's attempts to respond to calls for greater political participation in the 1960s. Such demands emanated from within its own ranks as well as from activists outside the party. Indeed Herbert Morrison declared 'ballot box democracy' to be 'out of date' as early as 1948 and Tony Benn was complaining of election campaigns as 'vast marketing operations' twenty years later, well before the age of spin and focus groups. If Britain remained the most centralised of the democracies at the end of the 1960s the problem was at least becoming more clearly specified and the need for an 'active democracy' was acknowledged within Britain's principal party of the left.

Of course there was an argument within social democracy about these supposed transformations, just as there had been at the time of the first, Bernsteinian, revisionism of the 1890s. Many socialists refused to believe that capitalism had been tamed and continued to regard it as a source of poverty, unemployment, inequality, waste, irrationality and volatility. Talk of a 'social democratic consensus' was held to be phoney in such quarters, because it disguised the fact that right-wing opponents had not abandoned their mistrust of state intervention or their support for market forces. The supposed object of consensus *par excellence*, the welfare state, came under repeated attack from the Treasury in Britain and was subject to regular 'bouts of panic' about its allegedly bottomless cost (Timmins, 1996: 198–206). Socialists were also inclined to scorn aspects of mass consumerism. They connected it to a modern alienation and soulessness, to a cheap counterfeit culture and a technocratic disregard for social, economic and political morality. This suspicion was also not new. Commercial mass culture had been an object of fear and loathing to many socialists since the 1880s (Waters, 1990). It was seen as the enemy of creativity and participation and the source of passivity, vulgarity, homogeneity, false values and low critical standards. By the 1950s it was associated above all with the USA, the biggest and best capitalist state of them all and the one in which social democracy was conspicuously absent as a party with coast-to-coast support. American dominance in advertising, public relations, film, television and other branches of popular culture and consumption reinforced the connection. Deception, waste, conformity and exploitation were inscribed in these developments for many socialists. The new consumerism of the affluent society encouraged one-upmanship, acquisitiveness, narcissism, improvidence, indebtedness and dependency. The affluent worker might also be, or become, a natural Tory and the trend was certainly inimical to cultures of solidarity. The demise of street corner politics, falling attendances at public meetings, the decline in sales of left-wing newspapers and the perennial problem of bringing people into active politics could all be vaguely connected to the consumer society (Thompson, 1957; Black, 1999).

Not all these critical views were confined to the European socialist left, nor did they go uncontested within it. American liberals were prominent in the cultural critique of the affluent society. The world of consumer affluence was a world of alienation and vulgarity, regimentation and manipulation as analysed in such works as David Riesman's *The Lonely Crowd* (1950); Vance Packard's *The Hidden Persuaders* (1957) and *The Status Seekers* (1959); and William H. White's *The Organisation Man* (1956). J. K. Galbraith famously indicted the 'private affluence, public squalor' equation of 1950s America in *The Affluent Society* (1957). Aldous Huxley contributed *Brave New World Revisited* to the genre in 1959, while Richard Hoggart's *Uses of Literacy* (1957) worked within the British Leavisite tradition, at least to the extent of continuing its opposition to exploitative mass culture. Hoggart's celebrated analysis of 'working-class life, with special reference to publications and entertainments' complained about the 'regular, increasing, and almost entirely unvaried diet of sensation without commitment' that he found in the mass culture of the 1950s and the 'hedonistic but passive barbarians' that it produced (Hoggart, 1957: 246–50). He perceived 'spiritual dry-rot' among the teenagers who hung around the milk bars, young men who adopted an 'American slouch' and were destined to become the 'directionless and tamed helots of a machine-minding class'. Hoggart agreed with much of the left in perceiving mass-entertainments as 'anti-life', full of 'corrupt brightness, of improper appeals and moral evasions' and tending to a view of the world 'in which progress is conceived as a seeking of material possessions, equality as a moral levelling and freedom as the ground for endless irresponsible pleasure' (1957: 340). This 'vicarious, spectators' world', then as now, generated particular worries about the impact of modern media on the minds, above all, of children.

Ilaria Favretto (chapter 11) explains the trajectory of Italy's two main left parties in the post-war years as they battled with and finally succumbed to the pressures of an increasingly consumer culture. The mass Communist Party (PCI) which emerged after the Second World War was one of the most successful attempts in Western Europe to create a 'working class counter-hegemony', catering to a host of social needs of its constituency through the activities of its women's groups, youth organisations, peasants' organisations, publishing houses, libraries, film clubs, sports activities and a host of cultural activities and media. Both left parties regarded commercial culture with disdain and suspicion in the 1950s, perceiving consumerism as a new and subtle form of alienation. This critique gave way to a more conciliatory line in the later 1960s as the left came to terms with the power of these cultural trends and the need to win support across an increasingly affluent Italian society. Such concerns were not confined to the left, but it was the left which worried most about the pernicious influence of commercial interests in these media in the 1950s. When the Pilkington Report of June 1962 on the future of television was published in Britain it chimed in with such sentiments in its critique of populism and triviality, especially in independent commercial television. This was probably the high point of the left's identification with such issues in Britain. By the mid-1960s the most prominent campaigning against sex and violence in television was associated with the National Viewers' and Listeners' Association, headed by an old supporter of Frank Buchanan's Moral Rearmament crusade against Communism, Mary Whitehouse. Thereafter the British 'moral majority' against the permissive 1960s, or as near as there was to such thing in Britain, was firmly associated with the right.

In the 1960s left-wing analyses of popular culture began to emphasise its potential as an arena for contestation and resistance rather than simply a medium for the reproduction of the status quo. The intended audience for what Hoggart had called 'mass-entertainments' took on an active, differentiated character in such studies, rather than the passive receptacles stressed hitherto, and popular culture itself began to be seen as something more than mere escapism. The New Left of the late 1950s pioneered this turn, especially after the rediscovery of Gramsci's writings and the import of continental structuralist and semiotic approaches to cultural analysis. The Campaign for Nuclear Disarmament (CND) provided evidence that the 'apathy' of the 1950s was over and the young in particular could still be drawn into left politics. Though CND and the New Left had peaked by 1961 popular culture continued to provide evidence of an appetite for resistance and criticism, whether it was in the form of the American civil rights movement, opposition to the war in Vietnam, student radicalism, politicised popular music or the spirit of rebellion which permeated so many teenage sub-cultures. More important was the evidence that the left was being reinvigorated by movements of opinion with which the established social democratic and Communist parties were uncomfortable. Among these 'new social movements' one can count second wave feminism, anti-racism, opposition to 'Atlanticism' and the received accounts of the Cold War's origins, the peace movement, environmental politics, and a concern for north–south issues which renewed and revived the old critique of imperialism. Originating outside the left parties this was an agenda which challenged the culture of contentment and proposed new ways of doing politics, with an emphasis on participation and direct democracy. Such developments also challenged the centrality of class as an organising principle for social analysis and political action. John Callaghan (chapter 12) looks at the contribution of the new social movements to the ongoing programmatic renewal of social democracy since the 1970s, with special reference to environmental politics, and the argument that the Third Way, by freeing social democracy from old workerist values, clears the path for an appropriate modernisation capable of facing current problems. Holger Nehring (chapter 13) focuses on the peace movements in Britain and West Germany and their relationships to the principal left parties and each other, arguing that the failure to establish a transnational community of protestors derived from different national cultural traditions in social democracy. In this, as in so many other issues addressed by this volume, strong continuities with the past of social democracy are as evident as the new and the unforeseen.

References

Albert, M. (1993), *Capitalism against Capitalism*, London, Whurr.

Anderson, P. (1965), 'The Left in the Fifties', *New Left Review*, 29.

Black, L. (1999), 'The Political Culture of the Left in "Affluent" Britain, 1951–64', PhD thesis, London, Guildhall University.

Crossland, C. A. R. (1952), 'The Transition from Capitalism', in R. H. S. Crossman (ed.), *New Fabian Essays*, London: Turnstile Press.

Dahrendorf, R. (1990), *Reflections on the Revolution in Europe*, London, Chatto and Windus.

Durbin, E. (1940), *The Politics of Democratic Socialism*, London, Routledge.

Giddens, A. (1998), *The Third Way: The Renewal of Social Democracy*, Oxford, Oxford University Press.
Gray, J. (1996), *After Social Democracy*, London, Demos.
Hoggart, R. (1957), *The Uses of Literacy: Aspects of Working Class Life with Special Reference to Publications and Entertainments*, London, Chatto and Windus.
Orwell, G. (1948), Review of T. S. Eliot's 'Notes Towards a Definition of Culture', *Observer*, 28 November, in *The Collected Essays, Journalism and Letter of George Orwell, volume 4*, edited by Sonia Orwell and Ian Angus, Harmondsworth, Penguin, 1970.
Thompson, E. P. (1957), 'Socialism and the Intellectuals', *Universities and Left Review*, 1.
Timmins, N. (1996), *The Five Giants: A Biography of the Welfare State*, London, Fontana.
Waters, C. (1990), *British Socialists and the Politics of Popular Culture, 1884–1914*, Manchester, Manchester University Press.
Western, B. (1995), 'A Comparative Study of Working Class Disorganisation', *American Sociological Review*, 60, April.
Wolfe, A. (1978), 'Has Social Democracy a Future?', *Comparative Politics*, 11, October.

Part I
One hundred years of social democracy: an overview

1

Socialism in the twentieth century: a historical reflection

Donald Sassoon

Introduction

Those who venture to discuss the meaning of socialism confront two distinct but not incompatible strategies: the essentialist and the historical.

The essentialist strategy proceeds in conventional Weberian fashion. Socialism is an ideal-type, empirically deduced from the activities or ideas of those commonly regarded as socialists. Once the concept is constructed, it can be used historically to assess concrete political organisations, their activists and thinkers and measure the extent to which they fit the ideal type, why and when they diverge from each other, and account for exceptional behaviour. This procedure, of great heuristic value, is still broadly accepted and widely used, even though its theoretical rigour is highly dubious as the analysis rests on a somewhat arbitrary selection of the 'socialist' organisations and individuals used to produce the ideal-type concept of socialism.

This procedure has the added disadvantage that, if strictly adhered to, it does not allow for historical change. Once the ideal-type is defined, novel elements cannot easily be integrated into it. However, life must go on, even in sociology. So when something new turns up, such as a revisionist interpretation, all that is required is to hoist the ideal-type onto the operating table, remove – if necessary – the bits which no longer fit, and insert the new ones. Thus rejuvenated, the concept of socialism can march on, rich with new meanings; social scientists, armed with a neatly repackaged ideal-type, acquire a new lease on life, produce more books on the new socialism and make academic publishers happier still.

Alternatively, sociologists may defend the old ideal-type, pronounce the new revisions incompatible with it and declare socialism dead. They can then write more books on the death of socialism and make academic publishers happy.

Activists, unconsciously Weberian, proceed in the same essentialist fashion, either exalting the new revisionism and its intelligent adaptation to the realities of an ever-changing world, or bitterly recriminating the changes which have occurred, evidence of yet another dastardly betrayal of the old faith. In so doing they keep 'socialism' (i.e. their idea of socialism) alive, its body on a life-support machine, waiting for better times. Such clash between modernisers and fundamentalists is a regular fixture of political movements, especially where ideologies and values are of central importance – as is the case in socialist and religious movements.

It is evident from the tone of the above remarks that I favour the second strategy, the historical one, though this has problems too. Its opening move is the same as that of the essentialists: one selects the organisations and thinkers which self-identify as socialists and tell their stories in a conventional empirical fashion, highlighting similarities and differences. However, no definition of socialism is required: socialism becomes what socialists do. No prediction can be made: the death of socialism, like that of feudalism – can only be declared when it is universally acknowledged and no longer a matter of dispute, that is, when there are no socialists left except for the usual cranks, who, along with flat-earthers, may have some remaining anthropological interest.

While the essentialist strategy is overwhelmingly concerned with the question of definition, the historical one is obsessed with change and causality – why do socialists behave as they do? – and hence with the context within which organisations and thinkers act as they do. This method, far from discounting the importance of ideology, regards it as an integral part of the history of the movement. What is of interest here is the connection between the particular ethical view of the world championed by socialists and their action in the domain of practical politics. How such theory and such practice are modified over time is thus the central preoccupation of the historical approach.

This procedure, with its emphasis on the inevitability of historical change, is clearly less judgemental than the essentialist one. However, like all historicist narratives, it suffers the persistent hazard of falling into a determinist version of events: whatever happened had to happen. It is useful to be conscious of this and be aware that, within determinate circumstances (this is not a minor proviso), things could have proceeded differently. In particular, it is worth reminding ourselves that while it is true that the socialist movement arises with the inception of industrial society and tracks its development, it is never a necessary component of it. There have been, there are and, in all likelihood, there will be industrial societies without a significant socialist movement. Similarly, there have been societies with a powerful socialist movement where the process of industrialisation had barely begun.

The two socialisms

At the beginning of the twentieth century socialists knew that their movement was contingent to capitalist society. It is true that the version of Marx's theory most of them adhered to implied that socialism was a state of affairs that would succeed capitalism, but they had noticed that the fastest growing capitalist society in the world, the USA, did not have a socialist movement. They were also equally aware that the most developed capitalist state in Europe, Great Britain, home of powerful trade unions, had, at most, only an embryonic socialist party. From their point of view, Britain was an advanced capitalist society with a backward socialist movement. Conversely, some of the still mainly agrarian societies of Europe – such as Italy and Finland – had fairly strong and electorally successful socialist parties.

In Russia the movement appeared divided – like the whole of the Russian intelligentsia, between westernising and slavophile tendencies (see for instance, Venturi, 1960). The westernisers assumed that the duty of socialists was to accelerate the development of capitalism, because only capitalism could provide the terrain for a further advance towards socialism. The slavophiles surmised that Russia would be able to skip western-style capitalism. Populist anti-capitalists – such as V. Bervi-Flerovski, author of *The Situation of the Working Class in Russia* (1869), a book much praised by Marx – held the view that the *mir*, the Russian peasant commune, provided communal principles which could and should be made universal. Russia could avoid the iniquities of capitalism and offer the rest of the world the example of a superior social system based on nation-wide solidarity and co-operation. This mirage of overtaking and outstripping the West remained a fundamental feature of nearly all revolutionary Russian beliefs. A century later, the abandonment of this 'Great Idea' coincided with the collapse of the entire communist system.

The westernising and slavophile positions converged towards a notable consensus: the real problem facing Russian society was one of modernisation which was then regarded as being co-terminous with industrialisation. The issue was whether this should be left to the capitalists themselves or should be undertaken directly by socialists. Those who held the second view were inevitably pushed towards the proposition that to achieve socialist-led industrialisation it was necessary to be in charge of the political apparatus itself, that is, to be in command of the state. It did not follow that the state should necessarily own the means of production. There were various possibilities: the state could substitute itself for a class of capitalists visibly unable to perform its historical task; alternatively the state could encourage the capitalists and help them to industrialise the country or, again, it could stimulate some entrepreneurs, for instance in agriculture or in new or/and smaller concerns, or it could provide financial incentives to a managerial class operating in a quasi-market even where private property had been abolished. The appropriate mix of state and market was never an issue settled once and for all and it certainly did not follow inevitably from the October Revolution. After all, much of the subsequent history of Russia – from war communism, to the New Economic Policy, to Stalin's five-year plans, to the limited and inadequate economic reform of the 1960s and 1970s – can be seen as a dispute over the relationship between markets and politics.

This version of socialism or *developmental socialism* can be described as an ideology of modernisation or development. Though its final goal is a socialist society, its practical tasks consisted in developing an industrial society under conditions where it was felt that if socialists did not do it either no one would (and the country would stagnate) or foreigners would do it (and the country would be like a colony). This kind of socialism – one is tempted to define it as capital-building socialism – coincides, more or less, with communism and its state socialist variants.

The other variety of socialism – the main concern of the rest of this essay – can be conceived as a form of regulation of capitalism (Sassoon, 1997). Its task is not to develop an industrial society; the capitalists themselves are busy doing just that. Far from requiring any 'help' from socialists, they can do it better and faster without them – as nineteenth-century Britain and twentieth-century America and Japan amply demonstrate.

This coincides with what came to be known as social democracy. The contrast between developmental or modernising socialism and socialism as capitalist regulation is, of course, far more profound than this. The former, whether in the USSR or in Cuba or in China and North Korea exhibited marked authoritarian features and intolerance of dissent and of pluralism which matched and in some cases exceeded those of capitalist authoritarian regimes. The latter brand of socialism co-existed, in all instances, with democracy, pluralism, and human rights. Such a comparison is often, quite legitimately, made by social democrats themselves who point out that developmental socialism (i.e. communism) was never liberal while social democracy was never dictatorial. It is tempting to agree, to follow convention by distinguishing communism from socialism, and to leave it at that.

Unfortunately, this would leave a number of problems unsolved. The passage from pre-modern to modern society, at least in its initial phase, has seldom been accompanied by democracy and human rights in their twentieth-century meaning. Even in Britain or the USA, not to speak of Germany and Japan, the pattern was one in which the suffrage was non-existent or severely restricted, freedoms were seriously limited, trade unions were banned or subjected to harsh control (Mazower, 1999). In some instances the process co-existed with slavery and genocide (the USA), racism, colonialism, rigid authoritarianism (for instance in Japan) and one-party rule (for instance in Taiwan and South Korea until relatively recently). Full democracy and human rights were established later. They were, in other words, the outcome of a *political* struggle, and not an imperative accompaniment of the first phase of the process of modernisation. Social democracy, where it existed at all, was in the forefront of the political struggle for democracy and human rights, goading along the liberal parties, then far less democratic, and even the conservative parties, then barely democratic, towards political reforms.

Social democrats, however, when capitalism was not fully developed, were usually in opposition. The modernisation of the country, the development of capitalism, its profitability and productivity were not their concern. They came to power only when the first phase of industrialisation was over, unlike the communists who came to power facing the problem of industrialising the country (with a few significant exceptions such as Czechoslovakia and East Germany). It does not follow from this that the degree of authoritarianism exhibited by communist rule was justifiable or inevitable. In principle, other, less harsh and cruel forms of modernisation could have been devised. The point is that the two forms of socialism which have characterised the twentieth century are not comparable. Ideologies are shaped by the kind of societies within which they operate and the relationship they have to political power, that is, to the state. Social democrats ruled only when capitalism was well established and democracy had become the common property of the main political parties. Communists had to develop an industrial society. Social democrats (or socialists, I shall use the two terms interchangeably) had to manage it. Communists prevailed in less developed societies, socialists in developed market economies.

Individualism and collectivism

One of the many paradoxes confronting the historian of socialism is that the notion of managing market societies was not part of the ideological armoury of socialists although this is what they all ended up doing. At the turn of the century, socialist ideology distinguished between an end-goal and short – or medium-term demands. The end-goal was a socialist society vaguely defined as the abolition of private property. The short-term demands were varied but, on the whole, they aimed at achieving three aims: the first was the democratisation of capitalist society, the second was the regulation of the labour market (for instance, the eight-hour day) and the third was the socialisation of the costs of reproduction of labour: free medicine, pensions, national insurance – in short, costs which would have had to be absorbed by individual workers. This third goal is what we now call the welfare state.

The values which informed this politics were those of equality, social solidarity and the establishment of minimum standards of life. If all citizens were to be of equal worth, they all (including women) had to have the vote, had to be treated equally, and have the same rights. Illness, unemployment and old age were to be protected by a common fund, centrally administered and financed. The definition of what would be the minimum standards of civilised life could not be left to the sphere of civil society, that is to the arbitrariness of the market. It had to become a political matter. The state was to be called upon to enforce a system of protection which would not exist or would exist in a rudimentary form if left to market forces. This was the basis for subjecting the conditions of work to state regulation: health and safety procedure were to be strengthened and enforced and a limit placed on the length of the working day. To force the state to operate in this way, it was necessary to democratise it, i.e. to detach it from the exclusive control of the dominant classes. I take this to be the essential meaning of T. H. Marshall, *Citizenship and Social Class and Other Essays* (1950).

The extension of democracy socialists advocated was not based on class principles but on the principle of individual rights. Universal suffrage, after all, assumes that all individuals have exactly the same worth when voting: each, literally, counts as one. The ballot had to be secretly cast by a lone individual making an individual choice. In the domain of politics, social-ists, far from being class-conscious, were staunch individualists. It is worth reminding ourselves of such unexceptional views, historically well docu-mented, at a time when socialists are criticised (and supinely acquiesce in being criticised) for their alleged class-collectivist position. Those who, at the turn of the century, defended a class conception of democracy were the liberals and the conservatives, not the socialists. Liberal or conserva-tive parties defended an electoral system that allocated votes in terms of the wealth possessed or earned by each individual. Throughout Europe they also accepted and defended an upper chamber that over-represented or represented only the members of the upper classes. As I write, such an insti-tution still exists, incredibly enough, in Britain, the 'mother of democracy'. Furthermore, liberal and conservative parties were not only guilty of 'class-ism', but also of sexism. Not only did they oppose the enfranchisement of the working class, they also opposed that of women. Their opposition to working-class suffrage may have been based on opportunism: workers, they felt, would have increased the electoral weight of dangerous socialists. Women, on the other hand, were believed to be more likely to vote for conservative and traditional parties, yet these resisted female suffrage – a rare instance of ideology and principle prevailing over self-interest.

Socialists, of course, often did not fight for female suffrage with great vigour, but this had little to do with principle. Some were moved by their commitment to gradualism and moderation (the modern requirement to keep everyone happy, jolly them along, upset no one and remain united). It was thus essential to proceed by stages and to achieve full manhood suffrage before extending it to women. Other socialists were moved, quite simply, by political opportunism: it was clear to them that the enfranchisement of women would give a distinct advantage to religious parties. When it came to principles and values, however, all socialist parties stood firmly on the side of real universal suffrage.

Thus socialists were far more consistent defenders of individual democratic rights than liberals and conservatives. However, in the pursuit of their second aim, the regulation of the working day and, more generally, the regulation of the conditions of work, socialists took a clearly collectivist position. The contractual relation which associated capitalists and workers was one of individual to individual. In exchange for agreed wages, each individual worker undertook to perform a determinate operation, in determinate conditions and for a determinate length of time – a situation Marx and his followers described as 'formal' equality, meaning that such agreement was between juridically equal parties, a contractual relation between equals which disguised a massive inequality in power. Furthermore, capitalists had substantial advantages, especially where there was a considerable surplus of labour which, in the initial stages of industrialisation, was the norm.

The formation of trade unions was a collective means of redressing this inequality of power. Their chances of success depended on a variety of factors the most important being the absence of legal impediments to their effective functioning. Here, the unions were in favour of retrenching the state and might well have adopted the latter-day slogan of 'getting the state off their backs'. When it came to the political enforcement of minimum standards, however, the unions were in favour of bringing the state back in to create – to use, once again, modern terminology – a level playing field among entrepreneurs, preventing them from competing at the expenses of the workers.

The third aim, the creation of what was later called the Welfare State, entailed the socialisation of some of the costs of reproduction of the working class. The collective tax fund (to which the middle classes were expected to contribute disproportionately) or the forcible extraction of contributions from the capitalists could be used to help finance pensions, national insurances and medical expenses. This would have had obvious beneficial effects for the workers and their families, but it also allowed the entrepreneurs to pay them less. While wages are necessary for the reproduction of the working class, the development of non-wage benefits meant that monetary wages (as opposed to real earnings) could be lower than they would have been if there were no other benefits.

The success obtained in reaching these aims differed from country to country. Much depended on the relative strength of the two contending classes, capitalists and workers, the wealth of the economy, the power and dominance of landed aristocratic interests, the prevailing political ethos, the position of the Church. For instance, at the turn of the century, the USA had the most rapidly developing economy in the world, but wave upon wave of immigrant labour acted as a break on the formation of powerful politically inclined trade unions, and the competition among capitalists enabled some to opt for a high wage strategy (Fordism) which helped prevent the formation of a larger market for consumer goods than would have been the case otherwise. While the American political elites were also largely impervious to trade union pressures, they were less resistant to those stemming from the large class of small farmers. The ensuing polarisation more or less isolated the trade union movement and weakened its political progress, hence the development of a peculiar anti-big business populism.

Britain followed a different path. In the nineteenth century its working class was large and well organised, and had, by the standards of the time, a long history of struggles and militancy. No established party could ignore the workers. The religious fragmentation of the country and especially of the working class contributed to preventing the formation of a confessional party along the lines of continental Christian democracy. The result was that, in the second half of the nineteenth century, Liberals and Conservatives competed with each other for the support of the labouring classes and incorporated in their own programme aspects of a social democratic platform before that could find an outlet as an organised political party. This helped delay the formation and growth of a large British socialist party along the lines of the SPD. On the continent, a similar process of cooption was under way: nation-building required the incorporation of demands emerging from the lower classes and took the form of what was called in Germany a form of 'state socialism' – built by Bismarck and supported by the socialist leader Ferdinand Lassalle. Liberal, conservative and nationalist parties were in the forefront of this movement. They were eventually joined by Church-based parties particularly when the Roman Catholic Church abandoned its intransigent defence of the ancient regime and adopted a new position towards what it called the 'social question' with the publication in 1891 of Pope Leo XIII's encyclical *Rerum novarum*.

Socialists, liberals and the state

By the beginning of the twentieth century the three key aspects of the medium-term programme of social democracy could be found in some form in other parties. It follows that it was no longer possible, if it ever was, to establish a clear and permanent distinction between socialists and non-socialists in terms of practical policies.

There were, of course, also massive differences: socialists remained committed to the long term aim of achieving a post-capitalist society, possessed a set of distinctive symbols, advanced their demands in a more radical way, pursued and explored new forms of struggle, such as the political strike, remained opposed to overt co-operation with other parties, and, with the exception of Britain, expounded anti-clericalism. In other words socialists tried to distinguish themselves in all possible ways from what they persisted in regarding as a monolithic bourgeois bloc.

The continuous attempt by anti-socialist forces to incorporate socialist demands should be regarded as evidence of the success of socialists and of their ability to shape and influence political developments. But it also makes it impossible to construct a foolproof definition of socialist policies.

The extension of democracy, the institution of the welfare state, the control of the working day, were socialist aims and policies, but one can always find, at any moment, similar demands advanced and implemented by non-socialist parties, be they right, centre, conservatives, liberal, Christian or nationalist. From the outset, 'socialism' was not the prerogative of socialists (Baldwin, 1990).

It is true that socialists were forced, in their everyday practice, to trim their demands and accept compromises, but so were the conservatives and liberals. The extension of democracy and the advance of mass society meant that no political party could hope to obtain sufficient support either by defending the status quo *in toto* (the essential conservative position) or by proposing to return to the status quo ante (the essential reactionary position). Reformism triumphed. It was adopted by the most varied forces: in Germany by Bismarck and the later Wilhelmine nationalists as well as the 'social' Christians of the Zentrum party; in Italy by the majority wing of the Liberal Party (Giovanni Giolitti) and the emerging forces of political catholicism; in France by the Radicals of the Third Republic; in Britain by both Disraeli's and Salisbury's conservatives as well as Joseph Chamberlain, Gladstone, the New Liberals, Asquith and Lloyd George; in Austria by the antisemitic Social Christians of Karl Lüger and in Holland by the new confessional parties in alliance with the more enlightened Liberals.

The impact of this turn to the social was more visible at the local level than at the national. Local authorities were busy devising imaginative schemes to improve the social conditions of urban life through public health programmes, housing developments, slum clearance, poor relief – that is by developing an important local public sector. This evolving 'municipal socialism' was seldom, if ever, the work of socialists. The success of reformist socialism, like the success of all political ideologies, lay in the fact that it did not have a monopoly of what it stood for. In politics success consists in ensuring that what one thinks as normal or desirable or possible becomes the shared attitude, the common property of the entire polity. To achieve this, however, it is necessary to formulate demands which are detachable from the ideological package (the symbols and language) which accompanies it. This can only be realised when the connection between ideological values and practical policies is vague and loose, and thus ready to be endlessly renegotiated. It is precisely because it is perfectly possible to be in favour of adequate pensions without signing up to the end goal of socialism that adequate pensions can be fought for by liberals and conservatives. Consistency and coherence may enable small political sects to survive indefinitely, but they spell certain ruin for parties and movements with real hegemonic ambitions.

Approaching socialism as a political programme that overlaps with that of other parties helps to highlight the importance of the long-term aims, of the symbols used, of the privileging of a particular class. Socialist parties, like other parties, had to advance contradictory positions. On the one hand they put forward a realistic programme that could appeal to as many people as possible; on the other, they stressed what was absolutely distinctive and unique. They knew successful policies were likely to be imitated and popular demands taken over. To counter the probable dispersion of support, socialists presented themselves as the authentic champions of reforms. At the same time, they emphasised that these were not ends in themselves but steps to a situation – socialism – where they would no longer be necessary because the social problems had been eliminated. Thus the insistence on the final end was not only part of a recruitment strategy aimed at intellectuals and others with millenarian aspirations. It was also a convincing way of reinforcing the appeal of what might otherwise appear as limited reforms. Similarly, the insistence on the working class was not just derived from Marxist theory – the non-Marxist British Labour Party was a far more vociferous advocate of a 'proletarian' consciousness than most of its continental counterparts. It was the recognition that that particular social group represented the most likely source of support for social and economic reforms.

The struggle for democracy, for the welfare state and for the regulation of the working week thus created a wide arena of struggle in which all the main parties participated. It also brought about a fundamental feature of twentieth-century socialism: its *étatism*. It is only relatively recently that socialists themselves have come to question it. The growth of an exceptionally strong centralised state in the USSR and the development, between the wars, of so-called totalitarian states offered those opposing socialism an ideal platform. Fascism, nazism and stalinism may have been extreme forms of state-worship, but did not socialist thought itself come perilously close to it? Had not socialists developed a 'love affair' with centralised control. Was not the welfare state itself – often depicted as the product of a compassionate and socially concerned ideology – but the moderate face of an obsession with controls, bureaucracy, and top-to-bottom direction? Was it not in fact a systematic onslaught against individual freedoms and incentives? (von Mises, 1981).

Socialists have now accepted, partly out of political opportunism, partly out of conviction, partly out of that chronic ignorance of their own history that blights modern political movements, that there is an element of truth in such criticisms. In fact étatisme was an inseparable and inevitable part of the practice of socialist (i.e. of reformist practice) but not of its ideology (i.e. of its revolutionary commitment to a socialist end-goal).

Throughout the nineteenth century, when socialists were in opposition and the movement in its infancy, socialism was against the state. The reasons are so obvious and have been investigated so thoroughly that here they can merely be restated: the state was – to Marxists and non-Marxists alike – a bourgeois state which deprived workers of the right to vote and produced legislation which, by and large, favoured the entrepreneurs, the aristocracy and the middle classes far more than the workers. The anti-state position of the socialists had some substance. For similar reasons the European confessional parties, where they existed, and the Roman Catholic Church also regarded the state as an alien force. It was, after all, in the hands of disbelievers and rationalists (as in France and Italy) or 'state-worshippers' (Bismarck and German nationalists). The Church realised perfectly well what liberal propaganda has always attempted to disguise, namely that the power of the state was usually the inevitable counterpart of the cult of the individual. In the nineteenth century the state was regarded by Liberals as the essential means with which to break down the resistance of traditional privileges, or local power and clear the way for the development of national markets and hence for the accumulation of capital. Similarly, conservatives regarded the state as the main instrument to be used to slow down the advance of liberal reforms. The real *étatistes*, in the nineteenth century, were the liberals and the conservatives.

Gradually, at first imperceptibly at the beginning of the twentieth century, more overtly between the wars and conspicuously after the Second World War, socialists came to recognise that the state was the best political weapon available for the implementation of the three components of the original political programme – democracy, welfare and regulation of labour market.

It is rather surprising that this acceptance of the state – not just the state as a concept, but the state as a machine, as a coercive apparatus – came so late in the development of twentieth-century socialism. There was, in the years before the First World War an optimistic view of the possibility of forcing the bourgeois state to implement the socialist reform programme. In principle they were not wrong. Without the state there could not have been a socialisation of some of the cost of reproduction of the working class (the welfare state) and a regulation of the working day. Powerful trade unions, without a political party, could have struggled alone and negotiated with employers over the length of the working day, the conditions of work, holiday pay etc. They could have acted as a pressure group and wrested concessions from governing political parties. This was, prior to the Second World War, the British experience. Two patterns emerged: on the continent, the length of the working day and similar labour market regulations were obtained from the state; in Britain these were left to the 'class struggle', that is to the trade union's confrontation with the employers (Cross, 1989).

The continent followed the principle of universal rights: where the eight-hour day was won, it was won on behalf of all citizens. In Britain any gain would be confined to union members.

The endorsement of the state was thus not part of the ideology of socialism. It was instrumental to the achievement of their medium or short-term aims. The commitment of socialists to the state grew as these aims became more significant and as the final aim of a post-capitalist state receded ever more into the future. Universal suffrage made the state more receptive to the demands made by the socialists on behalf of all citizens. It also made it more legitimate and hence more powerful. It enabled socialists to achieve political power by 'capturing the state machine'. This facilitated the implementation of the rest of their reform programme – the regulation of the working day and the socialisation of some of the cost of production and reproduction. This transformed industrial society.

Socialists and liberals shared equally positive assumptions about industrialism, but had different views on what the relationship between the political system and industry should be. As far as Liberal *theory*, as opposed to its practice, was concerned, the purpose of the state was to remove obstacles to the advance of industrial society. Once this was achieved, industry – as part of civil society – should be allowed to develop without interference. It is noteworthy that this was precisely the position reached by some of the early socialists, in particular Saint-Simon.

The socialists were ambivalent about civil society. On the one hand, they wanted to be as free as possible to organise and use collective action to achieve their demands, thus joining with the liberals who wanted broad market freedom. On the other hand, they viewed civil society as a space where the distribution of power and money was so uneven as to dilute considerably the equality of rights achieved in the political arena.

After the First World War

Socialists thus regarded the state either as an alien force or as machine which could be used for the redistribution of power. They hoped that they could control capitalism and eventually replace it. What they did not assume is that they could manage capitalism. And here lies the other substantial zone of agreement between socialists and liberals. Before the First World War, no socialists, whether Marxist or non-marxist, moderate or authoritarian, contemplated a planned economy. How socialism should be organised was an issue on which socialist parties were quite silent, or resorted to vague generalisation of no practical value. The intellectuals were of no help. Marx somehow thought that the socialist economy would run itself, it would be 'the administration of things' whatever that meant. Lenin piously suggested that a cook would be able to run it. Kautsky, like most social democrats of the time, simply believed that the question could be resolved only when capitalism had fully developed and when the working class had acquired a superior culture and intellect. Bernstein, as he declared more than once, was not much interested in a socialist society, preferring to fight for the improvement of the conditions of the working class under capitalism. There were no plans to create a large public sector, or to nationalise the economy (Geary, 1987; Tudor and Tudor, 1988).

The war changed matters and not only for socialists. Politically it broke the isolation of socialists from bourgeois parties in all the contending countries, as socialists in France and Germany put the defence of 'their' state over international solidarity. In economic matters, states were forced to manage the economy, regulating labour markets, production and distribution to an unprecedented extent. The idea of managing the capitalist economy was firmly installed on the agenda of liberals, conservatives and socialists alike.

In Russia the collapse of tsardom and the ensuing military debacle created a power vacuum which allowed the Bolshevik seizure of power. Even then the automatic response of the Bolsheviks was not the abolition of private property and the construction of a planned economy. During the civil war the forcible top to bottom control of the economy was due to requirements of the military situation, not to ideological preconceptions. The 'step back' towards the adoption of the New Economy Policy was seen as a return to a market economy, not as the harbinger of new forms of economic management. The planning mechanism installed by Stalin in the late 1920s was not the inevitable consequence of the Bolshevik victory (ten years after their seizure of power!) but the outcome of a vigorous political conflict which saw the victory of the planners over their more gradualist opponents. In other words, even in what had become the USSR, socialism had not been always identified with the abolition of market forces or with a state monopoly of the economy.

Elsewhere in Europe, socialists turned out to be reluctant economic interventionists. One of the effects of the Russian revolution was to remove from socialist parties their more radical cadres who formed communist parties. Nowhere were these able to secure the support of a majority of the socialist electorate, even where, as in France, they had been able to rally the majority of party activists. The upshot was that some socialist parties, though radicalised by the war, were freer to pursue more conciliatory policies towards parties of the centre and the centre-left. Before the war all socialist parties, without exception, accepted the political principle that under no circumstances would they cooperate with 'bourgeois' parties. During the war and even more so afterwards this principle was abandoned. In the 1920s and 1930s socialists were finally able to achieve political power and to form governments. In all instances they were able to do so only in alliance with other parties: in Sweden, in France, in Germany, in Britain, in Spain (Miller and Potthoff, 1986; Koblic, 1975; Skidelsky, 1967; Pimlott, 1977; Jackson, 1988).

Some of the ideological barriers which had been erected to distinguish socialists from the rest came tumbling down. As we have seen, in terms of practical politics, these barriers had been flexible all along. After the war and particularly in the 1930s, key aspects of the reform programme of social democracy came to be accepted by other political forces. Radical organisations of the right (fascists and right-wing populists) incorporated some of the social demands of the left, including major features of welfare reform, but rejected the democratic politics which accompanied them. Liberal, Catholic and centrist forces accepted the principles of universal suffrage, though in some cases (France, Belgium and Switzerland) still excluded the female half of the population. The principle of the regulation of the working day became almost universally accepted.

The incorporation of some aspects of the welfare state while repressing the political forces which most strongly advanced it became the hallmark of the populist authoritarian regimes which prevailed in areas of central, southern and eastern Europe such as those of Fascist Italy and Nazi Germany. In some of the remaining democratic states of Western Europe a period of uneasy compromise between labour and capital characterised the interwar period.

The existence of a communist movement forced the socialist parties to develop ideological barriers to their left. They did so by stressing the importance of political democracy. This they no longer regarded only as the best political shell for the implementation of their economic and social demand but also as the thing that fundamentally distinguished them from the communists. Socialists, however, were also influenced by key aspects of the new communist ideology, namely the importance of the expansion of state ownership. The regular re-interpretation of the famous Clause Four of the Labour Party is emblematic. Adopted in 1918 almost as an afterthought, it vaguely referred to the 'common ownership' of the means of production, distribution and exchange. How this would work in practice remained unclear. To some, it referred clearly to a socialist future. To others it became part of a gradual process towards a socialist society: capitalism would eventually be abolished as firms and entire industries came to be absorbed into an ever-expanding public sector. To others again, public ownership would compensate for market failures, eliminate inefficient firms, prevent private monopolies.

The process of osmosis between left and right which had started before the First World War continued and was accelerated by the crisis of 1929. Liberals were no longer so certain that the state which interfered the least was the best. The rapidly developing unemployment which had de-stabilised Germany and threatened France and Britain was seen as evidence that the socialists had been right at least on one point: market forces did not naturally lead to an equilibrium but to chronic instability. In Italy the fascist regime reacted to the crisis by taking over most of the banking system, but limited state intervention became acceptable even in liberal and conservative Britain.

Nevertheless, the old pre-First World War view that capitalism and socialism were rigidly separated – one shared with the communists – remained in place almost everywhere between the two wars. When socialists came to power they refrained from extending the public sector, and did not attempt to direct the economy. Capitalism, they believed, could not be managed except by capitalists, hence the respect for orthodox economics exhibited by socialists in Weimar Germany after 1928, in Britain when Labour was in power in 1929–31, and elsewhere, such in Belgium and in the Scandinavian countries. The most that could be done was to set up systems of conciliation and negotiation between capitalists and trade unions, one of the many schemes of 'partnership' between the two sides of industry which are still – at the beginning of the twenty-first century – hailed as the *dernier cri* in socialist modernity: from the Stinnes–Legien pact of 1918 which established in Germany the joint labour-management board for economic regulation, to the 'Whitley Councils' in Britain, from the Matignon Accords of 1936 following the victory of the Popular Front in France, to the National Recovery and Wagner Acts of 1933 and 1935 in the USA, from the Saltsjöbaden agreements in Sweden (1938) to the Main Agreement in Norway (1935). Nevertheless, to most socialists, then as later, practical socialism meant protecting the workers and their families by developing the tried and tested policies of welfarism and regulation of the conditions of work. The victory of the Popular Front government in France was a clear sign that whenever they could socialists should 'occupy power' – and implement needed reforms – even though the time had not come for the 'exercise of power' to use Leon Blum's famous distinction. In opposition some socialists advanced schemes for planning the economy – as in Belgium with Hendrik de Man's *Plan du travail*, or, to use its more appropriate Flemish title, the *Plan van den Arbeid* – and advocated a mixed economic system including, in addition to a private sector, a nationalised sector consisting of credit institutions and former private monopolies (Hansen, 1978). This obviously required a strong and efficient state. Conservatism, right-wing authoritarianism, the technocratic liberalism of Keynes and Lloyd George and all shades of socialism converged on this. The only main ideology still defending the minimal state, classical liberalism was on the run, after the collapse of 1929, even in its Anglo-Saxon heartland.

After the Second World War

After the Second World War, European social democrats became leading contenders for power in virtually all the democratic countries of Western Europe. Of their three-pronged platform, the first – universal suffrage – had become the unquestioned basis of all politics with some significant exceptions which all occurred where socialist parties did not wield any powers: the southern states of the USA which, until the early 1970s, deprived blacks from exercising their right to vote in most elections, Switzerland where many cantons (in which socialists were weak) restricted suffrage to men only until 1971 and South Africa where – until the collapse of the apartheid regime – a multi-party system excluded blacks from effective political participation.

So strongly recognised was the principle of universal suffrage that it was adopted or maintained – albeit in principle only – in most of the newly decolonised countries and in all communist states; dictatorial rule was secured not by disenfranchisement but by the elimination of all effective political opposition.

The principles of welfarism and full employment never had such universal legitimacy. They became state policies prevalently in Western Europe and where socialist parties were strong such as in Australia. As for the public sector, it was expanded throughout Western Europe, but there was little connection between the extension of the public sector and the strength of socialists. Post-war nationalisations occurred under the impetus of conservatives (Gaullism), Christian Democrats in Austria and Italy, socialists (in the UK). One of the smallest state-owned sectors in Europe was in the social democratic Nordic countries.

No common foreign affairs principle was adopted in the post-war period. The pre-First World War rhetorical commitment to pacifism remained, after the Second World War, a sub-culture within the socialist parties. These were divided between Atlanticists and neutralists and between those in favour of the political integration of Europe and those who remained committed to a national conception of socialism. Only in the 1990s did Europeanism became a factor uniting all socialist parties – unlike Atlanticism which, even after the collapse of the USSR and the eastward expansion of NATO, was not accepted by major socialist parties such as those in Sweden, Finland and the Austria.

The international organisation the socialist parties had formed was never more than a symbolic forum. Its pronouncement simply reflected in general terms a vague consensus on matters of principles. In fact each socialist party behaved strictly as a national organisation whose priority was to safeguard its own national polity and, consequently, the requirements of its own national capitalism.

As we have seen, the connection between modern socialism and its state and hence with its own capitalism had started to be established towards the end of the last century. It is thus hardly surprising that, as socialists proved successful in reforming their capitalist societies, they were reluctant to let go of the existing regulatory institutions: a large public sector, a powerful central bank, a mechanism of exchange control, a complex system of subsidies and regional policies, an intricate mechanism for the control of the labour market. This regulatory aspect became the fundamental relation between socialism and capitalism and further reduced the importance of the older goal of abolishing capitalism. This, in fact, had become largely of symbolic value. It stood to represent that, however indispensable was a thriving economy for the success of all other intermediate socialist goals and however distant were the prospects for a post-capitalist society, socialists still stood in an antagonistic relationship to capitalism. However, the popular appeal of this symbolic message had been much reduced. The prosperity associated with capitalist growth, the establishment of full employment, the protective apparatus of the welfare state, the patent incapacity of communist states to develop a consumer society comparable to those in the west, had almost eliminated the deep-seated antagonism against capitalism which had existed previously. Other political parties, such as those committed to Christian and conservatives values, who, in the past, had not been major proponents of capitalism, discovered its virtues. The socialists did the same. Thus, gradually but constantly, at varying speeds depending on differing political conjunctures and, above all, on electoral vicissitudes, the parties of the left dropped their radical anti-capitalist symbols. This process, generally referred to as revisionism, accelerated in the late 1950s with the German SPD Bad Godesberg Congress. It continued in all parties, dividing both activists and leaders amidst the indifference of the electorate at large whose remarkable electoral stability is one of the most significant factors of post-war West European history.

The victory of revisionism was almost inevitable. We have just alluded to one of the reasons: the left's electorates were never seriously concerned with the long-term aim of abolishing capitalism. They were far more interested in medium-term demands, and in a generic social justice particularly in education and health. Consequently the revisionists, even when weak inside their parties, had always a fairly strong following among voters. This could not fail to have an impact on those radical activists who wanted their parties to maximise the chance of winning elections. There were, however, other reasons for the victory of revisionism. In almost all instances, socialists could only hope to achieve power by forming a coalition with parties of the centre. Such accords would have been more difficult if socialists had persisted with their anti-capitalist rhetoric and radical schemes of redistribution (which would require high levels of taxation). There were, of course, instances where socialists could achieve power only by reaching an understanding with parties to their left – for instance in France in the 1970s between socialists and communists. Here the agreed manifesto was radical, but the French socialists were able to use other symbolic events to signal that they would be the dominant partner and that they would be able to keep the communists under control – which is indeed what has occurred.

More generally, revisionists could always mount a successful challenge because they always enjoyed a vital advantage: their conservative opponents (the parties to the right) and the media and power structures which backed them could always be relied upon to stigmatise the radical left as hopelessly out of touch with modern realities. In other words revisionism had the advantage that all centrist positions have: they can play a game on two fronts. As part of the left they can denounce capitalist iniquities; as part of the centre they can distance themselves from radicalism.

This underlines the main ideological achievement of modern socialism and also its failure. The achievement lies in the fact that free untrammelled market capitalism has never been able to establish itself as the dominant ideology of European politics. It manifestly failed to do so throughout Catholic Europe (Spain, Portugal, Italy, Austria and southern Germany) where the leading non-socialist ideologies have always taken a traditionalist form (Christian democracy) or a national-popular one (Gaullism) or an authoritarian-populist one (fascism). It also failed to do so in protestant Nordic countries where the agrarian parties actively co-operated in the establishment of social-democratic hegemony. Only in Britain – the original home of laissez-faire ideology – did free market conservatism gain a position of relative hegemony during the 1980s. Yet, even there, it did so only almost by stealth thanks to an electoral system which worked to the advantage of the largest party, disarray in the left and centre, and retreat of traditional 'one-nation' conservatism.

The main ideological failure of social democracy is linked to one of the causes of its original success: having correctly identified the state as the principal regulator of the capitalist economy it sought, successfully, to democratise it and use it. As long as the state held that position, social democratic strategy retained its full coherence. But as various aspects of capitalism (especially its financial organisation) developed in a global direction, this state-oriented strategy began to falter. Social democrats and the larger communist parties of the west remained wedded to a nationalist conception of politics and reinforced it constantly, ring-fencing their achievements (welfare, education, civil rights) within the territorial boundaries of the state, while capitalism set out to stride the globe.

Conclusion

To predict whether socialism has a future is a futile exercise which is nevertheless undertaken with astonishing regularity by intelligent and well-informed people. As we have seen, what socialism 'really' is has always been a matter of dispute; as its precise meaning can be endlessly redefined and renegotiated, there is no reason why the term could not be used indefinitely – or at least as long as capitalism exists. The only condition for its survival is the existence of significant political forces ready to associate themselves with it. As long as the term 'socialism' is used to denote any forms of political regulation of capitalism, socialism will live on, frightening some, comforting others, regularly dying and yet reviving, the endless centre of debates and disputations.

Socialism as an anti-capitalist force, aimed at overcoming the present economic arrangements of society and establishing an alternative social order where resources are allocated on the basis of need, has been a dead force in Western Europe for decades.

The claims of socialism to be a modernising force (socialism in its communist guise) able to catch up with capitalist industrial societies has been completely routed since the late 1980s. The collapse of the USSR constituted the most conspicuous evidence of this defeat. Developments in China, where a communist party is striving to establish capitalist relations, further confirms the historical collapse of the idea of communism.

At the beginning of the twenty-first century, socialism as a distributive force aimed at allocating vital resources, such as health, culture and education, outside of market mechanisms and on the basis of social citizenship, that is, without excluding anyone, is still surviving with no loss of support. Its electoral successes may be seen as a conscious or unconscious recognition by a majority of voters of the necessity of some kind of re-negotiation with a new kind of capitalism, more assertive, more confident, more powerful, more global. And a tacit acknowledgment that it may be better to entrust such re-negotiation to political forces that, historically speaking, have always been suspicious, if not hostile, to the ideology of the untrammelled market.

The difficulty facing those who still call themselves socialist is that, while they need capitalism and the economic growth and prosperity which it can generate, capitalism does not need them. Capitalist societies can be organised in an economically sustainable way by offering only minimal protection to some marginal groups (the USA) or by devolving welfare activities to organisations of civil society such as large firms, families and social groups (Japan). These alternative models, particularly the American one, whose capacity to use each crisis to re-emerge greatly strengthened is striking, have good prospects of a victorious outcome. Such expectations are greatly strengthened by the increasing reluctance of socialist leaders and followers to identify themselves with the term socialism.

Such reluctance is a reflection of the uncontrollable multiplicity of meanings the term has been encumbered with, and of the incapacity of socialists to produce their own dominant meaning of the term. It is as if they had accepted that the 'hegemonic' definition of socialism is that which has been given by its enemies, one which disparages socialism for its alleged illiberalism, statism, anti-individualism and dogmatism; for rewarding inefficiency and mortifying initiative.

No ideology can survive for long if its followers are embarrassed to identify themselves with it.

Note

This chapter first appeared in the *Journal of Political Ideologies* (2000), vol. 5, pp. 17–34.

References

Baldwin, P. (1990), *The Politics of Social Solidarity: Class Bases of the European Welfare State 1875–1975* (Cambridge: Cambridge University Press).

Cross, G. (1989), *A Quest for Time: The Reduction of Work in Britain and France, 1840–1940* (Berkeley: University of California Press).

Geary, D. (1987), *Karl Kautsky* (Manchester: Manchester University Press).

Hansen, E. (1978), 'Hendrik de Man and the Theoretical Foundations of Economic Planning: The Belgian Experience, 1933–1940', *European Studies Review*, Vol. 8, No. 2.

Jackson, J. (1988), *The Popular Front in France: Defending Democracy, 1934–38* (Cambridge: Cambridge University Press).

Koblic, S. (ed.) (1975), *Sweden's Development from Poverty to Affluence 1750–1970* (Minneapolis: University of Minnesota Press).

Marshall, T. H. (1950), *Citizenship and Social Class and Other Essays* (Cambridge: Cambridge University Press).

Mazower, M. (1999), *Dark Continent* (New York: Knopf).

Miller, S. and H. Potthoff (1986), *A History of German Social Democracy: From 1848 to the Present* (Leamington: Berg Publishers).

Pimlott, B. (1977), *Labour and the Left in the 1930s* (Cambridge: Cambridge University Press).

Sassoon, D. (1997), *One Hundred Years of Socialism: The West European Left in the Twentieth Century* (London: Fontana).

Skidelsky, R. (1967), *Politicians and the Slump: The Labour Government of 1929–1931* (London: Macmillan)

Tudor, H. and J. M. Tudor (eds) (1988), *Marxism and Social Democracy: The Revisionist Debate 1896–1898* (Cambridge: Cambridge University Press).

Venturi, F. (1960), *Roots of Revolution* (New York: Grosset and Dunlap).

von Mises, L. (1981), *Socialism* (Indianapolis: Liberty Fund).

2

A case of lost identity? A long view on social democracy worldwide

Marcel van der Linden

Introduction

There have been many debates on the differences between social democratic and other parties. I will not go further into this matter, but I will work on the assumption, that all parties in the Socialist International (SI) are part of international social democracy. On the basis of this supposition I should be able to make some observations on social democracy's world-wide development. Table 2.1 shows the regional spread and development of the SI since the mid-1970s.

What we have here is nothing less than an organisational explosion. Within a quarter of a century, the number of countries with SI members has increased by 147 per cent, and the number of member parties has increased even more, by 169 per cent. This tempestuous growth is especially remarkable, because the membership of the SI has been rather stable during the preceding decades. During the first twenty-five years of its existence (the period 1951–76), the number of affiliated parties had always fluctuated between 34

Table 2.1 Countries represented in the Socialist International by full members (number of member parties in brackets)

	1977	1981	1986	1992	1998	2003
Africa	2 (2)	3 (3)	3 (3)	6 (6)	9 (9)	18 (19)
Asia	5 (6)	3 (4)	4 (6)	4 (6)	5 (6)	8 (9)
Australasia	2 (2)	2 (2)	2 (2)	2 (2)	2 (2)	2 (2)
Europe	20 (22)	21 (23)	20 (23)	28 (32)	33 (38)	38 (45)
Latin America & Caribbean	5 (5)	12 (12)	10 (10)	17 (17)	18 (21)	21 (27)
North America	2 (2)	2 (3)	2 (3)	2 (3)	2 (3)	2 (3)
Total	36 (39)	43 (47)	41 (47)	59 (66)	69 (79)	89 (105)

Sources: *Socialist Affairs*, 1977/2, 1981/2, 1986/4, 1992/3, 1998/2, and www.socialistinternational.org/2Members/who.html
Note: Israel has been counted in Asia, Turkey in Europe.

(at the foundation in Frankfurt) and 39 (*Socialist International Information*, I/27–8 (7 July 1951): 36–7).

How can we explain the SI's global expansion in the second quarter century of its history? How was it possible, for instance, that many political forces in former colonies suddenly felt drawn towards social democracy, while in the 1950s and 1960s they considered European social democratic parties as allies of the colonisers? (This was an understandable attitude, in view of the actions taken, for example, by the British, French and Dutch labour and socialist parties in India, Algeria and Indonesia.)

It is very likely, that several factors have contributed to this reversal (both on the 'supply' and 'demand'-side, so to speak). Here I would like to focus on *one* element that seems to be crucial for any explanation that we try to give. My hypothesis is that the worldwide growth of social democracy was rendered possible by the increasing vagueness of the social democratic political profile. In other words, the gradual disappearance of social democracy's identity was a *necessary*, but not a *sufficient* condition for its global expansion.

If we take a long view and sum up the development of international social democracy of the last hundred years, then we may distinguish four different party-types.

First, the old social democratic parties in Europe, whose development started in the last decades of the nineteenth century. Many of these parties have known a more or less continuous development, although there have been violent interruptions of varying duration (12 years in Germany, 33 years in Italy, 36 years in Spain). This 'family' of parties can of course be subdivided (e.g., North versus South).

Second, the social democratic parties in settler colonies which also had an early start and have seen a rather continuous development until the present (Australia, New Zealand, to a certain extent also the USA).

Third, the social democratic parties in settler colonies that had an early start but disappeared after a few decades (Argentina, for example).

Fourth, the parties that were *not* social democratic from the start, but transformed themselves into social democratic parties at a later stage of their development. This category comprises transformed communist parties (such as the Italian PDS, several parties in Eastern Europe), former liberation movements, and others.

The first category (the European parties) have dominated the Socialist International from the beginning. The Canadian Assistant General Secretary Robin Sears was justified in saying in the mid-1980s:

> One should not overestimate the change [of the SI], by claiming that because the majority of member parties of the SI are now non-European the centre of political gravity has shifted south or west. It hasn't . . . [F]or the reasons of history, scale, collective cohesion internally and with each other, the political weight of Europe within our ideological family will not soon be shifted. (*Socialist Affairs*, 1985/4: 32)

Therefore, we will only be able to explain the transformation and expansion of the SI if we understand the developments in Europe. I have argued before, that European social democracy has gone through two important metamorphoses since the late nineteenth century (van der Linden, 2003: 95–116). Here I will restrict myself to a quick summary of the transformations of the nine parties in countries north of the Alps (Scandinavia, [West] Germany, Great Britain, the Netherlands, Belgium, Austria, and Switzerland) – the developments in Southern Europe (France, Spain, Portugal, Italy) had similar outcomes but followed different courses.

The northern parties differed not only politically from most other parties, but also culturally. At an early stage the parties had established a broad network of affiliated organisations everywhere: sports associations, women's clubs, organisations for nature lovers, consumer cooperatives, newspapers, theatre groups, and the like. The parties obviously maintained close ties with the social democratic trade unions as well. Only Great Britain deviated from the norm. Although such organisations existed there as well, they were less *directly* linked to the party than in other countries. This old network remained provisionally intact after the metamorphosis and benefited party stability immeasurably. Provided the party not only influenced its members in purely political respects but also controlled their daily life in countless other ways, the bond between the 'foundation elements' and the 'upper crust' remained rock solid. Theo Pirker aptly noted that German social democracy long 'withstood the most violent literary and factional strife, prevailed over breakaway factions, and carried out the most unlikely reunifications because the workers movement was not merely contingent upon theory and ideology but was an extensive network of associations and relationships between individuals and groups within and outside the working class' (Pirker, 1984: 45).

These subcultural ties remained in existence when the parties went through their first metamorphosis. That was during the 1930s and 1940s, when they gave up the socialist ultimate goal (in those cases in which they had had such a goal), accepted Social Keynesianism, and thus changed from reformist workers' parties to reform parties with workers' support. Social Keynesiansm's attractiveness was the fundamental cause of this major change. Social Keynesianism's attraction proved strong, even irresistible. The old reformism, which had assigned workers' interests first priority in its basic programme and ultimate objective and had considered capital an adversary from which progressively greater concessions were to be exacted, made way for a political practice that pursued *systematic cooperation* with that very capital. From a social democratic perspective, Keynesianism offered several major advantages:

1 It seemed to allow control over the economy via the state from above. Reconciliation between socialism and the market became possible by

managing the unemployment rate and the income distribution notwithstanding the perpetuation of private ownership of production means.
2 It justified the egalitarian outlook by showing that increasing consumption
   among broad segments of the population stimulated economic growth.
3 It provided for a fast capital accumulation *and* reconciliation between
   entrepreneurs and workers.
4 It enabled governments – without disrupting the economic balance – to
   spend part of the social product on expanding social services.

Capitalism's unprecedented growth until the early 1970s, social
Keynesian policy's corresponding apparent 'fairness', and the cohesion of
social democratic networks generally ensured reasonable success for the social
democratic parties, despite their diverging fates.

The socio-economic factors responsible for social democracy's relative
success in its second stage eventually backfired. The extended and propi-
tious capital accumulation of the 1950s and 1960s dramatically altered
public regard for the operating environment of the parties, gradually at first
and then spectacularly from the early 1970s onward. At least five major
changes occurred:

1 Economic internationalisation, manifested by the continuously growing
   importance of cross-border trade, migration and capital transfers, reduced
   the control of national governments over their economies. Some years
   ago, Belgian social democratic minister Louis Tobback described the new
   situation as follows: 'Ministers no longer possess the instruments to define
   their national economies. We lack a hammer. We lack a sickle. We are
   even without a saw. Inside Belgium – or the Netherlands – interest rates
   are beyond our control. So is inflation. So are energy prices . . . Belgian
   ministers today have as little power as Antwerp's aldermen thirty years
   ago. While our hands are not entirely tied, our potential range of achievements is modest. We can distribute umbrellas against the rain and screens
   against the sun. We cannot, however, determine what the weather *will
   be*' (*Vrij Nederland*, 13 August 1994).
2 The declining, and in some cases even stagnant or briefly negative
   economic growth, which made its first worldwide post-war appearance
   during the oil crisis in 1973, considerably reduced the share of the social
   product available for redistribution. Decreasing tax revenues and increasing government spending gave rise to a fiscal crisis. As a result, painful
   cutbacks became inevitable within the system's logic.
3 The class composition in the highly developed capitalist countries
   changed: the 'traditional' working class's share in the labour force
   decreased progressively from the 1950s onward, while 'new' groups of
   wage dependants rapidly expanded.
4 Post-war capitalism brought about dramatic cultural shifts. In addition
   to a historically unique standard of living among large segments of the

wage-dependent population, the fast increase in purchasing power led to essential socio-cultural and psychological changes. An entirely new type of individualisation became apparent, women and young adults acquired a new awareness of their role in society, etc.
5 From the 1960s onward, the unforeseen and negative effects of the turbulent economic growth, such as the dramatic rise in pollution, gradually became more obvious.

These changes carried over to the social democratic parties: not at equal rates everywhere but nevertheless in a single direction. The socio-cultural and economic reversal toppled both 'pillars' of the social Keynesian stage, as the networks fell to pieces and social Keynesianism became less feasible.

The *social democratic networks* disintegrated because the affiliated organisations collapsed or became autonomous – a process that penetrated a variety of fields. The usual singing, drama, sports, and nature associations were forced into a losing battle against individualisation and the new popular culture; they lost touch with the younger generation, exchanged their traditional repertoire for more modern practices, or abandoned their direct association with the parties entirely. The recession also caused a rift between parties and trade unions.

This last observation leads to the second of the progressively collapsing pillars: *social Keynesianism*. From the mid-1970s onward, the old policy pursuing a 'top-down' redistribution lost much of its credibility. Although this list of problems was already quite impressive, more problems awaited: an entire series of *qualitative new political 'issues'* emerged, ranging from the democratisation movement and the protests by young adults to the second feminist wave and the environmental issue. These new themes – obviously sources of tremendous concern and insecurity in other established political movements as well – revealed a field of problems for which no convincing answers were available. One example of social democracy's helplessness is the rise of the 'green' political movements, which often involved extremely tense relations between adherents to the different ideologies.

All these changes are interrelated. The medical term for the pattern is a syndrome, which comprises a collection of concurrent symptoms. The social democratic parties thus faced a great many challenges that had to be met more or less simultaneously. The parties were forced to maintain their reputation as social reformers despite the progressively diminishing policy scope for 'nice things and good deeds'. Traditional centralism had to be reconciled with basic democratic movements and feminism with the conventional androcentric culture. Moreover, the environmental movement needed to be taken seriously without abandoning the pursuit of economic growth (the condition for social redistribution in a capitalist context).

In addition to this need to reconcile the myriad conflicting interests, the changed party culture complicated efforts to draft a coherent strategy. This aspect surfaced both in the erosion of the traditional individual network and in internal party relationships. Overall, the bond between the rank and file and the parties weakened. The remarks quoted above regarding the reduced dedication among the 'regular members' reflect this trend. Another indication is the tremendous increase in the group of voters floating its loyalties from one party to another. The ageing membership is also relevant. Finally, the decreasing number of members offers a clue: while the decline in some countries (e.g. Denmark) started in the 1960s, with other countries following much later (e.g. Sweden from 1984 onward), the trend is universal. Moreover, the influence of the proletarian members has virtually disappeared; they account for fewer than ever of the participants in branch meetings and are rarely represented in the party's upper echelons any more.

Little wonder that the tremendous weight of all these problems has given rise to widespread dissent and insecurity within social democracy. The parties are undeniably undergoing a second metamorphosis. They are progressively abandoning the stage of reform parties with worker support and are assiduously searching for a new identity.

Now, let me come back to my original question. It was precisely during the second metamorphosis, that the worldwide expansion of the Socialist International took off. Several authors have pointed out that the 1970s were characterised by a peculiar political conjuncture (Mujal-Léon and Nilsson, 1995: chs 1 and 2; Seidelmann, 1983; Vellinga, 1993):

- both the USA and the USSR had lost much of their credit on the left (Vietnam, Czechoslovakia, etc.);
- the Cuban model had got stuck;
- the rise of Eurocommunism facilitated a *rapprochement* between some communist and social democratic parties;
- Social Keynesianism still seemed to work;
- and Social Democracy had supported the struggle against military dictatorship in Latin America and elsewhere.

But these observations are only small pieces of the puzzle. After all, most of the parties which joined the SI after 1976 did not fit the organisation's old profile. Before the mid-1970s nobody would have considered ex-guerilla movements like the Popular Movement for the Liberation of Angola (MPLA), and the Sandinista National Liberation Front (FSLN), or the autocratic Democratic Action in Venezuela as Social Democratic parties (Levitsky, 2003: 235–6). Such organisations could *only* find a home within the SI, because the SI's profile was fading. Alex Fernandez Jilberto has rightly observed, that the SI's growth

> has neither generated truly social democratic parties of the past, nor created new ones . . . What did take place was the linking of Latin American parties and movements, whose political natures could not be defined as social

democratic, to the Socialist International. This includes populist currents as well as national parties and movements of an anti-imperialist and anticapitalist definition. (Fernández Jilberto, 1993: 169)

Naturally, the SI itself has seen this clearly. That is why the adoption of a new 'Declaration of Principles' at the Eighteenth Congress in Stockholm in 1989 was so important. This declaration acknowledges the existence of 'differences' in members' 'cultures and ideologies', but emphasises at the same time that the SI's core values (peace, freedom, justice and solidarity) 'originate in the labour movement, popular liberation movements, cultural traditions of mutual assistance, and communal solidarity in many parts of the world' (www.socialistinternational.org/4Principles).

Our conclusion has to be a paradox: the Socialist International could only grow so dramatically, *because* the classical social democratic parties were in a deep identity crisis.

References

Fernández Jilberto, Alex (1993). 'Internationalization and Social Democratization of Politics in Chile', in Menno Vellinga (ed.), *Social Democracy in Latin America: Prospects for Change* (Boulder: Westview Press), 163–85.

Levitsky, Steven (2003). *Transforming Labor-based Parties in Latin America: Argentine Peronism in Comparative Perspective* (Cambridge: Cambridge University Press).

Linden, Marcel van der (2003). *Transnational Labour History: Explorations* (Aldershot: Ashgate).

Mujal-León, Eusebio and Ann-Sofie Nilsson (1995). *Die Sozialistische Internationale in den 80er Jahren: Dritte-Welt-Politik zwischen den Blöcken* (Paderborn: Ferdinand Schöningh).

Pirker, Theo (1984). 'Vom "Ende der Arbeiterbewegung"', in Rolf Ebbighausen and Friedrich Tiemann (eds), *Das Ende der Arbeiterbewegung in Deutschland?* (Opladen: Westdeutscher Verlag), 39–51.

Seidelmann, Raimund (1983). 'Le renouveau de l'Internationale Socialiste (1972–1981)', in Hugues Portelli (ed.), *L'Internationale Socialiste* (Paris: Les Editions Ouvrières), 101–36.

Vellinga, Menno (1993). 'The Internationalization of Politics and Local Response: Social Democracy in Latin America', in Menno Vellinga (ed.), *Social Democracy in Latin America: Prospects for Change* (Boulder: Westview Press), 3–20.

3

Missing in action: the New Deal legacy in American politics

Norman Birnbaum

Introduction

As Europe in the 1930s struggled with depression and fascism, the United States was a source of hope. Auden's 'low dishonest decade' was less low, less dishonest, in the United States. I grew up in New Deal New York. We were aware of the terrors actual and impending in Europe, of the flagrant injustice of much of our own national life. Still, we had a sense of battles joyfully joined, of solidarity in a new politics. Franklin Roosevelt, with his robust imagery, his biting contempt for greed and reaction, his rejection of fear and passivity, was our charismatic leader. The patrician New Yorker led Catholics, Jews socially engaged Protestants and secular modernists in a common effort to reclaim radical republicanism. Thousands of activists in the government agencies and millions in social movements struggled to achieve New Deal reforms.

The New Deal was the result of fifty years of social thought, institutional experimentation, and political mobilisation. It had three major currents. The Progressives, middle-class reformers repelled by the corruption and vulgarity of late nineteenth- and early twentieth-century capitalism, were attentive to the social achievements of imperial Germany and Lloyd George's United Kingdom. With their President, Theodore Roosevelt, they instituted regulation of the market and an American welfare state. They co-existed ambivalently with the Populists, strong in the west and south amongst farmers opposed to metropolitan capital's control of credit, transport and markets. The Progressives concentrated on reform of the expanding urban society that the Populists distrusted. They were mainly northern European Protestants distant from the new urban working class of recent immigrants – many of them Catholic. The urban social movements were divided. Socialists of European inspiration were allied with homegrown radicals. The urban Catholics supported social reforms but abjured socialism. The trade unions concentrated on immediate gains in the workplace.

Woodrow Wilson's wartime government of 1917 and 1918 temporarily stilled these conflicts. The trade unions collaborated with capital and the intelligentsia served as bureaucrats and propagandists. The technocratic tendencies of American social reform were greatly reinforced. The war also made possible the near destruction of the socialist movement – which opposed it. Henceforth, American expansionism would be inextricably connected to American social reform. Franklin Roosevelt served in the Wilson government as an Assistant Secretary of the Navy. Like his elder cousin, he was later Governor of New York – a state which functioned as a laboratory of social reform. Franklin Roosevelt was an anti-imperialist with a conviction of US culpability in the western hemisphere. The New Dealers evinced a sense of American world mission all the more acute because of their own social ascent in the nation. The New Deal involved a continuous alternation between the reconstruction of the domestic social order and geopolitical and ideological engagement abroad in the rest of the world. That it was transmuted into the theory and practice of a warfare-welfare state is not the least of our national tragedies.

The New Deal began in 1933 with emergency support programmes in the Depression. Its subsequent legislation included Social Security (old age and disability pensions), the Wagner Act, which facilitated unionisation, and Federal supervision of banking, commerce, and the stock market. There were major public works projects (dams, waterways, urban infra-structure) and programmes of price support and technical aid for agriculture. In 1938 a counter-attack (by both Republicans and southern Democrats) brought its forward movement to an end.

The New Deal in the decades that followed legitimated economic intervention by Federal and state government. As the nation urbanised, the New Deal brought city dwellers (many offspring of immigration from Europe) into the centre of American politics. New Deal jurisprudence, the work of the legal realists, undermined doctrines of 'Freedom Of Contract' which reified capitalist power. New Deal culture was radical populism. Its ethos of social experiment provided space for modernism. (Chaplin, a New Dealer, combined both, and *Casablanca* was a product of New Deal internationalism.)

The New Deal empowered a greatly expanded union movement. An intelligentsia (economists, historians, lawyers, political scientists, social policy experts, publicists, writers) in and out of government gave it intellectual substance. The New Deal anticipated the black and feminist movements of the 1960s by the widening of legal and social possibility in the 1930s and 1940s. The war of 1941–45 brought full employment. Later forced out, women entered the labour force in large numbers. Black militancy won Afro-Americans access to industrial employment. Price controls and rationing induced some distributive equality. Unions gained members and a share of governance of the war economy. Mixing across ethnic and regional (if not racial) lines expressed the New Deal's idea of one nation. An undertone of American millennialism hardened later into the imperialist triumphalism of the Cold War. The intelligentsia, aware of its indispensability, became more open to collaboration with capital. The capitalists learned that there was an alternative to demonisation of the state: its colonisation in capital's interests.

In the post-war decades, capitalists initially accepted Keynesian investment responsibilities and a social contract, a rising standard of living for a nation of consumers. Governmental policies greatly enlarged home ownership. A new middle-class labour force was created by a university scholarship programme for returning members of the armed services. National health insurance, however, failed of enactment. Systematically, organised capital used the Republican Party and a large segment of the Democrats (particularly but not exclusively the southern ones) to contain New Deal initiatives – and to prepare for an eventual return to the sovereignty of the market. The highest echelons of capital were quite capable of pursuing this design while compromising or temporising with the extant New Deal forces.

With the internationalist segments of American capital, the New Dealers initiated the Cold War. In the new consumer's republic, it had something for everybody: chauvinist frenzy for the primitives, doctrines of American exceptionalism for many, and millennial tasks, paid in earthly coin, for the intelligentsia. Arms production was a permanent Keynesian stimulus in the domestic economy, and the dominant American role in international financial institutions extended the domestic class compromise abroad. Occupation officials in Germany and Japan, and administrators of the Marshall Plan in Europe were predominantly New Dealers. A minority opposed the militarised internationalism of anti-Communism, but they were defeated in the domestic persecution of Communists or those designated as such. The American Communist Party in the 1930s and early 1940s, strong in the cultural industry and the unions, was part of the left wing of the New Deal. Its elimination was used to delegitimate much of the New Deal tradition itself – not Stalinism but social democracy.

How much of the New Deal's moral energies were expressed through an American version of social realism, a narrative in which the people (good) confronted capitalists (evil)? Roosevelt described his adversaries as 'economic royalists', evoking the American Revolution. Certainly in its iconography and serial narrative structure, much of the art of the New Deal period owed more to Dickens and Zola than to Joyce or Mann. Yet the sense of new possibility of the New Deal also encouraged modernism. The great American cultural review of mid-century, *Partisan Review*, sought to reconcile modernism and Marxism. In the post-war period, the proponents of high culture abjured social realism as philistine. More recently, academic students of mass culture have reinterpreted it as actually or potentially critical of society.

The religious groups allied politically in the New Deal now confront each other as adversaries. The Protestant Evangelicals and Fundamentalists who were originally populists, the Protestant modernists of Progressivism,

argue over how much of Enlighenment culture to accept. If fitfully champ
pioning the workers who were its members, American Catholicism is
divided between its traditionalist and reformist segments. The millennial
drives of Judaism contributed much to the New Deal. The very integration
of the Jewish community as well as guilt and horror at the Holocaust have
made support for Israel the major preoccupation of many American Jews.
In the 1930s and 1940s, a largely religious nation set aside its theological
quarrels to bring the Kingdom of Heaven on earth somewhat nearer. For
the past decades, however, the separate American faiths agree that the United
States is so close to sacredness as to render its deficiencies secondary.

Now, there is no one American nation but a kaleidoscope of ethnic,
generational, regional, racial and religious perspectives. What has been lost
is what Dos Passos portrayed, the nation itself. There is a parallel between
art and the use of focus groups to generate electoral strategies: no one thinks
a general narrative applies. The single most important American contribution
to world culture, jazz, was born in the tormented depths of the nation.
It is impossible to say the same of the post-war productions of film, television, music. They are designed for specific segments of the market, or
vacuously generalised for a broad market. They usually reproduce the appear-
ances of everyday life and purposefully avoid going beneath the surface.
There have been critical films and television dramas – which touch nerves
precisely because they refer to conflicts in the public's ken. So much denial
is cultivated in the products of the cultural industry, that even an approx-
imation of reality is radical. The culture of the New Deal, in films and
novels and theatre, did show open struggles against wealth and power. Some
film directors and novelists still do, just as there are still plenty of radical
social scientists in the universities. Both groups have been marginalised. The
partners of the entertainment entrepreneurs in their willed frivolity are the
conservative intellectuals in their seriousness. For each, the New Deal vision
of social transformation has been replaced by defence of the prosperity and
power in which they share.

The intellectuals are not alone in having an altered vision. The great wave
of unionisation under the New Deal was the work of men and women
engaged in a larger project of social reconstruction. The high wages and
job security in the unionised industries, their social benefits, reconciled the
working class with capital. The unionists largely voted for the Democrats
until 1952. Dwight Eisenhower in his 1952 and 1956 campaigns made
inroads into trade union voting blocs, and Nixon in 1968 and 1972 and
later Reagan in 1980 and 1988 widened the opening. Racial conflict was
one cause of the shift, and a rejection of the 1960s protest movement was
another. The unions, and an American social democratic project, already
suffered three great defeats in the early post-war period. In 1947 the
Republican majority in Congress (and Democrats allied to capital) replaced
New Deal legislation which facilitated union organising with a law which

made it much more difficult. The unions' efforts to organise the south failed, in part because of southern whites' fears of wage equality for blacks. The south became the destination of choice for American firms seeking cheaper labour – and the asocial nature of the entire political climate there was reinforced. Finally, the most forceful and reflective of American unionists, Walter Reuther of the United Automobile Workers, failed to obtain a share for workers in the governance of the larger automobile firms, making an American version of co-determination impossible.

The unions then concentrated on maximising benefits and wages, on struggles for some control of the work process. They collaborated with management in imposing very demanding workloads. The unions did raise the standard of living of an appreciable segment of the American labour force (at the time of the Johnson Presidency, a third of American workers were unionised.) The unions were the strongest advocates, within the Democratic Party, of a social wage – universal health insurance, decent levels of unemployment and disability insurance – and of public investment. They educated their members, politically: states with unionists were the strongholds of American social democracy. That much said, they accepted an idea of the US as a republic of consumption, in which citizenship gave way to an economic definition of social personality. In a Darwinian society, the unions did what they could to strengthen the capacity of their members to conduct the struggle.

The United States from 1973 onward entered a period of de-industrialisation, and increasing inequality. The large industrial unions were forced onto the defensive. An increase in unionisation amongst public service workers and in education did not stem the decline in unionisation. Unions have since 1953 lost two-thirds of their effectives. No union represents even half the workers in any one industry. Only 9 per cent of private-sector workers are unionised; some 16 per cent of public sector workers are organised. Meanwhile, American workers work longer hours than their European counterparts, enjoy far less vacation time, and have far less access to public goods.

In this desperate situation, the leadership of the AFL-CIO passed in 1995 to John Sweeney, who has a large attachment to Catholic social doctrine, and an acute appreciation of the ravages of American economic Calvinism. Sweeney has a long-term strategy, its central element the retention of the Presidency and Congressional majorities by the Democrats – so that the state would once again aid unionisation. The failure of his political strategy has accentuated the continuing decline in union numbers and influence. It is difficult, however, to see what other strategy would have had success. Now the union movement has fractured, with a large faction insisting that organising in the service sectors (from which jobs cannot be exported) has priority. Whether this strategy will alter the balance of forces in the labour market is a very open question.

The United States is a nation in which movements of social protest often erupt, alter the course of history, and can then be found only in history texts. Perhaps the very heterogenous and loose alliance of groups protesting capitalist models of globalisation will constitute the next vanguard of American radicalism. They, and the unions, have made 'free trade' a political issue – with immense help from the unashamedly rapacious behaviour of American capital. Under Clinton, this alliance achieved a notable political victory, blocking Congressional ratification of the Multilateral Trading Agreement.

Some of the leaders of the American organisations opposing capitalist globalisation were, when younger, activists of the 1960s. Then, they held that the New Deal had been deformed into 'corporate liberalism' and were particularly enraged with Franklin Roosevelt's protege, Lyndon Johnson, and his Vice President, Hubert Humphrey. The social achievements of the Great Society did not for them outweigh the moral and social costs of the Vietnam war. Still, George McGovern had been a professorial specialist on the agricultural policies of the New Deal, and Jimmy Carter recalled electricity being brought to his family's farm by a New Deal agency. Meanwhile, Edward Kennedy remains a permanent witness to the tradition in his forty-year Senate struggle for an American welfare state, and a relatively rational foreign and military policy. A new generation of black legislators led by veterans of the civil rights movement entered the Congress, and more recently, a group of Congresswomen and Senators have sought redistribution and social regulation. It took Kennedy decades (well into the eight years of the Clinton Presidency) to obtain a modest increase in the statutory minimum wage. There is a division of labour: the social movements act in the public sphere, the New Deal's legislative heirs struggle in government itself.

Nothing has so haunted the US public sphere for the past generation as the memory of the movements of the 1960s. The black struggle for civil rights was almost entirely black until repression in the segregationist states of the south mobilised a party of conscience amongst whites there and in the rest of the nation. The decision of the Supreme Court abolishing segregation in 1954 was the culmination of a half century of struggle by the black community itself. The black churches are the bearers of black historical consciousness, expressed in biblical imagery.

Dependent upon the Democratic white vote in the segregationist states, where blacks did not vote, Franklin Roosevelt feared for the entire New Deal programme were he to move against segregation. So great was the New Deal paralysis on race relations that he accepted the initial exclusion of agricultural and domestic labour from the Social Security system – insisted upon by southern white legislators fearful of black economic independence. The demand for labour in the northern factories after the outbreak of war in 1941 initially was of no help to black workers, who had migrated from the south in search of employment. The black leaders threatened Roosevelt with a march on Washington and he barred Federal contracts for firms refusing to employ blacks. Later, under Truman, Kennedy and Johnson, measures to ensure equal rights were frequently justified as indispensable to the standing of the US in the struggle against Communism. Truman (opposed by the then Chief of Staff, Dwight Eisenhower) desegregated the armed forces – which have since functioned as an institution of integration for black citizens.

Truman left the Presidency in 1953, and Eisenhower held it for eight years thereafter. Truman as a Senator was a considerable antagonist of the power of the large corporations. John Kennedy left his Massachusetts Senate seat to become President in 1961, a child of the New Deal. His father had been Roosevelt's first Wall Street regulator. He was especially suited for the post as a financial pirate himself – and, as a Catholic, especially antagonistic to the Protestant club that was Wall Street. John Kennedy understood that the white working class was his electoral base – and was very reluctant (for fear of losing votes in the south) to take up the cause of black rights. The rhetoric of the New Frontier ('Ask not what your country can do for you, but what you can do for your country') was intended to apply to the US world role. Many younger Americans supposed it meant that they had tasks of domestic social reform. By the end of his presidency, having saved the world from destruction by ignoring the advice of the Cold War managers, in the Cuban missile crisis, Kennedy turned to domestic matters. What might have become of his presidency is a matter of speculation. The Vice President who succeeded him in 1963, Lyndon Johnson, was despite the catastrophe of Vietnam, a great domestic reformer.

In his Great Society programme he sought to make good the deficiencies of the New Deal itself. His remark as he signed the Civil Rights Act of 1964, that the white south would be lost to the Democrats indefinitely is invariably cited. The enormous pressure of protest apart, Johnson himself grew up in abysmal poverty. Whatever the balance of conscience and calculation in his decision (if the white south was lost, the black south and blacks elsewhere were won), he was a New Deal traditionalist in making benefits universal. The Civil Rights Act benefited by extension children, Latinos, welfare recipients, and women. Johnson initiated medical insurance for elderly citizens and the impoverished – again, universal measures. He began a very large programme of Federal aid to schools. Johnson's War On Poverty had been anticipated, in fact, by Kennedy – influenced by an American socialist of Catholic theological origins, Michael Harrington. It was Johnson, however, who funded it generously. He was, in his belief in the socially constructive powers of government, the last New Dealer.

The other category of Americans whose situation had not been directly improved by the New Deal was women. Roosevelt appointed the first woman cabinet member, Secretary Perkins at the Labor Department. Mrs Eleanor

Roosevelt was an omnipresent champion of the excluded, impoverished, neglected and oppressed. The New Deal generated torrents of activism. Just as the labour movement of the 1930s originated in the struggles of the unions earlier in the century, the women leaders of the New Deal epoch looked back to the battles for suffrage and economic and social protection. The dominant figure of the New Deal epoch remained, however, the white male worker and head of family. The wartime male labour shortage opened opportunities: many women developed a self-sufficiency denied by traditionalised gender concepts. They were sent home after the war. Women's employment gradually increased, but in lower paying jobs. The unions insisted that the standard wage should be sufficient to support an entire family and were opposed to measures which would grant women formal equality in the labour market. The complaints of educated women excluded from managerial and professional careers contrasted with the sufferings of tens of millions of their working-class sisters employed under conditions of discrimination in wages, harassment and insults to their dignity. The unions did do something to remedy the situation, but where women workers were in a minority position amongst unionised males, they were not spared culturally legitimated abasement. Lyndon Johnson's Civil Rights Act of 1964 provided the legal basis for active intervention by the Federal government to enforce rights for women. Since then, more women than men voters have supported Democrats in national elections – until 2004.

In the period since Lyndon Johnson's Presidency, the Republicans have held the White House for some twenty-five years (Nixon and Ford, 1969–77, Ronald Reagan, 1981–89, George Bush Sr, 1989–2003, George Bush, Jr, 2001 to date: 2006) and the Democrats for twelve (Carter, 1977–89, Clinton, 1993–2001). The Senate has had Republican majorities from 1981 to 1987 and from 1995 to 2001 and again from 2003 to date. The House has had a Republican majority since 1995. In this period, the Democratic majorities were reduced from year to year. Equally, the Republicans in the period gradually won a majority of Governorships, majorities in a majority of state legislatures, and occasional mayoralties in Democratic strongholds, the larger cities. Entire areas of the nation (much of the white south, and the far west, and many of the metropolitan suburbs on the east and west coasts) became permanently Republican. Democrats in more closely contested districts or states frequently took their distances from the traditions of the New Deal. Those who remained loyal to it acted to defend the immediate interests of their constituents. When small Democratic majorities in the House and Senate faced Republican Presidents, the latter could count on conservative Democrats to achieve their legislative programmes. Democratic Congressional majorities blocked repugnant federal agency, cabinet or judicial appointments. They traded their budgetary powers, usually, for limited goals of great importance to their voters: educational, health and welfare benefits. That made it possible for the adversaries of the welfare state to claim, with some plausibility, that its 'entitlements' were inflexible. The proponents of the welfare state were unable to advance new projects. They had to expend their political capital warding off efforts to dismantle what had already been achieved.

No Republican President, before the present incumbent, was more disliked by the Democrats than Richard Nixon. Still, Nixon actually enlarged the Great Society and the role of government as an agent of redistribution. His innovations included revenue sharing, by which the Federal government turned funds over to the states for specified programmes – a move which integrated the functions of the Federal state with the workings of the state governments in ways unattainable by the early New Dealers.

Reagan voted for Franklin Roosevelt four times, and as a leader of the Screen Actors' union, joined the iconic figures of the New Deal tradition in 1947 to found the most prominent lay movement in the New Deal church, Americans for Democratic Action. He abandoned his beliefs in the benign functions of government, to replace them with faith in the efficiency and justice of the market in a society of responsible individuals. The anti-Communism of the Cold War and shock, more real than feigned, at the rejection of American society by its favoured children in the students' revolt completed his ideological conversion. When he came to Washington as President, he had been Governor of the nation's largest state, California, and had wrested it from the Democrats by mobilising the fears of newly prosperous citizens. Like Thatcher, he insisted on deregulation of the market, but he installed in the Federal state a generation of colonisers whose aim was a symbiosis between capital, state and society.

New Deal liberals and radicals complained of the intellectual counter-offensive of the right, designated neo-conservatism. It had several distinct elements. One was an unapologetic eulogy for American power, closely connected to the assertion of the superiority of the American model of society. This supposedly consisted of autonomous citizens integrated in the institutions of civil society: family, neighbourhood, church. American religion assumed the importance attributed to it by President Eisenhower, who declared that every citizen ought to have a religion – and that he did not care what it was. The promulgation of these ideas was entrusted to an ideological cottage industry with quite exceptional capacities for growth. The production of books and journals, the staffing of centres of research and university departments, the disbursement of fellowships and grants, editorial posts and writing assignments in major magazines and newspapers, and posts in Republican governments, constituted careers open to many talents. The American intelligentsia, in the Cold War, had shown its acute sense of opportunity in accepting covert funding from the CIA for its contributions to the struggle of a free and plural society against state socialism. As the Cold War wound down, the next generation (some figures provided a familial connection between the generations) showed that it too could sell its talents on the cultural market. One of the strengths of neo-conservatism was that it drew very able recruits from those raised in the New Deal tradition. Some, in their youth, had even been socialists.

A note of triumphalism was marked in Catholics and Jews who had grown up as outsiders, but who now found themselves with elite status. Perhaps this was what accounted for an acerbic tone when the new ideologues confronted the nation's older social critics. They were dismissed as hopeless pessimists or fanatic utopians – or both – because of their explicit belief that the US was exceptional only in its wildly exaggerated selfcongratulation. Their alleged addiction to arcane and senseless doctrines and methods (deconstruction, multi-culturalism, neo-Marxism, structuralism) – especially suspect because imported in some cases from France – was evidence of their utter failure of rootedness. In time, the attitude generated grotesque episodes like the criticism of an exhibition at the Museum of American History in Washington, because it intimated that the conquest of the American west was accompanied by a certain amount of environmental destruction, ethnic cleansing, and economic exploitation. These ideologies were also voiced inside the Democratic Party.

A schematic image of a typical (white male) Democratic voter was constructed and critics were instructed that to fail to acknowledge his sensibilities was a form of elitism. That the stereotype recalled no one as much as Archie Bunker, the prejudiced and stupid anti-hero of the television series *All In The Family* was not, it seemed, snobbery but an expression of moral solidarity with the American working class. From the 1960s onward, three inter-connected streams of debate agitated and divided the Democrats. The first was broadly cultural: could a party espousing a pluralist and secular conception of American life mobilise voters who were deeply religious and who had little or no tolerance for feminism, homosexual rights and modernism generally? The second was economic: the Democrats as a party of redistribution was depicted as the representative of parasitic groups whose values were not shared by those Americans who were hard working. 'Tax and spend' was a charge levelled at the Democrats by the Republicans, There was no point to objecting that educational and social investment were important – if ordinary citizens, like the Californians who joined the tax revolt that ruined that state's ability to pay for public services, thought first of all of their own incomes and not in larger terms. The third argument concerned the necessity for the nation to be 'strong' in terms of military resources and the readiness to use them. Distinctions were made, but they were not always luminously consistent. Democrats willing to accept US sponsorship of the Pinochet regime in Chile were eloquent advocates of putting maximum pressure on the USSR to obtain freedom of emigration for Soviet Jewry.

These contradictions racked the party in the period of the Nixon–Ford governments, and when Watergate proved too much for the American electorate, an unprepared Governor of Georgia, Jimmy Carter, became President. He was a southern Christian, given to using a moral language (quite effective when as Governor he rejected Georgia's legacy of racial segregation). That did not protect the party from the systematic attacks of the Republicans portraying it as anti-Christian (a phrase often offered spontaneously in contemporary interviews with supporters of the present President, viewed as 'a good Christian'). As the deferred bill for the Vietnam war became due, as deindustrialisation proceeded at a rapid rate, as the foreign trade deficit increased, his government was charged with responsibility for both inflation and unemployment. Lacking a coherent economic strategy, he turned to the financial elite. The presence of a Wall Streeter at the Treasury or at the head of the Federal Reserve offers reassurance that Democrats will not take redistribution or economic planning seriously. (John Kenneth Galbraith as John Kennedy's former Harvard tutor and campaign adviser was sent ten thousand miles from Washington to serve as Ambassador in New Delhi – and a Republican was made Kennedy's Secretary of the Treasury.) The third problem for Carter was his inability to decide what to do about the empire. A former naval officer (on submarines equipped with nuclear weapons), he was inclined to seek a different American relationship to the world. That was the view of his Secretary of State, Cyrus Vance, but not of his National Security Adviser, Zbigniew Brzezinski. He had, therefore, two foreign policies. Vance resigned after his advice not to undertake the disastrous Iran hostage rescue mission was ignored. Brzezinski succeeded in igniting a war between the USSR and the Islamists in Afghanistan and so gave us the Taliban. The miseries of the domestic economy and the embarrassment of the hostage situation in Teheran so undermined Carter that he lost to Reagan. Senator Edward Kennedy had attempted to replace him as the party's candidate, but the Democrats feared his person and policies even more than they disliked Carter.

By the end of the Carter Presidency, most of the elements of our current situation were visible. One is the systematic ignorance, inauthentic chauvinism, and total servility to corporate capitalism of the media. The intelligentsia and the university are divided, and those who think the US can be changed for the better are increasingly remote from politics. So far from being 'liberal', the American synonym for leftist modernism, the universities are in fact ruled by technocrats like the President of Harvard, Lawrence Summers.

Meanwhile, in the larger society, the idyllic picture of middle-class life defended by the ideologues of American contentment is falsified by the inner and outer travails of: depression and familial conflict, alcoholism and drug addiction, and of course economic insecurity. Church and family are unable to bear the strains of a privatised society. In the upper-middle reaches of society, psychotherapy, self-help groups, and the cults of personal growth are responses to the commodification of existence. Below that, in many of the churches which draw one of two or six of ten Americans to weekly services, apocalyptic imagery provides narratives which purport to make sense of history. How much of American life is lived in private hells is unclear – but to judge by demand for surcease, these hells abound. The familiar picture of the division of the US into two cultural blocs, modernist and traditionalist, is excessively simplified but there is something to it, especially if we acknhowledge that each of the blocs is peopled by very troubled humans with not much energy for actual citizenship.

The absurd notion of American middle-class normalcy was the dominant ideology when Governor Dukakis of Massachusetts opposed Reagan's Vice President, George Bush Sr, in 1988 for the Presidency. Dukakis began by saying: 'This election is not about ideology, it is about competence.' When very late in the campaign he evoked issues of redistribution, of social investment and social benefits, he made large gains – too late to win. Opposing factions of Democrats drew opposite conclusions from his defeat. Some argued that Dukakis was hopelessly compromised by the party's record of 'weakness' in foreign policy – a fictive concept brandished by the Democratic proponents of confrontation with the Soviet Union to beat down their inner party opponents, and used by the Republicans to delegitimate the entire party. Others argued that Dukakis, since he came from Massachusetts, represented the wrong values – exemplified by the fact that his wife admitted that she had been treated for depression. Dukakis was also charged with having presided over a prison system which released a man who subsequently murdered someone, and a black man at that. The New Deal Democrats argued that they had almost won, that many segments of the electorate if not immune to issues like abortion and the death penalty were more interested in obtaining economic benefits and social protection and thought that only government could help them. The party could not agree on a common denominator.

Bill Clinton in his electoral campaigns was aided by a split in the potential Republican vote caused by the candidacies in 1992 and 1996 of the eccentric millionaire, Ross Perot. Clinton was a southerner and a Christian, but these characteristics endeared him more to blacks, with whom he had a special rapport, than to southern whites. It is difficult to say what his basic convictions were. He was as President much more intellectual than any predecessors since Wilson, he had an instinctive grasp of the limits of the office in a period in which change was difficult to articulate, let alone master. He was greatly helped by the sordid tactics of the Republicans in the matter of his sexual conduct, especially since the Republican leaders themselves were not obvious candidates for sainthood. Their failure to oust him was hardly a permanent defeat for the late model Puritans. Bush has combined theological rhetoric and federal subsidies of the churches to great electoral effect.

The unstable mixture of class alignment, and cultural choice of modern American politics became especially pronounced in the Clinton years and is with us still. The Republicans are dominant in the south and parts of the west, in many of the suburban areas elsewhere too, and apart from the proprietors and senior employees of capital, include small businessmen, a large number of persons for whom their church identity is important, gun owners, anti-tax fanatics, exponents of traditional gender roles and (especially important in the US) persons rendered uncomfortable by both heterosexuality and homosexuality. The Republicans can count upon those who regard questioning the statement 'ours is the greatest nation on earth' as close to treason, or at least pathological rootlessness. Latinos, environmentalists, feminists, unionists, and the smaller and less organised advocates of a demilitarised and anti-imperialist foreign policy join the black churches and community organisations in backing the Democrats, who also win the support of the public interest organisations of the best educated part of the electorate. The Republicans, with more and denser ties to capital, can generally outspend Democrats in elections by a ratio of two or three to one. The Democrats are not inclined to practice voluntary poverty, however, and their own excellent connections to the cultural industry, financial capital and retailing enable them to raise very large sums of money.

Two additional points are important. With electoral participation usually at only 50 per cent (40 per cent in Congressional election years when the Presidency is not at stake) the influence of particular interest groups and lobbies is all the greater. Since what counts in the presidential election are electoral votes won state by state and not national vote totals (Gore had more votes than Bush, but still lost), national campaigns on national themes are very difficult. The other point is that any important issues of the role of the state are left to the courts to decide. We have experienced a judicialisation of politics, making struggles over the nomination and approval of Federal judges in the Senate that much more important.

The Democrats' alliances with Wall Street, rather than any serious ventures in historical and political analysis, accounted for the eagerness with which Clinton and the somewhat more ambivalent Al Gore (the son, after all, of a New Deal contemporary of Lyndon Johnson and John Kennedy in the Senate) embraced the doctrines of the Third Way. In the Democrats' case, this entailed the adoption of the view that budget deficits were intrinsically bad and that as a consequence, social spending had to be curtailed. It also meant a vague ideology of 'personal responsibility', particularly applied to impoverished recipients of social assistance – obliged to work to qualify for welfare. The ensuing bargain with Wall Street and the Chair of the Federal Reserve Bank, Greenspan (whose fiscal rigour disappeared with a Republican President in office and his own re-appointment in the balance) led to low rates of interest. This in turn enabled tens of millions of householders to re-finance their homes at lower rates and to use the gains for consumer expenditures. Combined with a boom in technology, the increase in household debt led to a rise in the price of equities, which added to what was a speculative bubble. It is true that millions of jobs were created under Clinton, but large social needs (in education, health, infrastructure) continued unmet. Clinton did attempt a reform of health insurance – but not by instituting a single-payer system which would have eliminated the swollen administrative costs and profits of the private sector. The project was defeated (Hillary Clinton, who was in charge of it, told me that she was deeply disappointed at the way in which the large insurance corporations broke the terms of a political bargain the White Hoiuse had negotiated with them). The Democrats had no coherent ideological and political defence against the onslaught of the Republicans. The Presidency passed with a good deal of argument between Clinton and the New Democrats and the trade unions and the New Deal remnant on 'free trade'.

A Democratic Presidency, even when Republicans control both chambers of the Congress, makes a difference. At the very least, certain things do not happen. Environmental and labor laws, social legislation of all kinds, are not eviscerated by administrative action or inaction. Extremely important in the US system, where the Federal Appeals Courts and the Supreme Court act as political instances, entirely reactionary judges are not appointed; sometimes judges with a reasonable social conscience make it to the bench. A US President appoints, initially, some four thousand officials to policy making posts: under the Democrats, some of these (younger as well as older) think of themselves as in the New Deal tradition. The two major American political parties are each forced to unite, or pretend to unity, when contending for the Presidency. Still, even under a Democratic President, the House and Senate Democrats are sharply divided and responsive less to a central party ideology than to their own financial backers and constituencies. When Gore ran for President, he did so in utterly schizophrenic fashion – one day he was the son of a New Dealer, the next he was a New Democrat abjuring 'big government'. Despite that, a very considerable degree of mobilisation by blacks, environmentalists and trade unionists won him a majority of the votes. Why not? Polling studies conclude that despite the even division in the active electorate, a majority of all eligible voters consider that government has responsibility for minima of economic and social decency. Gore's defeat in the electoral college can be ascribed in some part to the 3 per cent of the vote he lost to the authentic antagonist of capital, Ralph Nader.

The United States is a continental nation; it is also an imperial power, the armed defender not only of its own geopolitical interests (which are, in the view of US imperial managers, limitless) but the ally, protector and sponsor of a quite striking variety of nations. The consolidation of democratic institutions and the observance of human rights are not the primary ends of US foreign policy. The US has sought stability, understood as an unerring constancy in alignment in questions large and small with the US – not least, access to cheap raw materials (as with oil) for the US and the opening of foreign markets (including financial markets and now, services) to US firms. There have been strenuous debates in the US on foreign policy since the 1950s, but only recently have some advocates of American power dared to state what many of its critics have thought obvious: the US world role entails a constant striving for hegemony. The Democrats have been at least as responsible for the US imperial position and the development of imperial structures as the Republicans. The dysfunctions of empire – deformations in resource allocation, the inequality of the risks of military service and in bearing the costs of domination, the encouragement of a chauvinistic idea of national superiority which is the direct successor of now embarassing ideas of Anglo-Saxon moral and racial virtue, the development of a corps of imperial bureaucrats and ideologues who live not for but from the US empire and are correspondingly unable to criticise its existence and working – are as visible under Democratic Presidents as under Republican ones. Theologically speaking, empire tempts Americans to indulge in the sin of pride. It is true that towards the end of his life, John Kennedy in his speech at American University in June of 1963 called for a reconsideration of, even an end, to the Cold War: that may have been connected to his assassination. America's development of a dualistic morality, in which the government and its agencies are allowed criminality of every kind outside US borders has been as much a part of the ethos of the Democratic party as of the Republicans. Worst of all, America's global involvements have been conducted in imperial structures which have merged with domestic ones to consolidate and deepen the democratic deficit of US institutions, as in the supreme disregard for constitutional liberties and the recognised norms of international law by the Bush government. The mobilisation of the society for tasks which reflection suggests it might be better off without, under the leadership of persons of a striking degree of authoritarianism and arrogance, are major sources of the attenuation of the New Deal legacy. Franklin Roosevelt was an internationalist: he would not have wished for the world the US has now made.

That is the world, however, that John Kerry supposed he could not change. His campaign against Bush tried to use the nation's scepticism about the President but the President was able to focus the nation's doubts on his challenger. Kerry made it easy for him by firmly taking all sides of major issues. The war in Iraq was a mistake, but he supported it and would conduct it more successfully. He was 'not a redistributionist' but somehow would protect average Americans from the impersonal savagery of the market. Kerry was supported by a considerable mobilisation by public groups and party factions which disagreed with him, but wanted Bush out. They succeeded in bringing their adherents to the polls, but the Republicans had even greater success with their tactics – emphasising Bush's 'steadiness' as opposed to

Kerry's fictive ambiguity in defending the nation. A majority, in fact, believed that the President's falsehoods about Iraqi weaponry and the purported alliance of Baathists and Al Qaida were true. The cultural divisions war within the US also worked in Bush's favour, helping him to win a majority amongst white males and eliminating previous Democratic gains with women voters. Despite a miserable campaign, administrative hindrances to voting by Democratic constituencies, and the problems suggested by electronic voting machines under supervision of local Republican authorities, Kerry did win 48 per cent of the vote. There remains a large potential bloc of voters favouring an American welfare state and distrustful of US imperial managers and the very idea of American empire. It remains to be seen if the class biases, corruption, dishonesty and incompetence and of the Republican White House and its Congressional majorities will so delegitimise the Republican project that the Democrats will turn to their past for inspiration. The grandchildren and great grandchildren of the New Deal will have to strike out on as yet unmapped roads to achieve its ends in very altered historical circumstances. First, they will have to wake from the moral amnesia which has rendered them so passive.

References

Bacevich, A. J. *The New American Militarism: How Americans Are Seduced by War.* Oxford University Press, Oxford and New York, 2005.

Birnbaum, Norman. *The Radical Renewal: The Politics of Ideas in Modern America.* Pantheon Books, New York, 1988.

Branch, Taylor. *Parting Waters: America in the King Years, 1954–1963.* Simon & Schuster, New York, 1988.

Branch, Taylor. *Pillar of Fire: America in the King Years, 1963–1965.* Simon & Schuster, New York, 1998.

Dallek, Robert. *Lone Star Rising: Lyndon Johnson and His Times, 1908–1960.* Oxford University Press, New York, 1991.

Dallek, Robert. *An Unfinished Life: John F. Kennedy, 1917–1963.* Little, Brown, and Co., Boston, 2003.

Dallek, Robert. *Lyndon B. Johnson: A Portrait of a President.* Oxford University Press, New York, 2004.

Dionne, E. J. *They Only Look Dead: Why Progressives Will Dominate the Next Political Era.* Simon & Schuster, New York, 1996.

Edsall, Thomas Byrne and Edsall, Mary D. *Chain Reaction: The Impact of Race, Rights, and Taxes on American Politics.* Norton, New York, 1991.

Fraser, Steve and Gerstle, Gary. *The Rise and Fall of the New Deal Order, 1930–1980.* Princeton University Press, Princeton, 1989.

Hacker, Jacob and Pierson, Paul. *Off Center: The Republican Revolution and the Erosion of American Democracy.* Yale University Press, New Haven, 2005.

Hoff, Joan. *Nixon Reconsidered.* Basic Books, New York, 1994.

Isserman, Maurice. *The Other American: The Life of Michael Harrington.* Public Affairs, New York, 2000.

Isserman, Maurice and Kazin, Michael. *America Divided: The Civil War of the 1960s.* Oxford University Press, New York, 2nd edn, 2004.

Kazin, Michael. *The Populist Persuasion.* Basic Books, New York, 1995.

Kennan, George. *American Diplomacy.* University of Chicago Press, Chicago, 1984.

Kennedy, David. *Freedom from Fear: The American People in Depression and War, 1929–1945.* Oxford University Press, New York, 1999.

Leuchtenburg, William Edward. *Franklin D. Roosevelt and the New Deal, 1932–1940.* Harper & Row, New York, 1963.

Lichtenstein, Nelson. *State of the Union: A Century of American Labor.* Princeton University Press, Princeton, 2002.

Matusow, Allen. *The Unravelling of America: A History of Liberalism in the 1960s.* Harper & Row, New York, 1984.

Mills, C. Wright. *The Power Elite.* Oxford University Press, New York, 1956.

Mills, C. Wright. *White Collar: The American Middle Classes.* Oxford University Press, New York, 50th anniversary edn, 2002.

Patterson, James. *Grand Expectations: The United States, 1945–1974.* Oxford University Press, New York, 1996.

Patterson, James. *Restless Giant: The United States from Watergate to Bush v. Gore.* Oxford University Press, Oxford and New York, 2005.

Pollin, Robert. *Contours of Descent: U.S. Economic Fractures and the Landscape of Global Austerity.* Verso, London and New York, 2003.

Schlesinger, Arthur Meier. *The Age of Roosevelt.* Houghton Mifflin, volumes 1, 2 and 3. Boston, 1957–60.

Schlesinger, Arthur Meier. *The Cycles of American History.* Houghton Mifflin, Boston, 1986.

Skocpol, Theda. *Diminished Democracy: From Membership to Management in American Civic Life.* University of Oklahoma Press, Norman, 2003.

Steinfels, Peter. *The Neoconservatives: The Men Who Are Changing America's Politics.* Simon & Schuster, New York, 1980.

Teixeira, Ruy and Judis, John. *The Emerging Democratic Majority.* Scribner, New York, 2002.

Williams, William Appleman. *The Contours of American History.* New Viewpoints, New York, 1973.

Wills, Garry. *Nixon Agonistes: The Crisis of the Self-Made Man.* New American Library, New York, updated and expanded edn, 1979.

Wills, Garry. *Reagan's America.* Penguin Books, New York, 1988.

4

Writing the comparative history of social democracy: a comparative look at Britain and Germany

Stefan Berger

Introduction

Any kind of history writing is always also a political act. What is being remembered and what is being forgotten has political implications. How something is remembered and in which way it is being written about has political consequences. The close relationship between politics and history writing is particularly evident in the case of social democracy. In what follows I would like to sketch a comparison of the evolution of the comparative historiography about social democracy in Britain and in Germany from its beginnings in the nineteenth century to the present day. After briefly describing the difficulties of labour historians in both countries in getting the subject the attention they thought it deserved, the essay outlines the breakthrough to an academically based historiography of social democracy. After the subject area blossomed in the 1960s and 1970s interest among historians began to decline in the 1980s. The turn to comparative history was one answer to this crisis. Has it been able to rekindle interest in the history of social democracy? Or is the history of social democracy also facing an irreversible decline at a time when social democracy, as we knew it for well over one hundred years, is said to have come to an end (Moschonas, 2002)?

Coming of age: the historiography of Social Democracy from the late nineteenth century to the 1960s

In the decade before the First World War social democratic mass parties had been successful in capturing the imagination and loyalty of European voters to varying degrees. German and Czech-speaking Central Europe and Scandinavia had the biggest and most successful social democratic parties in Europe, and the German Social Democratic Party (SPD) in particular was widely regarded as a model for others to emulate and follow (Nettl,

1965). German social democrats felt strongly that theirs was a historical movement meant to capture political power, end the toil and suffering of the working classes and bring about a fair and just society. Karl Marx and his historical materialism provided, in its Kautskyist variant, social democracy's rationale for existence.

Given the importance of history to the social democratic project it cannot be surprising that the earliest historians of social democracy came from within the social democratic movement. Eduard Bernstein wrote a history of social democracy as well as other historical works (Bernstein, 1893, 1910, 1930) and there were many other autodidacts in the party who tried their hand at history – preferably the history of their own movement. Max Beer (1921a), for example, wrote the history of the early socialist movement in Britain as well as a sketch about the life and teachings of Karl Marx (1921b). Beer worked as a journalist for the SPD's main daily newspaper, *Vorwärts*, in London before the war. There he knew most of the British social democrats who were divided into several different political groupings. The Labour Party, founded by some of these groupings in alliance with sections of the trade union movement in 1900–06, was successful in establishing itself electorally, although it found it difficult to develop a distinct left-of-centre profile against a reform-enthusiastic Liberal Party in the years preceding the Great War. The attitude of German social democrats towards the British Labour Party depended largely on the ideological stance of the observer: the reformist and revisionist wings of the SPD tended to admire the pragmatic and non-ideological character of the Labour Party while the more orthodox Marxist wing criticised Labour for not being committed to the theories of Marx and for not possessing a body of theory and a sense of its historical mission. Members of the Labour Party, having a much less developed sense of history and of their party's historical mission, indeed did not see the need to write its own history with the same degree of urgency as their comrades in Germany.

It is certainly hard to find the autodidacts in the British Labour Party who were engaged in writing the history of British socialism. The nearest equivalent to the Bernsteins and Beers in Germany were perhaps the Webbs, who, as founders of the London School of Economics, and middle-class intellectuals and civil servants, were, however, far closer to the academic establishment than would have been the case for the social democratic historians of social democracy in Germany. The Webbs' writings were also characterised by a strong interest in comparison. They were keen to learn about conditions elsewhere, because they thought it might shed light on possibilities in Britain. As Sidney Webb wrote in the introduction to a little booklet by W. S. Sanders (1916: 4) on German trade unionism: 'There are many lessons in this book for British Trade unions.' In their more universal and cosmopolitan interests the Webbs resembled the German Socialists of the Chair (*Kathedersozialisten*) – liberal academics with an interest in the social question and the early labour movement. In Germany, Lujo Brentano in particular portrayed British industrial relations as a model for Germany and studied closely the British trade union movement in order to draw lessons for the organisation of a German equivalent (Hennock, 1993). And Werner Sombart pursued his famous question why there was no socialism in the United States of America (Sombart, 1906). But the scholarly interests of those liberal academics were not representative of the wider community of professional social scientists and historians. As civil servants, who often felt a special loyalty to the imperial German state and the Hohenzollern dynasty, they did not regard the history of social democracy as a topic worth studying. Social democrats were, after all, widely typecast as 'fellows without a fatherland' and an intensely nationalist historical profession distanced itself politically from the SPD to such an extent that it also regarded its history as anathema for study.

The historical establishment in Britain was, of course, no beacon of progressivism before the First World War. Labour studies, including labour history, was very much an interest of outsiders, and it was not by chance that it flourished especially well at the newly created London School of Economics (LSE), where special attention was paid to economic and social developments. Early on in the life of the LSE, Bertrand Russell (1896) gave a cycle of six lectures on German social democracy, introducing the topic to the students of the LSE. In the inter-war years the history of social democracy was, above all, written at the LSE, but it was also possible for a leading historian of European social democracy to establish itself at the very heart of the British academic establishment, as the case of G. D. H. Cole at Oxford University demonstrates.

The integration of social democratic historiography into the academic mainstream in Germany was far more problematic and uneven. It remained more isolated within the social democratic milieu and contributed to the self-sustaining and closed communities of solidarity formed by German social democrats. In Britain it was also the occupation of academic outsiders, but those outsiders managed to found an academic institution and were more easily accepted among academics than was the situation in Germany. The case of Gustav Mayer demonstrates the continued non-acceptance of historians of social democracy among academic historians in the inter-war period. In 1917 Mayer's *Habilitation* had been jeopardised by a fronde of ultranationalist professors in the Humanities Faculty of Berlin University. When, as a result of his growing reputation as one of the pioneers of labour history, he finally got a chair in 1923, he remained a social outcast among his fellow professors and was one of the first to get sacked in 1933, when the Nazis came to power (Prellwitz, 1998). Mayer's oeuvre subsequently was so forgotten that, by the late 1960s, it had to be literally rediscovered and republished by a new generation of labour historians in Germany.

Under Nazism, no historians of social democracy could practise their trade in Germany and many, including Beer and Mayer, went into exile. Yet ironically the advances of the racist 'people's history' (*Volksgeschichte*) under Nazism introduced new social science methods and new themes, including an interest in social structures and social formations. It appealed in particular to a group of younger historians, including Werner Conze and Theodor Schieder, who, after the Second World War, did much to integrate social history into the mainstream of the West German academic establishment. They also actively promoted an interest in the history of the German labour movement among their own PhD students. It was among this next generation of West German historians, including, among others, Hans-Ulrich Wehler, Jürgen Kocka, and Hans Mommsen that the history of social democracy became a key concern. They were immensely successful in establishing a social science oriented school of history writing (sometimes referred to as 'Bielefeld school') in West Germany. They founded key journals and book series which were to have an extraordinary impact on re-orienting West German historical science from the 1970s onwards.

As far as the history of social democracy is concerned, they entered into an alliance with the Institute for Historical Research at the Friedrich–Ebert Foundation (FES) – a political foundation financed generously from public money with close ties to the SPD. The FES had not only its own historical institute and vast archives, but they also had their own publishing house, including a well-developed history list and one of the key social history journals, the *Archiv für Sozialgeschichte*. In their attempt to conceptualise the history of social democracy the new generation of West German labour historians had to contend with an extensive historiography on the German labour movement produced by historians in the German Democratic Republic (especially Geschichte der deutschen Arbeiterbewegung, 1966ff). In Communist Germany the history of the labour movement had become of prime importance and research was lavishly funded. West German social historians, by the early 1970s, were the first to draw attention to the rich vein of literature being produced here. While rejecting the Marxist–Leninist interpretations, West German social historians broke with the tradition of ignoring GDR historiography recognising that much important work was being done – especially in areas which had been traditionally weak in German historiography, such as labour history.

But West German social historians also had to contend with indigenous West German Marxist traditions. In the 1950s and 1960s, authors such as Theo Pirker and Wolfgang Abendroth heavily criticised the move of the SPD away from its Marxist roots and attempted to write a history of social democracy which would keep social democrats aware of their previous aims and ambitions (Pirker, 1965; Abendroth, 1964). Yet the Bad Godesberg turn of the SPD produced its own historiography, and it was the new social historians of the Bielefeld school in conjunction with the Friedrich–Ebert

Foundation which laid the foundations of such a re-writing of the history of German social democracy.

Towards the crisis of labour history

In the context of the 1960s student revolt, the topic of social democracy and the wider labour movement became extremely popular, and the 1970s saw the emergence of a whole string of studies. Not everyone was in agreement with the Bad Godesberg turn of the historiography of German social democracy. A younger generation of Marxist historians, such as Georg Fülberth and Jürgen Harrer (Fülberth and Harrer, 1974) advanced a more orthodox Marxist understanding of that history which was, in some respects, closer to the interpretations which could be found among GDR historians of the German labour movement. More unorthodox Marxists, such as Detlef Peukert and Alf Lüdtke, dissatisfied with both the post-Bad Godesberg turn of social democratic history writing and its Marxist–Leninist variant in the GDR, called on historians to move away from their concern with the organisations of the labour movement and with formal politics and to explore the everyday lifeworlds of workers. The move towards history from below and oral history (Lüdtke, 1995) has since yielded pathbreaking new insights into workers' lives, but it has not yet built any bridges to the history of the organised labour movement. Although workers formed the backbone of the social democratic movement well into the 1950s, workers' history and social democratic history often co-exist without much overlap. If the 1980s saw the emergence of the great books of synthesis on the history of social democracy (Ritter, 1984), the same decade also saw a marked decline in interest among students. The flow of monographs on German social democracy slowed down as PhD students turned to other topics.

It was around the same time, the late 1980s and early 1990s, that British labour historians diagnosed a crisis. But the trajectory of the British historiography of social democracy was in many respects quite different from the German one outlined above. For a start, there was much more continuity, symbolised in the work of people such as Cole and institutions such as the LSE. After 1945 major works by Henry Pelling provided the seminal starting point for future generations of historians of British social democracy. Pelling's was a political history which interpreted the Labour Party as a reformist party seeking, with varying degrees of success to improve the social conditions of those it sought to represent: the British working classes (Reid, 2003). Arguably the most important Pellingite from the 1970s onwards was Ross McKibbin (Callaghan, 2003).

This non-Marxist political historiography was challenged by the New Left in the 1960s. Two seminal articles in the pages of the *New Left Review*, penned by Tom Nairn (1964), brought together most of the complaints that the Marxist left had with the history of the Labour Party, which it accused of betraying rather than furthering the interests of the British working class. Ralph Miliband (1961) held 'parliamentary socialism' responsible for the Labour Party's inadequate revolutionary fervour. In the heady days of the 1960s a lot of students in Britain, like in Germany, took to the history of the labour movement, and the Marxist *Zeitgeist* made many of them turn away from the Pelling school and take up the rallying cry of the New Left. A strong historiographical tradition emerged which was heavily critical of 'labourism' and the Labour Party's seemingly perennial reformism (Fielding, 2002).

The party itself had, as mentioned above, never been as interested in its own history as the SPD. Hence it never built up even faintly similar institutions to the historical research institute of the Friedrich–Ebert–Stiftung. It neglected its own archive, it had no interest in academic publishing and generally speaking, contact between the academics researching the history of British social democracy and the politicians framing the policies of British social democracy were remote by German standards. Hence there was little institutional and party political resistance to the onward march of a radical left-wing reinterpretation of the history of social democracy in Britain. On the other hand, one can also say that the history of Social Democracy was far less influenced by the British Labour Party than the history of the SPD was influenced by the SPD. But by the 1980s, when the heady optimism of the 1960s student radicals had given way to the brutal transformation of the very foundations of British society by Thatcherism, it was, like in Germany, more and more difficult to find young historians with an interest in the history of Social Democracy. New topics and themes, e.g. the question of British national identity came to the fore, the latter in particular in the wake of the Falklands war.

The crisis of labour history in Britain and Germany had a number of common transnational causes which also affected labour history in other parts of Europe and North America (van der Linden, 1993). Some of them were disciplinary, such as the rise of the new cultural history with its accompanying interest in subjectivities or the appeal of history from below. Others were political, such as the disillusionment of the student radicals of the 1960s. The intellectual challenges of poststructuralism and postmodernism were, above all, directed against the hegemonic set of modernisation theories, be they Marxist or Weberian. For the historiography of social democracy this meant that the predominant theoretical framework within which that history had been written began to look outdated.

The comparative method as as way out of crisis?

Labour historians came up with a range of suggestions all meant to alleviate the crisis. Arguably one of the more widespread and prominent suggestions involved the move of labour history towards comparative and transnational history writing (e.g. Cronin, 1993). How did British and German researchers of social democracy react to this call? For a start, it would be fair to say that both British and German historians of social democracy had written that history predominantly in national terms, often formulating national 'special paths', peculiarities or *Sonderwege* on the basis of very little actual comparison. On balance it would appear though that many more labour historians in Britain were interested in developing comparative perspectives earlier than was the case in Germany. Thus, historians such as Pelling (1956) and Harrison (1957) had an intense interest in the links between British and North American labour movements. Cole produced a seminal five-volume history of social thought (Cole, 1967–69). Eric Hobsbawm never restricted his gaze to a national perspective (Hobsbawm, 1964, 1984). In Germany Wolfgang Abendroth also contextualised the experience of the German labour movement in a wider European perspective (Abendroth, 1972). But thereafter, much of what appeared specifically on social democracy was on German social democracy only. While comparative history more generally did develop strongly from the 1970s onwards, with key practitioners of comparative history, such as Jürgen Kocka, Hartmut Kaelble, Heinz-Gerhard Haupt and Hannes Siegrist, playing a major role in advancing comparative history nationally and internationally, this only occasionally affected the historiography of social democracy.

In fact, much of the pioneering comparative work on social democracy was carried out by American scholars and published in the English language (e.g. Sturmthal, 1953, 1972; Mitchell and Stearns, 1971). Ironically two British historians of Germany took up the challenge of comparative labour history with considerable vigour: Dick Geary used the comparative method to investigate in particular the protest culture of the European labour movement between 1848 and 1939 (Geary, 1981, 1991). John Breuilly asked in particular about the relationship between social democracy and liberalism in Britain and Germany (Breuilly, 1992). In Germany Gustav Schmidt, in an early essay from the 1960s, had also treated the relationship between organised liberalism and the labour movement in comparative perspective (Schmidt, 1966), but it was not until the 1980s that two edited collections brought comparative labour history more firmly onto the agenda of German historical research (Kocka, 1982; Tenfelde, 1986).

In the 1990s a whole range of monographs and edited collections explored diverse aspects of the history of social democracy in comparative perspective. The early, artisanal phase of social democracy, is increasingly analysed as an altogether separate phenomenon which cannot be reduced to a mere pre-history to the rise of mass social democratic parties (Lenger, 1991; Rule 1985). Several authors, such as Keller (1994), Kirk (1994, 2003) and Berger (1994, 1995) concerned themselves with questions of mutual influences of social democratic parties and the notion of typologies and exceptionalism, both in European and more global perspective. They contributed to a comprehensive critique of the notion of exceptionalism, be it German, British or American, and it is now rare to come across unreflected statements about the peculiarities of a particular social democratic movement.

Ideology time and again finds the attention of comparative labour historians. Steenson (1991), for example, seeks to establish where in Europe the reception of Marxist political thought was strongest among the social democratic parties. Lipset (1983) has analysed the factors which made working-class parties opt for reformist or for more radical ideological orientations. Mann (1995) argued that the conservative counter-attack summoned the themes of religion, nationalism and technology in order to defeat the challenge posed by social democratic parties in the first half of the twentieth century. Horn (1996) argued that the impact of the struggle against fascism in the 1930s had a radicalising effect on European social democracy. But after the Second World War, as Orlow (2000) points out, the move to postindustrial societies had wide-ranging implications for the organisational set-up and ideological orientation of social democratic parties. They moved from their traditional self-understanding as class parties to advertising themselves as catch-all parties. Some were obviously quicker than others, and Hodge (1993, 1994) as well as Nicholls (1994) have explored the reasons which made social democratic parties adopt reformist strategies more quickly under the general conditions of the Pax Americana after 1945. James Fulcher analysed the reasons for the relative failure of corporatism in Britain by comparing it with Sweden (Fulcher, 1991). And by the late 1990s and early 2000s, a range of excellent synthesis of the comparative history of Social Democracy began to be published (Kitschelt, 1994; Sassoon, 1996; Bartolini, 2000; Callaghan, 2000).

Overall then, as far as the comparative history of social democracy is concerned, there exists a very healthy balance sheet since the 1990s in Britain and Germany. The increasing number of works putting the history of social democracy in comparative perspective (of which only a small selection could be mentioned here) has much to do with the by now formidable opportunities for scholars to use diverse exchange and mobility programmes to travel and spend time in different national surroundings. What, however, still needs developing is the transnational history of social democracy. As has been pointed out by the critics of comparative history, it tends to isolate its units of comparison, as though there were no relations and no mutual influences between the units of comparison. This, however, was clearly not the case. Comparing social democracies without taking into account that, of course, these social democracies and their exponents knew of each other, visited each other and attempted to adapt and adopt what was regarded as good and beneficial. Any comparison that ignores those points of contact runs the risk of producing a heavily lopsided comparison. Hence the well-developed comparative history of historiography needs to take into account, more than it has done so far, the relational history of social democracy and the history of cultural transfer. An early and unsurpassed master in tracing these relations is the late Georges Haupt (1986), whose work concentrates in particular on the relational history of social democrats in South-eastern Europe. Some other important work in this area has been done: Christine Collette (1998), for example, has explored the networks of William Gillies and other Labour leaders in the interwar period with continental European socialists. Anthony Glees (1982) has analysed at some length the strained relations between the Labour Party and the German SPD in exile during the Second World War. Isabel Tombs (1996) has also traced the multitude of relations that political exile from Hitler's Europe forged in wartime Britain. And Julia Angster (2003) has argued convincingly that only the extensive networks between German social democrats and representatives of the American labour movement after 1945 can explain the rapid ideological transformation process of the SPD which paved the way to the party's famous Bad Godesberg programme of 1959. Van der Linden (2003) has emphasised the importance of overcoming the Eurocentric orientation of research on social democracy, pointing out that the move towards a genuinely transnational labour history will have to lay open a range of multipolar developments in different parts of the globe and establish to which degree they have been a feature of similar underlying processes.

While the comparative history of social democracy has made vast strides since the 1990s, the transnational history of social democracy is now developing well. There still exists a healthy institutional basis for research into the history of social democracy. The International Institute for Social History in Amsterdam as well as several major national research archives and libraries such as the Friedrich–Ebert Foundation in Bonn, the Institute for Social Movements in Bochum, the Arbetarrörelsen Arkiv in Stockholm and the International Association of Labour History Institutions (IALHI), founded in 1970, are all examples of the strong and successful institutionalisation of labour history writing. Such institutionalisation is comparatively weaker in Britain, but the Labour History Society, various thriving regional societies for the study of labour history and the publication of important research in a range of journals dedicated to labour history have also produced a strong and steady stream of labour history

If there has indeed been a decreasing interest among younger scholars in the history of social democracy, this can also be seen as normalisation of the level of interest after an unusual period of intense politicisation had produced extraordinary streams of research in the 1960s and 1970s. Such normalisation can also be an opportunity to move away from the heavily charged interpretations tinged with particular political objectives and ideological predilections. In other words, it should be grasped as an opportunity to shed ideological baggage and move towards a genuine historisation of the history of social democracy.

Where does comparative labour history go?

The major task for the future is to move the comparative history of social democracy from its traditional focus on organisations, ideologies and institutionalised politics to a cultural history of social democracy, i.e. integrating the methodological arsenal developed by historians from below and cultural historians: we need to ask more specific questions about the making and remaking of social democratic subjectivities and identities, and the place of religion, ethnicity, class and gender in the make-up of these identities (Voss and van der Linden, 2002; Geary, 1999). The world of the workers and the everyday needs to be related to the world of social democracy and organised politics (van der Linden, 1995). There is already a host of promising comparative work being carried out in these areas. They include work on the relationship between nationalism and social democracy (e.g. Schwarzmantel, 1991; Garscha and Schindler, 1994; Berger and Smith, 1999), on the impact of ethnicity on the identities of labour movements (e.g. Alexander and Halpern, 2000), on the impact of religion on social democracy (e.g. McLeod, 1996; Strikwerda, 1988) and on the particular way in which social democracy was a gendered phenomenon, often making it difficult for women to negotiate feminism and socialism within the labour movement (Gruber and Graves, 1998; Walsh, 1999). Autobiography has been an important means of analysing the subjectivities and identities of labour leaders (Maynes, 1995; Berger, 2000). And poststructuralist and culturalist approaches have also been trying to reconfigure the area of labour history – even if few labour historians have completely accepted the theoretical presuppositions of poststructuralism (Croll, 2002; Berlanstein, 1993; Belchem and Kirk, 1997; Geary, 2000). And yet the comparative study of the history of social democracy has been moving away from the overarching interpretations provided by Marxist or Weberian theoretical frameworks. The new research on the identities and subjectivities and the new approaches to labour history have been most widely integrated into the masterly synthesis by Eley (2002). And yet, one might ask, whether it is already time for synthetising the existing research. More and more historians are sceptical of such synthesis attempting to provide systematisation and typology. Instead there is, by now, an important body of work which has emphasised the heavily contingent and heavily local circumstances of the success or failure of social democracy (Tanner, 1990; Williams, 1996; Welskopp, 2000). Over the coming years, historians will increasingly reassess the history of social democracy from this local perspective. Was it really industrialisation and the set of social and economic conditions associated with it, which led to the emergence of social democratic movements? How much about social democracy was determined by universal processes of industrialisation? And how much was conditioned by specifically local circumstances? Which interests did social democracy represent in those local circumstances? But arguably, a comparative and transnational perspective will still be invaluable to come to perhaps less crude and finer typologies of social democratic movements in Europe and the wider world.

References

Abendroth, W. (1964), *Aufstieg und Krise der deutschen Sozialdemokratie*, Frankfurt/Main.

Abendroth, W. (1972), *Sozialgeschichte der europäischen Arbeiterbewegung*, 8th edn, Frankfurt/Main.

Alexander, P. and Halpern, R., eds, (2000), *Racialising Class. Classifying Race: Labour and Difference in Britain, the USA and Africa*, London.

Angster, J. (2003), *Konsenskapitalismus und Sozialdemokratie: Die Westernisierung von SPD und DGB*, Munich.

Bartolini, S. (2000), *The Political Mobilisation of the European Left 1860–1980: The Class Cleavage*, Cambridge.

Beer, M. (1921a), *History of British Socialism*, 2 vols, London.

Beer, M. (1921b), *The Life and Teaching of Karl Marx*, London.

Belchem, J. and Kirk, N., eds, (1997), *Languages of Labour*, Aldershot.

Berger, S. (1994), *The British Labour Party and the German Social Democrats: A Comparison*, Oxford.

Berger, S., ed., (1995), *European Labour Movements and the European Working Class in the Twentieth Century*, Oxford.

Berger, S. (2000), 'In the Fangs of Social Patriotism: The Construction of Nation and Class in Autobiographies of British and German Social Democrats in the Inter-war Period', *Archiv für Sozialgeschichte* 40, pp. 259–87.

Berger, S. and Smith, A., eds, (1999), *Nationalism, Labour and Ethnicity 1870–1939*, Manchester.

Bernstein, E. (1893), *Ferdinand Lasalle as a Social Reformer*, London.

Bernstein, E. (1910), *Die Arbeiterbewegung*, Frankfurt/Main.

Bernstein, E. (1930), *Cromwell and Communism*, London.

Berlanstein, L. R., ed., (1993), *Rethinking Labor History: Essays on Discourse and Class Analysis*, Urbana.

Breuilly, J. (1992), *Labour and Liberalism in Nineteenth Century Europe: Essays in Comparative History*, Manchester.

Callaghan, J. (2000), *The Retreat of Social Democracy*, Manchester.

Callaghan, J. (2003), 'Ross McKibbin: Class Cultures, the Trade Unions and the Labour Party', in John Callaghan, Steven Fielding and Steve Ludlam, eds, *Interpreting the Labour Party: Approaches to Labour Politics and History*, Manchester.

Cole, G. D. H. (1967–69), *A History of Social Thought 1789–1939*, 5 volumes, 2nd edn, London.

Collette, C. (1998), *The International Faith: Labour's Attitudes to European Socialism, 1918–1939*, Aldershot.

Croll, A. (2002), 'The Impact of Postmodernism on Modern British Social History', *Mitteilungsblatt des Instituts für soziale Bewegungen* 27, pp. 137–52.

Cronin, J. (1993), 'Neither Exceptional nor Peculiar: Towards the Comparative Study of Labor in Advanced Society', *International Review of Social History* 38, pp. 59–74.

Eley, G. (2002), *Forging Democracy: The History of the Left in Europe 1850–2000*, Oxford.

Fielding, S. (2002), ' "New" Labour and the "New" Labour History', *Mitteilungsblatt des Instituts für soziale Bewegungen* 27, pp. 35–50.

Fülberth, Georg and Harrer, Jürgen (1974), *Die deutsche Sozialdemokratie 1890–1933*, Darmstadt.

Fulcher, J. (1991), *Labour Movements, Employers and the State: Conflict and Co-operation in Britain and Sweden*, Oxford.

Garscha, W. R. and Schindler, C., ed., (1994), *Arbeiterbewegung und nationale Identität*, Vienna.

Geary, D. (1981), *European Labour Protest 1848–1939*, London.

Geary, D. (1991), *European Labour Politics from 1900 to the Depression*, Houndmills.

Geary, D. (1999), 'Working Class Identities in Europe, 1850s–1930s', *Australian Journal of Politics and History* 45, pp. 20–34.

Geary, D. (2000), 'Labour History, the "Linguistic Turn" and Postmodernism', *Contemporary European History* 9, pp. 445–62.

Geschichte der deutschen Arbeiterbewegung (1966ff), 8 vols, Berlin – East.

Anthony Glees (1982), *Exile Politics During the Second World War: The German Social Democrats in Britain*, Oxford.

Gruber, H. and Graves, P., eds, (1998), *Women and Socialism. Socialism and Women: Europe Between the Two World Wars*, Oxford.

Harrison, R. (1957), 'British Labour and the Confederacy: A Note on the Southern Sympathies of some British Working-class Journals and Leaders during the American Civil War', *International Review of Social History* 2, pp. 78–105.

Haupt, G. (1986), *Aspects of International Socialism 1871–1914*, Cambridge.

Hennock, E. P. (1993), 'Lessons from England: Lujo Brentano on British Trade Unionism', *German History* 11, pp. 141–60.

Hobsbawm, E. (1964), *Labouring Men*, London.

Hobsbawm, E. (1984), *Worlds of Labour: Further Studies in the History of Labour*, London.

Hodge, C. C. (1993), 'The Long Fifties: The Politics of Socialist Programmatic Revision in Britain, France and Germany', *Contemporary European History* 2, pp. 17–39.

Hodge, C. C. (1994), *The Trammels of Tradition: Social Democracy in Britain, France and Germany*, New York.

Horn, G.-R. (1996), *European Socialists Respond to Fascism: Ideology, Activism and Contingency in the 1930s*, Oxford.

Keller, K. (1994), *Modell SPD? Italienische Sozialisten und deutsche Sozialdemokratie bis zum ersten Weltkrieg*, Bonn.

Kirk, N. (1994), *Labour and Society in Britain and the United States 1780–1939*, 2 vols, Aldershot.

Kirk, N. (2003), *Comrades and Cousins: Globalisation, Workers and Labour Movements in Britain, the USA and Australia from the 1880s to 1914*, London.

Kitschelt, Herbert (1994), *The Transformation of European Social Democracy*, Cambridge.

Kocka, J., ed., (1982), *Europäische Arbeiterbewegungen im 19. Jahrhundert. Deutschland, Österreich, England und Frankreich im Vergleich*, Göttingen.

Lenger, F. (1991), 'Beyond Exceptionalism: Notes on the Artisanal Phase of the Labour Movement in France, England, Germany and the United States', *International Review of Social History* 36, pp. 1–23.

Lipset, S. M. (1983), 'Radicalism or Reformism: The Sources of Working-class Politics, *American Political Science Review* 77, pp. 1–18.

Lüdtke, A., ed., (1995), *The History of Everyday Life: Reconstructing Historical Experiences and Ways of Life*, Princeton.

Mann, M. (1995), 'Sources of Variation in Working-class Movements in Twentieth Century Europe', *New Left Review* 212, pp. 14–54.

Maynes, M.-J. (1995), *Taking the Hard Road: Life Course in French and German Workers' Autobiographies in the Era of Industrialisation*, Chapel Hill.

McLeod, H. (1996), *Piety and Poverty: Working-class Religion in Berlin, London and New York, 1870–1914*, New York.

Miliband, R. (1961), *Parliamentary Socialism*, London.

Mitchell, H. and Stearns, P. (1971), *Workers and Protest*, Itasca, IL.

Moschonas, G. (2002), *In the Name of Social Democracy: The Great Transformation 1945 to the Present*, London.

Nairn, T. (1964), 'The Nature of the Labour Party (Parts 1 and 2)', *New Left Review* I:27 and 28, pp. 38–65 and 33–62.

Nettl, P. (1965), 'The German Social Democratic Party, 1880–1914 as a Political Model', *Past and Present* 30, pp. 65–95.

Nicholls, A. J. (1994), 'Zwei Wege in den Revisionismus: die Labour-Partei und die SPD in der Ära des Godesberger Programms', in Jürgen Kocka, Hans-Jürgen Puhle and Klaus Tenfelde, eds, *Von der Arbeiterbewegung zum modernen Sozialstaat. Festschrift für Gerhard A. Ritter zum 65. Geburtstag*, Munich, pp. 190–204.

Orlow, D. (2000), *Common Destiny: A Comparative History of the Dutch, French and German Social Democratic Parties 1945–1969*, Oxford.

Pelling, H. (1956), *America and the British Left from Bright to Bevan*, London.

Pirker, T. (1965), *Die SPD nach Hitler: Die Geschichte der Sozialdemokratischen Partei Deutschlands 1945–1964*, Munich.

Prellwitz, J. (1998), *Jüdisches Erbe, sozialliberales Ethos, deutsche Nation: Gustav Mayer im Kaiserreich und in der Weimarer Republik*, Mannheim.

Reid, A. J. (2003), 'Class and Politics in the Work of Henry Pelling', in John Callaghan, Steven Fielding and Steve Ludlam, eds, *Intepreting the Labour Party: Approaches to Labour Politics and History*, Manchester.

Ritter, G. A., ed., (1984), *Über das Projekt: Geschichte der Arbeiter und der Arbeiterbewegung in Deutschland seit dem Ende des 18. Jahrhunderts*, Bonn.

Rule, J. (1985), 'Artisan Attitudes: A Comparative Survey of Skilled Labour and Proletarianisation before 1848', *Bulletin of the Society for the Study of Labour History* 50.

Russell, B. (1896), *German Social Democracy: Six Lectures*, London.

Sanders, W. S. (1916), *Trade Unionism in Germany*, Westminster.

Sassoon, D. (1996), *One Hundred Years of Socialism: The West European Left in the Twentieth Century*, London.

Schmidt, G. (1966), 'Politischer Liberalismus, "Landed Interests" und organisierte Arbeiterschaft, 1850–1880. Ein deutsch-englischer Vergleich', in Hans-Ulrich Wehler ed., *Moderne deutsche Sozialgeschichte*, Berlin, pp. 266–88.

Schwarzmantel, J. (1991), *Socialism and the Idea of the Nation*, London.

Sombart, W. (1906), *Warum gibt es in den Vereinigten Staaten keinen Sozialismus?*, Tübingen.

Steenson, G. P. (1991), *After Marx, Before Lenin. Marxism and the Socialist Working-class Parties in Europe 1884–1914*, Pittsburgh.

Strikwerda, C. (1988), 'Catholic Working-class Movements in Western Europe', *International Labor and Working Class History* 34, pp. 70–85.

Sturmthal, A. (1953; 1972), *Unity and Diversity in European Labor*, Glencoe: IL.

Tanner, D. (1990), *Political Change and the Labour Party 1900–1918*, Cambridge.

Tenfelde, K., ed., (1986), *Arbeiter und Arbeiterbewegung im Vergleich*, Munich.

Tombs, Isabel (1996), 'The Victory of Socialist "Vansittartism": Labour and the German Question, 1941–5', *Twentieth Century British History* 7, pp. 287–309.

van der Linden, M. (1995), 'Keeping Distance: Alf Lüdtke's "Decentred" Labour History', *International Review of Social History* 40, pp. 285–94.

van der Linden, M. (2003), *Transnational Labour History*, Aldershot.

van der Linden, M., ed., (1993), *The End of Labour History?*, Cambridge.

Voß, L. and van der Linden, M. (2002), *Class and Other Identities. Gender, Religion and Ethnicity in the Writing of European Labour History*, Oxford.

Walsh, M., ed., (1999), *Working Out Gender: Perspectives from Labour History*, Aldershot.

Welskopp, T. (2000), *Das Banner der Brüderlichkeit: Die deutsche Sozialdemokratie vom Vormärz bis zum Sozialistengesetz*, Bonn.

Williams, C. (1996), *Democratic Rhondda: Politics and Society 1885–1951*, Cardiff.

Part II

Shaping the post-war 'social compromise'

5

Social democracy and class conflict in twentieth-century Europe

Nina Fishman

Introduction

It is an opportune moment to re-examine the changes in the balance of class forces in the four most populous, democratic states in Western Europe – Germany, Italy, France and Britain – during the twentieth century. Social scientists and political elites were pre-occupied for much of this time by escalating class conflict between large-scale industrial capitalists and their workers, who were also voting for social democratic parties with programmes committed to the expropriation of the means of production, distribution and exchange. Although economic struggles were subsumed by shared national interest at the beginning of the First World War, it swiftly became a battle of attrition, prompting outbreaks of class war in all four states. The immediate aftermath of the war's end in November 1918 was a renewed wave of intense strikes and lock-outs, including the victorious nations of Britain, France and Italy, and in Germany, a democratic revolution including the creation of revolutionary workers' councils.

A period of comparative stabilisation followed in western Europe, when a balance of class forces had apparently been struck. Social democratic parties gained ground in elections and confidence in government, proving capable of repelling political attacks from both conservative and communist political parties. European economies were, however, de-stabilised by the 1929 Wall Street crash and the protracted depression which followed in the domestic economy of the United States. In the most fragile states, Germany and Poland, political elites emulated Mussolini's fascist state, viewing the choice for their nation-states as fascism or a descent into permanent class conflict.

In the aftermath of the Second World War, Europe's future seemed more uncertain than it had in 1918, because the Germans had been defeated by an unlikely alliance of the chief capitalist and communist states. The re-drawing of political boundaries and installation of provisional governments precipitated civil war and the popular settling of ethnic and political scores, as well as large-scale movements of refugees fleeing from east to west, e.g. Lithuanians, Latvians and Estonians escaping from the newly legitimised

Russian hegemony; Sudeten Germans fleeing from popular Czech vengeance; ethnic Germans abandoning their land in what had been Germany and was now Poland; Prussian landowners and aristocrats fleeing from the Soviet occupied zone of Germany (SMAD) into the western zones occupied by Britain, the USA and France.

Widespread human suffering, economic dislocation and physical devastation made a return to normality impossible, and the political picture remained wholly unclear in Western Europe, despite Stalin's Potsdam's undertaking to abstain from political interference in western Europe. Potential political vacuums existed in Italy and France. The possibility of the breakdown of social order, followed by a communist seizure of state power, loomed large in politicians' calculations and the vagaries of popular imagination. The future geographic and political shape of Germany remained unknown until 1949. Veteran communists in the western zones of occupation were proving effective union and political leaders, earning respect from their role in the resistance and incarceration in concentration camps. They were also prepared to stand up to the occupation authorities for German workers' rights and better rations. In Italy and France, where popular disillusion with pre-war elites was strong, a critical mass of workers, small farmers and intellectuals might have welcomed a communist *coup d'état*, or at least not actively resisted it. The spectre of communism even haunted the British Labour government, despite the microscopic size of the British party (CPGB). Though Britain's state apparatus was intact and its material situation significantly better, people were exhausted and drained from six years of total war.

By the mid-1950s, however, the sustained activity of reconstruction had produced standards of living above subsistence for most, modest comfort for many workers. Capitalists embarked on new investment in heavy capital goods and the new consumer goods manufacturing sectors. Sustained economic expansion was fuelled by increasing levels of labour productivity, the fruits of which enabled unions to successfully press employers for higher wages and better conditions. Optimism gained ground as the social and political contours of cumulative prosperity became clearly visible.

Nevertheless, until the end of the 1960s, neither the participants in class conflict nor the social scientists observing them believed that class forces in western Europe had reached a stable equilibrium. Upsurges of union militancy, employers' intransigence and political turbulence fuelled the pessimistic prognosis that the protracted economic expansion would end precipitately and cause a crisis comparable to 1929–33. Unions and employers continued to engage in often intense economic struggle, clearly designed to weaken the other side, in the process exerting strong pressure on political parties and the government to intervene and take sides. Writing in 1999, Colin Crouch observed, 'The degree of unity that existed in pursuit of the social compromise model is easily taken for granted fifty years later, and we may not see the considerable tensions, almost contradictions' (Crouch, 1999: 35).

The moving balance of class forces

This chapter offers a historical analysis of the moving balance of class forces from the end of the nineteenth century. The extraordinary situation created by the economic imperatives of two total wars acted as a forcing house, encouraging the growth and developments in class relations which had begun in the 1890s. My purpose is not to re-tell the story, excellent narratives are already to hand, but to argue that 'the mid-century social compromise' was achieved because western European union leaders and social democratic party leaders pursued the goal of a fair and even balance of class forces self-consciously and determinedly throughout this period. There were, of course, other important contributory factors, e.g. the actions and political programmes of Christian democratic politicians, employers' associations, and communists.

Earlier descriptions of the emergence of the western European social compromise were necessarily distillations of the near past. Authors and readers were participants; their fortunes and vicissitudes formed part of the events they described. Their perspective was necessarily circumscribed by the collective *corpus* of public culture and private memory, both repeatedly rehearsed when family, friends, and work colleagues socialised. The passage of time and the principal actors makes it easier to perform the intellectual leap required to raise mental horizons above the minutiae of everyday events, and impose order on the mountain of surviving evidence.

Despite this navigational advantage, however, the end of the cold war has presented historians with an additional problem in interpreting post-1945 events. Their previous perspectives were shattered by developments in east-central Europe, beginning in 1989 on 7 July with the Warsaw Pact revoking the Brezhnev Doctrine, reaching a climax on 9 November with the opening of the wall dividing east and west Berlin, followed by the extraordinary, apparently inexorable denouement of the implosion of the USSR and the east-central European states linked to it. The Soviet Union was formally dissolved on 26 December 1991. Although the immediate results were self-evident, historians working today are divided on the underlying causes and also how this dramatic eighteen months affects longer narratives of the twentieth century.

A clearly visible continuity

From a post-cold war perspective, the 'almost contradictions' between unions and employers in the mid-twentieth century fit into a post-1890s pattern of Western European class conflict. Rapidly advancing technology and capitalist globalisation produced economic boom and increasing concentration of industry, accompanied by larger workplaces and increasing union density. International events, domestic political developments and economic conflicts were all moving the balance of class forces towards workers, away from its previous skew favouring capitalists. Throughout the period, countervailing tendencies acted to move the equilibrium back towards managerial prerogative. Before 1914, while many capitalists provided housing and social facilities for their workforce, managements expected to exercise unfettered prerogative in determining working conditions and intensity of production.

Nevertheless, union leaders found strong support from their members to challenge managerial absolutism in intense economic combat. Economic struggles were shaped by the tide of social democracy sweeping through states without universal male suffrage and the popular culture of militarism. Union leaders and their rank-and-file membership emulated the political elite's concentration on war-making, the arms race and marshalling a combat-ready conscript army. Employers responded in kind, mounting increasingly well-organised and intense resistance to the spirited battles conducted by union general staffs.

Before 1914, the balance of class forces remained skewed towards employers and outbreaks of large-scale industrial conflict continued. Nevertheless, unions and socialist parties were able to win important advances through economic conflict conducted on favourable terrain, i.e., in conditions of a tight labour market against employers who felt politically secure. Examples are the 1889 London Dock Strike and the national miners' strikes in 1892 and 1912 (in Britain), and 1894 and 1905 (in the Ruhr). In northern Italy, the intense, rapid industrialisation at the end of the nineteenth century produced comparably intense class conflict.

The pre-1914 elite consensus was that 'the democracy' (the term for the working classes in Victorian and Edwardian political idiom), were irresponsible, susceptible to subversive socialist propaganda, and generally not to be trusted. The liberal wing of the political establishment favoured a more equal balance, arguing that unions could never learn sound judgement, prudence and self-discipline until they were ceded a share of economic and political power. In Italy, Prime Minister Giolitti responded to the intensive industrialisation in the north with a programme ceding much ground to workers and unions. In 1912, he also gambled on democracy, reckoning that the provision of a broad male suffrage would draw the socialist party into the parliamentary political process.

But all Western European political elites remained alarmed by the possibility that strikes could precipitate general unrest, anarchy and revolution. Governments intervened, often deploying troops, to keep civil order and ensure that capitalists could continue their business unimpaired by enabling strike-breakers to get to work unimpeded by an army of striking workers. Nevertheless, reflective ministers also realised that their governments needed to make efforts to balance the contending claims of unions and employers. In an increasingly democratic political culture, it was unacceptable to be seen to always favour capitalists. Legislation was enacted, offering some statutory protection for unions and their members – including the right to strike – in return for which governments could hold union leaders to account when economic battles were apparently escalating out of control. A pattern of 'social compromise' appeared within which the state was critical in moderating the aggressive behaviour of both classes.

In contradistinction to this emerging trend, the Second Socialist International, founded in 1889, was committed to socialist revolution, expropriating the capitalist class. After the revolution, socialist society would contain neither aristocrats nor capitalists. Consequently, there would be no need for the state to impose a balance of class forces for the working class, small farmers and proprietors. This scenario was consistent with the Communist Manifesto and Marx's critique of the 1875 Gotha Programme of the German Social Democratic Party (SPD). However, it did not tally with either the reality of Europe in the 1890s or the actual experience of the great French Revolution – which Marx had systematically misinterpreted in 1848. (Socialists in France and Belgium drew different lessons from French experience than Marx, and were sceptical that revolution would inevitably produce socialism.)

The first Marx reviser

The new International need not have been handicapped by these unrealistic strictures. The emerging tilt towards workers in the balance of class forces had, not surprisingly, produced a turn towards Marx-revising from Eduard Bernstein, who shared the honour, along with Karl Kautsky, of being Marx's and Engels' chosen literary executor. Bernstein recognised that political revolution was *sui generis* incapable of producing socialism, he argued that advances away from capitalism and towards socialism would necessarily take place on economic and social terrain. It was impossible to predict an *a priori* end-point where socialism would begin and capitalism end. Experience showed that unions and socialist parties could exert influence on existing state *apparats* towards more democratic policies. The changing nature of capitalism meant that its relations of production were constantly modified, and in the process workers were able to gain significant material and social advances. Social democratic political and economic struggle should concentrate on achieving practical goals, and not attempt to predict or prescribe a socialist end-state. Socialism would exist when the balance of class forces tipped decisively towards the working-class side.

The evidence was in Bernstein's favour. In the French third republic, not only was there universal male suffrage, but socialist deputies had also held cabinet office. The historical reflexes of the French political elite encompassed a successful confrontation with Jacobinism, Robespierre and political terror. Consequently, they had greater confidence in being able to deal with any vicissitudes of the masses' behaviour. However, the fact that republican France was more open to socialist permeation (the British Fabian Society's tactic of winning political ground through evolutionary, incremental means), was dismissed as irrelevant by the new syndicalist unions, whose leaders regarded the state as an implacably bourgeois machine. Unlike Germany and Britain, the comparatively small numbers of French industrial workers meant that even disciplined voting behaviour by workers would not yield significant political rewards. French union leaders at the turn of the century were committed to a strategy of general strike, confident that it would precipitate the collapse of the political state. Bereft of their legal underpinning, syndicalists believed that employers would lose their battles with the more populous, resourceful and better organised union forces, enabling unions to assume the responsibility for organising production for the common weal.

In Germany and Britain, the considered tolerance of political elites towards limited union activity was tempered by their apparently implacable reluctance to surrender political prerogative to 'the masses'. The state *Apparat* in the Wilhelmine Reich functioned in tandem with the Prussian state, whose suffrage remained heavily weighted towards property. Executive power over the army and class conflict, as well as key foreign policy decisions, resided with Prussian ministers who were answerable only to the Kaiser, operating unrestricted by any kind of democratic check or balance. British historians rarely acknowledge that both countries possessed a power nexus, unusual in Western Europe, based on informal networks of the aristocracy, buttressed by the army, navy and heavy industry. It is hardly surprising that the commitment of the SPD, the Labour Party and unions towards the maintenance of the state and its established order remained ambivalent.

German union leaders and SPD politicians in liberal Baden and Württemburg were strong supporters of Bernstein's perspective. Along with his Fabian friends in London, they recognised their own behaviour in Bernstein's analysis. Critics on the left attacking their opportunism could be successfully refuted by reference to Bernstein's thesis that it was impossible to achieve socialism through political revolution. In Britain, a reforming Liberal government elected in 1905 opened the way to sweeping political and economic change. When the Liberal Prime Minister accepted the amendments put forward by the new Labour Party MPs to the government's Trades Disputes Bill, the resulting legislation was so radical that '[t]he Webbs were by no means certain that the provisions of the Act were all entirely in the interest "of the Movement"' (Saville, 1996: 39).

Socialist leaders evaded the negative consequences of their dogmatic Marxism by acting pragmatically. Nevertheless, they continually muddied the ideological waters to cover up their transgressions. The SPD leader, August Bebel was anxious to keep his left wing on board, and feared that Bernsteinian revisions bringing the party's programme into line with their practice would result in the party's fracture. He encouraged Karl Kautsky to spearhead the counter-attack against revisionism in favour of the authentic Marx. Kautsky spared no intellectual expense, popularising anti-Bernsteinianism with the reductive slogan 'Bernstein believes the end-point of socialism is unimportant, and the movement is everything'. The Second International swung into line.

Total war moves the balance towards unions

During the First World War, the balance moved more decisively towards unions in all four countries. Governments initially brokered no strike/no lock-out agreements. But by early 1915, the state's overriding need was to maximise production for reliable deliveries of military materiel and fuel. Union leaders used the dramatic expansion of war production and increases in labour productivity to obtain significant material concessions. Governments compelled employers to share substantial areas of managerial prerogative with union representatives. By 1917, politicians in Britain and Germany, and the army officers in charge of administering martial law in German industrial regions, had concluded formal working arrangements with unions and employers to secure continuity of production, social stability and minimise industrial conflict. Strikes in France in the first half of 1917 were settled by Clemenceau's decision to make substantial economic concessions (Kedward, 2005: 80).

In Britain, tripartite agreements invested shop stewards and coalmining lodge officials with delegated negotiating authority and sanctioned factory works committees and pit committees with equal representation for unions and management. In Germany, *Betriebsräte* (works councils), were established, with the concomitant union works councillors. Prussian precedents are frequently cited to explain this innovation. In fact, General Groener, the liberal military governor from Wurttemburg in charge of the Ruhr, was impressed by Lloyd George's successes, and sought to emulate the British example.

The government-brokered arrangements meant that union leaders, from the national to workplace level, became equal partners with employers. Shop-floor representatives used their membership of works committees and works councils to influence working hours, intensity of work and wages. Their efficacy made a strong impression on millions of politically disenfranchised men and women. They joined unions in large numbers and followed socialist political disputations with interest. Many national union officials regretted the expanded authority of workplace union representatives. But they acquiesced, recognising the importance of incorporating the growing battalions of union members. Union rules and institutions were adjusted accordingly. The new shopfloor representatives were assigned a legitimate, but subordinate, place in the organisational hierarchy. Although tensions arose between shopfloor and full-time officials, both remained loyal to the principle of workers' self-organisation and supported existing union structures.

Unions' cumulative success produced a strong sense of grievance among employers and a keen desire to retake ground conceded under duress. However, in November 1918, the political situation was so volatile that no government felt sufficiently secure to countenance restoring the pre-war skew towards employers. The capitalists' situation was most precarious in Germany, where the General Staff pressurised the Kaiser to abdicate before they concluded the armistice on 11 November. German employers and union leaders anticipated a collapse of the state and civil order. On 12 November, Carl Legien for the union leadership and Hugo Stinnes for the industrial capitalists concluded the *Zentralarbeitsgemeinschaft* (ZAG, Joint Industrial Alliance), a *concordat* by which both sides agreed to continue and extend the wartime co-determination (Feldman, 1992: 521–5; Moses, 1982: 218–23). (Feldman translates *Arbeitsgemeinschaft* as social partnership.)

There was no revolution in Britain. Somewhat nervously, the coalition government conceded universal male suffrage (increasing the electorate by 25 per cent), and gave votes to women over the age of twenty-nine. In the December 1918 general election the Labour Party vote increased from 7 to 22 per cent, and subsequently to 29 per cent in 1922. In 1919–20, widespread, high spirited strikes occurred in a wide variety of industries and conurbations, prompted by the swift transition to peacetime conditions and consequent release of tension and energy. The government enforced law and order with vigour whenever the conflicts threatened to spill over into civil unrest. However, Prime Minister Lloyd George took care not to inflame the militant mood of the millions of new union members. In the wake of the miners' demands for nationalisation, Lloyd George deployed his formidable political skills to pre-empt a full-scale battle between labour and capital.

There was an even more intense strike wave in northern Italy in 1920–21, where capitalists had responded to the demands of the total war economy with ingenuity and flair, presiding over an extraordinary expansion of high technology engineering and mass production. The labour force had also expanded, and the new industrial workers – both men and women – were enthusiastic about asserting their democratic rights at the workplace. In France, Clemenceau conceded the eight-hour working dayin a law of 23 April 1919, in a bid to pre-empt bids by the unions for more concessions and greater workplace power. Strikes by railway workers and miners in early 1920 were determined, but ended without any further ground being gained.

Inter-war oscillations in the balance

The post-war economic bubble burst abruptly in the second half of 1920, producing widespread unemployment and unrest. Many of the demobilised soldiers had still not been assimilated back into normal work and social life. Taking advantage of the opportunity, British employers and the Lloyd George government acted swiftly to push the balance back towards capital. They were keen to clip the unions' wings in good time, particularly when they looked nervously over their shoulders at events in Italy and Germany. Deprived of government backing, the mining unions were unable to stand up to the coal owners and were compelled to accept a worsening of both wages and working hours.

In Germany, the substantial transfer of power which had taken place in the war was not challenged. The Stinnes–Legien pact had ensured economic continuity and had also pre-empted any serious attempt by employers at counter-revolution. Neither the Council of People's Representatives, chaired by Friedrich Ebert, the SPD leader, nor the National Constituent Assembly, elected in 1919 to agree the Republic's constitution, had any reason to roll back the unions' wartime gains or undermine the *Zentralarbeitsgemeinschaft*. The Weimar constitution confirmed the wartime works councils with workers gaining effective workplace representation. Their importance has been obscured by hindsightism. Union leaders expected to remain employers' equals for collective bargaining and in economic consultations with government (Moses, 1982: 291–308). Unions' remarkable advance stood in marked contrast to the rest of Western Europe. Most German employers felt threatened, and an important minority resolved to redress the balance of class forces at the earliest opportunity.

However, in March 1920, German unions called a general strike in response to an appeal by SPD cabinet members to defend the republic against an attempted *putsch*, mounted by disaffected army officers and led by 'a not very distinguished East Prussian politician named Wolfgang Kapp'. The general strike foiled the *putsch* after four days, when 'the breakdown of public services and the signs of disaffection in some of the Berlin garrisons bewildered and defeated them [the Kapp government]' (Craig, 1985: 429–30). Leaders of the German ADGB (*Allgemeiner Deutscher Gewerkschaftsbund*) deployed their full force in order to restore the legitimate government. 'It was the ADGB . . . which seized the initiative and was in fact recognized by the majority of workers (as well as the rebels) as the real leadership . . . Their self-perception is eloquently illustrated by their initial proclamation: "Arise for a General Strike! THE GERMAN REPUBLIC IS IN DANGER . . . Absolutism both in the state and in the factory will be restored. The right of association, the indispensable precondition for all social betterment is being abolished"' (Moses, 1982: 325).

In Britain, Lloyd George's coalition was replaced by a Conservative government in 1922. Prime Minister Baldwin mounted a stiff resistance to the general strike called by the Trades Union Congress (TUC) General Council in May 1926 to support the miners' resistance to the coal owners' intention of ending the wartime national wages and hours agreement. It lasted ten days, during which strikers were well disciplined and effectively organised. The TUC's regional strike committees ensured food distribution and emergency electricity supplies in most industrial conurbations. Led by Ernest Bevin and Jimmy Thomas, the General Council's intention was to show that peacetime governments also had to take British unions seriously. They expected Baldwin to compel the coal owners to make a compromise settlement. Baldwin, however, responded to the party's electoral base and cultural heartland – capitalists and their retainers in the salariat to shop-keepers and those white-collar workers who emulated their 'betters'.

The skew towards workers

Bevin and Walter Citrine, the TUC's youthful acting general secretary, were buoyed up by the strike's success. They had displayed unions' immense power, but used it responsibly by withdrawing their support for the miners' union when it refused to negotiate a compromise settlement. Bevin's Transport and General Workers' Union gained members. Citrine concluded that no 'modern' government could function without the active participation of the unions, and was confirmed in his view that unions had a vital contribution to make in the operation of a 'modern' economy (Clegg, 1985: 461–4). The government was relieved that the spectre of class war had failed to materialise. Baldwin declined to satisfy vengeful Tory backbenchers and the tabloid press by enacting a law penalising unions for participating in a polit-ical strike. The 1927 Trades Unions and Trades Disputes Act disappointed reactionary expectations, and in practice made little difference to unions' interwar conduct. In 1928, progressive employers and representatives from the General Council met to discuss matters of mutual interest; Labour became the largest party in the May 1929 general election and formed a minority government. Although it was a casualty of the international capitalist crisis, the foundations of the 'mid-century social compromise' had been laid.

The French strike wave and occupation movement in the early days of the Popular Front government in June 1936 are comparable to the ADGB and TUC general strikes. But in contrast to their defensive nature, the French events were positive, precipitated by the national election victory of the socialists, communists and radicals. The 'unprecedented wave of strikes and occupations involving around two million workers' (Price, 1993: 242) were not planned, but union leaders were quick to seize the opportunity to open negotiations with employers. Three days after the Socialist, Leon Blum, became Prime Minister, the Matignon agreement was signed, conceding wage increases of 7 to 15 per cent and recognising unions' negotiating rights. The government legislated a fortnight's annual paid holiday and a forty-hour week. These advances were the first time the French working class had extracted major concessions from industrial capitalists and the state. Blum promised works councils (*comités d'enterprise*), but his government fell before passing the necessary legislation. Nevertheless, the Pétain government established them, formalising unions' legitimate place in the social order.

The Second World War and its aftermath

There was no comparable development in Italy. The political elite's gamble on Mussolini ended in 1926 with the destruction of the liberal state and the outlawing of independent political parties and unions. The conception of a balance of class forces with the government holding the ring was heretical to Italian fascism. German unions were subjected to the same fate by Hitler in 1933. Unions were also driven underground in France in May 1940, after the Petain government had concluded an armistice with the Germans. British unions operated freely during the war, and their leaders were determined to re-establish the commanding position they had occupied in 1914–18. After the Labour Party joined Churchill's coalition government, with Bevin as Minister of Labour, he secured the TUC's agreement to a raft of statutory arrangements, enabling him to direct labour, enforce arbitration and declare strikes illegal. In return he implemented material and political advances, including joint consultative institutions. German, French and Italian union activists had to operate clandestinely and precariously. Nevertheless, many remained secure at work, protected by workmates' silent collusion and managements' reluctance to lose scarce labour. In northern Italy and France, they organised underground nuclei and sought contact with resistance movements.

At the end of the war, these veteran activists led their workmates in ensuring that vital production was maintained. Their principal priority was to dismantle the total war economy speedily, and ensure that workers were not disadvantaged in the transition to 'normal' peacetime living. Because so many employers and management had been willing collaborators and sometimes enthusiastic allies, there were expropriations and nationalisation of firms whose owners were now pariahs. By virtue of their responsible social and economic positions in the war, employers and many managers in Germany and occupied Europe were summarily displaced and penalised, firstly in the immediate aftermath of German withdrawal and surrender and subsequently in the de-nazification process.

The vacuum was mainly filled by older men and women who had been union officials, works councillors, and works committee members before fascism and/or underground during the war. Leaders from the Christian democrats, radicals and Catholic trade unions had similar experiences. The dates of birth of the post-war union and political leadership are illustrative: Leon Blum, 1872; Hans Boeckler, 1875; Konrad Adenauer, 1876; August Schmidt, 1878; Leon Jouhaux, 1879; Ernest Bevin and Alcide de Gasperi, 1881; Clement Attlee, 1883; Herbert Morrison and Ernst Reuter, 1888; Arthur

Deakin, Charles de Gaulle, and Palmiro Togliatti, 1890; Pietro Nenni, 1891; Giuseppe di Vittorio, 1892; Arthur Horner, 1894; Kurt Schumacher, 1895; Carlo Schmid, 1896; Aneurin Bevan and Sam Watson, 1897; Luigi Longo and Maurice Thorez, 1900; Erich Ollenhauer, 1901; George Woodcock, 1904; Guy Mollet, 1905; Herbert Wehner, 1906.

They had been typically politically active and engaged in workplace and party political activity in the interwar period. Having weathered periods of extreme flux and uncertainty, they used their experience in dealing with the emergency situations of 1944–45. In France and Germany, they resurrected the remnants of their 1930s union structures and works councils, adding legitimacy to scratch arrangements. In northern Italy, a well developed resistance organisation inside factories played the same role.

Although some of this veteran cohort still maintained the dogmatic Marxist distinction between capitalism and socialism, others began to question its assumptions and re-consider Bernstein's ideas. Union leaders, both socialist and communist, made no attempt to use the favourable circumstances presented by ubiquitous dislocation and extreme hardship to seize state power and proclaim a socialist republic. Their intervention to take charge of production and distribution stemmed from different considerations: firstly, the need to maintain the means of life and ensure the society's survival; and, secondly, the determination to establish a balance of class forces favourable to unions and workers. They exercised an important restraining influence on younger workers who viewed the fluid situation as a fortuitous opportunity to expropriate capitalists and settle anti-fascist scores. In Italy, for example, the National Committee for the Liberation of Upper Italy (CLNAI) created councils of management which 'guaranteed discipline on the shop-floor . . . urged sacrifices on the workforce in the name of reconstruction and who had to choose which workers were to go once the veto on sackings had been lifted' (Ginsborg, 1990: 96–7).

By 1947, however, resistance leaders, works councillors and union representatives voluntarily relinquished prerogative, either to a new cohort of professional young managers, or some of the older cohort who had passed through a peremptory de-nazification. They had achieved their goals. There was no major breakdown in production or social life. A peacetime balance of class forces, which favoured the unions had been firmly established in Britain and France. Union rights and workplace representation remained problematic in Germany and Italy until the end of the 1950s.

The new workplace order

The new workplace order was permeated by the prevailing atmosphere of the United Nations with its member states' commitment to universal human rights, irrespective of class. Union leaders used the universality imperative to reinforce their claims for full-blooded social partnership in all four countries. British capitalists had played their patriotic part in the war effort, but Bevin had compelled them to surrender ground to unions in the wartime production drive. After Labour won the general election, they prepared themselves for a further erosion of managerial prerogative. In France, the Fourth Republic enacted the programme of the *Conseil national de la Résistance* (CNR), which laid down a comprehensive welfare system for the first time, as well as reviving the *comités d'enterprise*. These foundations survived the demise of the republic, and continue to provide the bedrock of the French state's relation to its citizens.

Union activists in France, Italy and Germany agreed that pre-war political and confessional divisions between socialists, communists, and Catholics were not only irrelevant, but dangerous, because they impeded unions' ability to affect the balance of class forces. Because of their prominence in resistance movements and in post-liberation governments, the French and Italian communist parties (PCF and PCI) gained a critical mass of young, enthusiastic members and votes from factory workers and small farmers. The French party built on its pre-war foundations, but its wartime record was critical in establishing the PCF as a powerful national institution, (Kedward, 2005: 279–89). The wartime political unity forged in the French and Italian resistance movements permeated their reconstituted unions. Similar co-operation had operated in German war factories and pits where pre-1933 union activists made attempts to maintain a rudimentary underground organisation (Major, 1997: 149–76).

The cold war imposed a new political imperative on union activists, however. By 1948, the French and Italian unions had re-fractured along political and confessional lines, with the communist-influenced CGT (*Confédération Générale du Travail*) and CGIL (*Confederazione generale italiana del lavoro*) remaining the largest unions throughout this period (Romero, 1992: 138–74). In Germany, those key union officials who were also prominent KPD members had been ejected from office by tactical voting, organised by an anti-communist alliance of social democratic and Catholic activists.

The imperatives of Cold War adversarialism operated for both sides: their non-communist rivals denounced the CGT and CGIL for subservience to the communist party line and obeisance to Moscow; the CGT and CGIL leadership accused the Catholic and secular unions of class collaboration. In practice, the CGT and CGIL pursued pragmatic, non-revolutionary goals. Their Catholic and secular counterparts could afford to be more militant because they were smaller and could rely on the CGT and CGIL to provide more responsible leadership in conflict situations. The most intense phase of the cold war in 1948–53 rendered both PCF and PCI ineffectual political forces. Their dogmatic insistence on the revolutionary transformation from capitalism to socialism was comparable to the SPD's dogmatic defence of Marx in the face of Bernstein's critique.

Neither West German nor British communist parties were effective political actors. In Britain, the CPGB leadership virtually supressed the party's separate political role to give Labour a clear run against the Conservatives. In west Germany, the KPD leadership were keen to maximise their political influence, but social democrats were determined to avoid the worrying fates of their colleagues in SMAD and Poland. Listening to the experiences of refugees from the east reinforced their anti-communist views.

Employers try to move the balance back

In the face of employers' demands and escalating inflation, successive French and Italian governments enforced low wages and workers' purchasing power suffered accordingly (Price, 1993: 307; Duggan, 1994: 252–3). West German wages also remained at 'a relatively low level: 47 per cent of GNP, while in Britain they were 58 per cent of GNP' (Sassoon, 1996: 200). The British Labour government used Marshall Aid to maintain working-class real wages and also to construct a comprehensive welfare state. Despite comparatively stable workplace conditions in all four countries, the febrile atmosphere created by Cold War propaganda produced a climate in which routine class conflict was viewed as threatening the social order. All unions, but the CGT and CGIL particularly, were suspected of pursuing other goals than their overt claims for better wages and conditions. Anti-communist intellectuals and eager revolutionaries prophesied a return to the intense economic conflict of the interwar period and the triumph of communism.

In Italy, fascist laws still in force were used regularly by magistrates anxious to minimise class conflict. Nevertheless, in 1945–46, employers conceded the *scala mobile*, 'a system to safeguard workers' real wages against the effects of inflation'. 'They feared the unpredictable consequences of galloping inflation, and viewed . . . the *scala mobile* as an instrument both to protect a weakened and numerically reduced working class, and to guarantee productivity' (Ginsborg, 1990: 97). In October 1949, the CGIL general secretary, Giuseppe di Vittorio, proposed a practical programme for economic development within the existing capitalist economy, making the strong political statement that national resources should be developed for the benefit of all classes. Though formally rejected by the political establishment, successive coalition governments nevertheless tailored their economic policies with an eye to its provisions, evidently keen to show their commitment to similar goals (Ginsborg, 1990: 188–9).

Within the newly sovereign West German state, the re-constructed trade union centre, *Deutscher Gewerkschaftbund* (DGB), was determined to regain the Weimar constitution provisions for works councils and co-determination. They succeeded to a remarkable degree. Employers and the Christian Democrat Chancellor, Konrad Adenauer, were equally determined to resist any skew towards unions. The DGB, led by general secretary Hans Boeckler, threatened a general strike in April 1951 which induced Adenauer to concede *mitbestimmung*, the election of equal numbers of worker and shareholder representatives on supervisory boards in coalmining and iron and steel manufacturing companies. In July 1952, the DGB reluctantly acquiesced in the dilution of parity for other industries, accepting Adenauer's final offer of 33 per cent representation for union representatives on the boards of other industries. Neither the government nor the prospering industrial capitalists tried to oppose the revival of *Betriebsräte*. The Christian Democrats insisted that works councillors should not be required to be union representatives, and the DGB chose not to resist this denial of corporate privilege to the last ditch. In practice, union activists were almost invariably elected as works councils, and used them to extend union membership and cultivate a strong union workplace culture.

The election of a Conservative government in October 1951 was a bitter disappointment for British union leaders and activists. They prepared to resist the anti-working class measures which they believed the Tories were bound to inflict. Had Churchill held onto power in 1945, his government would neither have nationalised the coal industry nor repealed the 1926 Trade Unions Act. But in 1951, Churchill was exceedingly careful not to disturb what the Labour Government had done. He and his emollient Minister of Labour treated the TUC as equal partners, with no hint of legislating to restrict its activities. The National Coal Board operated unchanged, with the National Union of Mineworkers maintaining its de facto position of co-determination.

The balance oscillates around a mid-point

Stalin's unwillingness to de-stabilise the political situation in Western Europe became obvious in June 1949 when he re-opened the land routes to West Berlin. His death in March 1953 produced a renewed optimism among many Western European social democrats that the Cold War divisions might lessen and working-class internationalism prevail. Although these sanguine sentiments proved unfounded, the balance of class forces in Western Europe had evidently reached a stable mid-point.

There had been an overheated wartime boomlet in Britain at the beginning of the Korean war in May 1950, but surprisingly little dislocation in the rest of Western Europe. Although raw material and steel prices had risen sharply in the world market, this hardly dented the continuing recovery in West Germany and accelerating industrialisation in France and Italy. Improving economic conditions created favourable circumstances for the working class to improve its material position. In France, militants from the secular anti-communist union, *Force Ouvrière*, led extensive public-sector strikes in the summer of 1953. Their protracted duration and extension to workers throughout the public sector were probably connected to the glorious weather. Nevertheless, the government made substantial concessions to ease a return to work (Rioux, 1987: 219–21).

Unions continued to organise economic conflict to ensure that employers surrendered substantial portions of their increased profits. Through *Betriebsräte*, works committees and *comités d'enterprises*, union representatives and a strong union workplace culture secured at least the status quo for working hours and intensity of effort in the labour process. Employers invariably offered resistance, but did not dispute the need to be seen to be sharing the fruits of production, if not equally, at least to award employees a substantial share.

By contrast, no western European social democratic party performed well. Neither the SPD nor the Labour Party gained significant ground in parliamentary elections during the 1950s. Nevertheless, these poor performances were marginal and contingent. No one great political issue, centred around class conflict, determined the Christian Democrats' and Conservatives' victories. Nor did their continuation in office result in any worsening of working-class conditions. Those most disadvantaged were the putative social democratic office-holders and their attendant bureaucracies.

Socialist electoral failures were explained by most contemporary participants and observers as being symptomatic of the systemic failure of socialism as a third way between communism and capitalism. An outpouring of revisionist political tracts followed from party intellectuals. In mid-November 1959, the SPD adopted a new programme, formally abandoning its more dogmatic Marxist past. A fortnight later, Hugh Gaitskell was rebuffed at the Labour Party conference in his ill-prepared bid to revise Clause IV of Labour's 1918 constitution, committing the party to the nationalisation of the means of production, distribution and exchange. But he declined to see his defeat as a resigning matter, and proceeded to lead the party as if Clause IV was a mere sacred cow, without practical implications. Party activists, for the most part, acquiesced.

The situation in Italy, with its smaller socialist party, paralleled West Germany and Britain. In July 1957, the Italian Christian Democrats, led by Amintore Fanfani, embarked on 'the opening to the left' initiative, with the possibility of including the newly re-unified Socialist Party in government for the first time since 1947. His move was taken without consulting the Vatican, and was widely interpreted as an appropriate response to the changes in Italian society as a result of rapid industrialisation. Socialists did not enter government until December 1963, under Prime Minister, Aldo Moro. In the interim, the socialist leader, Pietro Nenni, had engaged in protracted theoretical disputes to persuade his members to make the alliance with the Christian Democrats. In France, where the socialists were in a much stronger position, twenty out of the twenty-two governments of the Fourth Republic were 'a nucleus of ministers from the non-Communist left and the centre' (Kedward, 2005: 382). But the balance of domestic class forces was a comparatively minor problem compared with de-colonisation.

By the mid-1960s, the balance of class forces was oscillating around a mid-point in all four countries. Unions were maintaining their positions of influence both at the workplace and at the national level. Moreover, from 1968 to 1974, they fought and won national economic conflicts with strong rank-and-file support to extend their power at both levels. These successes were reflected in politics, where socialist parties in Britain, West Germany and Italy were acknowledged as legitimate governing parties. (In Britain, Labour's failure to win three successive general elections in the 1950s had seriously demoralised the party and the unions.) The Italian electorate's rejection of the *legga truffa* and the French electorate's rejection of de Gaulle's referendum are examples of an evolving popular commitment to a system in which a more equal balance of class forces was the norm.

In 1945, it was wholly uncertain that this outcome would be achieved. Employers and their political allies might have tried to regain a more favourable position. Union leaders, communists and social democrats might have over-extended their forces in an effort to achieve 'pure' socialism. The substance of the mid-century social compromise has continued to oscillate within historically determined limits. However, popular support for the principle of a balance of class forces remains undiminished. Anchored in the experience of the twentieth century, its health and utility in the twenty-first will depend on the impact of globalisation and American hegemony, and the response of politicians and people to them.

References

Clegg, H. A. (1985), *A History of British Trade Unions Since 1889, Vol. II: 1911–1933* (Oxford: Oxford University Press).

Craig, G. A. (1981), *Germany 1866–1945* (Oxford: Oxford University Press).

Crouch, C. (1999), *Social Change in Western Europe* (Oxford: Oxford University Press).

Duggan, C. (1994), *A Concise History of Italy* (Cambridge: Cambridge University Press).

Feldman, G. D. (1992), *Army, Industry and Labor in Germany 1914–1918* (Oxford: Berg).

Ginsborg, P. (1990), *A History of Contemporary Italy, Society and Politics, 1943–1988* (London: Penguin).

Kedward, R. (2005), *La Vie en bleu, France and the French since 1900* (London: Allen Lane).

Major, P. (1997), *The Death of the KPD, Communism and Anti-communism in West Germany, 1945–1956* (Oxford: Oxford University Press).

Moses, J. A. (1982), *Trade Unionism in Germany from Bismarck to Hitler, 1869–1933* (London: George Prior).

Price, R. (1993), *A Concise History of France* (Cambridge: Cambridge University Press).

Rioux, J. P. (1987), *The Fourth Republic 1944–1958* (Cambridge: Cambridge University Press).

Romero, F. (1992), *The United States and the European Trade Union Movement 1944–1951*, trans. H. Fergusson II (Chapel Hill: University of North Carolina Press).

Sassoon, D. (1996), *One Hundred Years of Socialism: The West European Left in the Twentieth Century* (London: I.B. Tauris).

Saville, J. (1996), 'The Trades Disputes Act of 1906', *Historical Studies in Industrial Relations*, 1, 11–46.

6

Social democracy in post-war East Germany

Gareth Pritchard

Introduction

Between 1945 and 1947 in the Soviet zone of occupation in Germany, members of the Social Democratic Party (SPD), in an often uneasy alliance with members of the Communist Party (KPD), attempted to reshape East German society along lines that seemed to have more to do with the radical-democratic inheritance of the Social Democrats than the authoritarian traditions of the Communists. Whilst implementing far-reaching reforms, such as land reform, nationalisation, educational and legal reform, the new civil authorities in East Germany, which were dominated from the start by the SPD and KPD, also pledged their commitment to finding a peaceful, democratic, 'German' road to Socialism. It was in part on the basis of this radical but reformist programme that the KPD engineered a merger with the SPD in April 1946 to form a new, united workers' party in the Soviet zone, the 'Socialist Unity Party' (SED), which was to remain in power until its ignominious downfall in the autumn of 1989.

For many Social Democrats in the Soviet zone, their efforts to bring about fundamental social change through peaceful and democratic means represented an attempt to realise the radical-democratic traditions that had dominated SPD politics before 1914, but which had been dislocated by the First World War and by the schism of the labour movement into Communist and Social Democratic wings. Between 1945 and 1947, much of the political programme of the pre-First World War SPD was actually achieved. From 1947, however, the progressive Stalinisation of East German society led to the complete extinction of the Social Democratic milieu in the Soviet zone of occupation.

Social Democracy at 'Zero Hour'

The SPD had deep roots in that part of Germany that fell under Soviet occupation. The Nazis, for all their brutality, had never been able to extirpate these traditions. Upon the collapse of the Hitler regime at 'Zero

Hour', Social Democrats throughout East Germany began to revive their party organisations at a grassroots level and to address the immediate political tasks that confronted them.

Unsurprisingly, the political aspirations and behaviour of Social Democrats in the immediate post-war period was deeply influenced by their traumatic experiences of the collapse of the Weimar Republic and of persecution at the hands of the Nazis. All Social Democrats were eager to revenge themselves on their former Nazi persecutors and to play an active role in the reconstruction of Germany along democratic and antifascist lines. Beyond these common goals, however, one of the most salient characteristics of the SPD at Zero Hour was political diversity. For many years, the majority of Social Democrats had been isolated, not just from their exiled party leadership, but from each other. In most towns and cities, all that remained of the party organisation by 1935 were isolated groups of individuals who were often ignorant of the existence of other resistance cells in neighbouring localities (Allen, 1986: 856). Given the isolation of most Social Democrats, and their lack of knowledge about events in the wider world, it was natural that their political development was determined above all by local circumstances and their individual experiences. Since circumstances and experiences varied considerably from one locality to another, and from one individual to another, the natural consequence was a multiplicity of views and orientations.

On the one hand, many of the Social Democrats who emerged from the rubble in 1945 manifested an unbroken commitment to the moderate, gradualist style of politics, focusing above all on the sort of parliamentary activities that had been pursued by the SPD leadership during the Weimar period. Normally, Social Democrats of this stamp vigorously defended the role played by the SPD before 1933, and refused to accept that the 'reformism' of Weimar social democracy had been even partly to blame for the debacle of 1933. Such individuals often expressed an affinity for the British Labour government, whose sweeping electoral victory in July 1945 provided them with a model that they wished to emulate, coupled with a distaste for the KPD that was often based on negative personal encounters with Communists and unsettled scores dating back to the Weimar period (Pritchard, 2000: 62, 74–5).

Other Social Democrats, by contrast, had developed in a very different political direction. Having witnessed the miserable failure of Weimar democracy, and having endured twelve years of oppression and six cataclysmic years of war, many Social Democrats had come to two conclusions that had an enormous impact on their political behaviour in the post-war period. Firstly, it was widely agreed in Social Democratic circles that the Nazis had only been able to come to power because of the schism in the German labour movement, and, consequently, that only a united working-class party could prevent a recrudescence of German militarism and reaction. Accordingly, throughout East Germany in May and June 1945, Social Democrats approached their neighbourhood Communists with a view to the immediate establishment of a united socialist party. At this stage, however, both the Russians and the KPD leadership regarded a rapid unification of the two parties as a threat to their political control, and all moves in this direction were firmly blocked, much to the disappointment of pro-unity Social Democrats (Naimark, 1995: 271–5; Malycha, 1996a: xxvi–xxxi; Rudolph, 1998: 173–5).

A second conclusion arrived at by many Social Democrats was that the disaster of Nazism had demonstrated beyond any doubt the bankruptcy of capitalism, and that only the rapid introduction of Socialism could rescue the Germans from the devastation and poverty that had been bequeathed to them by Hitler. The Social Democrats in the newly liberated concentration camp at Buchenwald, for example, produced a manifesto that called for the immediate creation of socialist economic relations and the establishment of 'a new type of democracy, which does not exhaust itself in empty, formalistic parliamentarism, but which enables the effective participation of the broad masses . . . in politics and administration' (SAPMO-BArch, DY28 II 3/8/1). As the leader of the Buchenwald Social Democrats, Hermann Brill, repeatedly stressed, the creation of a socialist society in Germany was 'not a question of the distant future, but an immediate task of the present' (ThHStA Weimar, BPA Erfurt, II/1-001).

Underlying the desire for both radical social reform and unity with the Communists was a profound nostalgia for the perceived 'golden era' of the SPD in pre-First World War Germany, when the forward march of a united working-class party, committed to a Marxist world view, had seemed unstoppable (Rudolph, 1998: 172). Rejecting both the reformism of the Weimar SPD and the pseudo-radicalism of the interwar KPD, many Social Democrats hoped to recreate the party of August Bebel and Wilhelm Liebknecht (Jodle, 1997: 76). As Karl Litke, a leading Social Democrat in Berlin, argued: 'The old Social Democratic [Party] stormed from success to success, so long as it was united and led in the spirit of consistent Marxism.' According to a group of party veterans, also from Berlin: 'We old ones still remember the time when a united and therefore strong labour movement under August Bebel led, with such great success, the fanatical struggle for the rights of working people' (SAPMO-BArch, DY28 II 2/10).

Social Democrats and the 'antifascist democratic transformation'

In some ways the situation in post-war East Germany presented the SPD with a unique opportunity for the implementation of a programme of radical reform. Ever since the party's creation in 1875, progress towards fundamental reform had been blocked by a hostile state machine. In 1945, however, the entire apparatus of the state had more or less collapsed and what remained of the German police, judiciary and civil service could no longer thwart the aspirations of Social Democracy. The ability of the far right to mobilise a large section of the population against 'Marxist' politics had been neutralised by the collapse of Nazism. There were thus no longer any major obstacles on the right to stand in the way of the kind of transformation of society aspired to by radical Social Democrats.

Nor, at least superficially, did there seem to be any remaining significant barriers on the left of the political spectrum. In the 1920s and early 1930s, the work of the SPD had been continually hampered by the ultra-radical antics of a Communist Party that explicitly rejected the principles of 'bourgeois' democracy. In 1945, by contrast, the KPD had apparently abandoned its revolutionary traditions, and was now arguing that conditions in Germany did not permit the proletariat to seize power for itself. Instead, the leadership of the KPD, freshly returned from exile in Moscow, insisted that it was the task of the working class, in alliance with the peasantry and the progressive bourgeoisie, to construct in Germany a parliamentary democracy in which civil and property rights would be guaranteed (Krusch, 1991: 616–22; Pritchard, 2000: 7–10). From the point of view of the Communists and their Soviet masters, there were good reasons for this apparent conversion to the principles of democracy. Throughout much of western and southern Europe, support for Communist parties had been massively swelled by the radicalising impact of the war against fascism. The East German Communists fondly imagined that, particularly with the energetic support of the occupying power, they would prove as popular as their French, German and Yugoslav counterparts.

On 11 June 1945, the KPD leadership in Berlin issued an *Aufruf* (declaration), in which it affirmed the party's commitment to radical change through democratic means. Four days later, the newly constituted Central Committee (*Zentralausschuss*) of the SPD in Berlin produced its own *Aufruf*. The two programmes were remarkably similar. Both called for far-reaching reforms to destroy, not just Nazism, but the structural roots from which it was believed that Nazism had sprung. Both emphasised the importance of working-class unity. Though the KPD programme was not as radical as that of the Social Democrats, there was enough common ground for close collaboration between the two parties and, over the following eighteen months, they implemented a whole range of measures that transformed the political and economic landscape of the Soviet Zone. One can question, of course, the sincerity of the Soviets and the KPD leadership in the carrying out of these measures. Wilfried Loth maintains that Stalin's commitment to the creation in Germany of an antifascist, democratic order was vague but nonetheless sincere (Loth, 1994: 33–4). Manfred Wilke, by contrast, argues that the Soviets and KPD leadership saw the establishment of a 'parliamentary-democratic republic' as little more than a 'tactical interim goal' (Wilke, 1993: 5). Whatever Stalin's long-term goals may have been, as far as the majority of Social Democrats were concerned, the purpose of the measures they were implementing was not to prepare the ground for Communist dictatorship, but to realise the traditional goals of the SPD in the construction of a new, democratic and socialist society.

Thus, from the very beginning of the party's history, the SPD had wished to break the semi-feudal power that the great landlords exercised on their estates. In post-war East Germany, this long-standing goal was at last achieved. In the autumn of 1945, 7,000 landowners were expropriated without compensation, and their land distributed to 500,000 small farmers, landless agricultural labourers, and refugees. It was a massive administrative exercise, and thousands of Social Democrats, sitting alongside their Communist comrades in the land commissions, played a crucial role in carrying it through (Naimark, 1995: 142–4, 150–4; Ross, 2000: 17–32).

An equally long-standing demand of German Social Democracy was that the commanding heights of the economy, along with essential public services, be taken into public ownership. This goal, too, was realised in the Soviet Zone in the immediate post-war period. Many East German enterprises in May 1945 were 'ownerless' (*herrenlos*), usually because the former owners and managers had blotted their copy books during the Nazi period and had fled from the Red Army. De facto control of such enterprises was exercised by the workers themselves, usually through their elected workplace councils (Suckut, 1982). Sometimes, as in the coalmines of the Oelsnitz district, the workers themselves declared their enterprises to be 'property of the people' (Rössler, 1965: 108). Through 1946, a large chunk of East German industry was nationalised on a more formal basis. In June 1946, for example, a referendum was held in Saxony on the issue of whether the enterprises owned by 'Nazis and war criminals' should be expropriated. After 77.7 per cent of voters gave their support for the proposal, appropriate legislation was passed in Saxony and in the four other states (*Länder*) of the Soviet Zone. The running of plants affected by the legislation was usually placed in the hands of trustees, most of whom were drawn from the ranks of the labour movement, and many of whom were Social Democrats.

Land Reform and nationalisation were perhaps the two most important reforms implemented during the 'antifascist democratic transformation' but there were many others. Social Democrats played an important role in the implementation of all of them. A school reform, for example, was introduced, in order both to democratise and secularise the East German education system. Such an overhaul of the education system was a traditional goal of Social Democracy, and the SPD threw its full weight behind it (SAPMO-BArch, DY 28 II 2/3). Another traditional demand of the SPD was a thorough reform of the legal system to bring it closer to the people and ensure that ordinary workers could get justice in the courts. After 1945, Social Democratic lawyers worked in the justice system to implement the desired changes. Ordinary working-class people, many of whom were Social Democrats, were sent on crash courses where they were trained as 'people's judges' (Wentker, 2001: 18–222).

Yet another important change witnessed during the 'antifascist democratic transformation' was the reconstruction of local, district and regional governments on antifascist lines. The German civil service had long been known for its reactionary traditions. In the first post-war months, a sweeping programme of de-nazification ejected tens of thousands of Nazi and reactionary officials from their positions. For the most part they were replaced by men and women from working-class backgrounds, the vast majority of whom were either Communists or Social Democrats. In terms of the class composition of government, this represented a revolutionary change. Never before in German history had working-class people held so many responsible positions in the state apparatus (Pritchard, 2000: 86).

Relations with the Communists

Though the SPD worked closely with the KPD in the implementation of such reforms, the relationship between the two parties was strained from the beginning and rapidly deteriorated. There were two main reasons for the increasing friction that characterised relations between Social Democrats and Communists in the months leading up to the unification of the two parties in April 1946.

Firstly, in many localities there was intense competition between the two parties for positions in local government, and Social Democrats complained bitterly that Communists had seized important posts for themselves and were systematically using their power to impede the organisational development of the SPD (Suckut, 2000: 27; Pritchard, 2000: 86–90). Typical is the example of Köpenick, where Social Democrats bemoaned the fact that their local Communists were as intolerant and fanatical as ever, and showed no willingness 'to break with the propagandistic methods of the past' (SAPMO-BArch, DY 28 II 2/11). In Grossvoigtsberg in Saxony, Social Democrats complained that the local KPD *Bürgermeister* was exhibiting 'dictatorial behaviour, indeed open hostility to our party', and accused him of employing 'fascist–Nazi methods' against the SPD (SStA Chemnitz, BPA Karl-Marx-Stadt, I-4/21). In Grosshartmannsdorf, also in Saxony, the SPD reported that the local KPD group was following a course 'that is reminiscent of the inglorious days of division of the pre-1933 period' (SStA Chemnitz, BPA Karl-Marx-Stadt, II-3/05). Such grievances are extremely common in the internal SPD documents that have come to light since the opening of the East German archives (Malycha, 1996a).

The second reason for deteriorating relations was the differing responses of the two parties to the more unpopular aspects of Soviet occupation. At least in public, the Communists justified the changes to the eastern borders of Germany that had been unilaterally imposed by the USSR. The KPD was equally dogged in its defence of the avaricious reparations extracted by the Soviets from their zone of occupation. With regard to the most sensitive issue of all, the attacks and rapes perpetrated by Red Army soldiers on German civilians, the KPD leadership variously ignored the problem altogether, or claimed that the level of attacks was massively exaggerated (SStA Leipzig, BPA Leipzig, I/3/28), or pretended that attacks were mainly carried out by 'bandits' dressed in Russian uniforms (Chemnitz, BPA Karl-Marx-Stadt, V/5/323), or argued that the Germans were simply paying the price for the bestial behaviour of the Wehrmacht and the SS in Russia (SStA Leipzig, BPA Leipzig, I/3/06).

The response of the SPD to the more unpleasant aspects of Soviet occupation was very different. Though Social Democrats, both in public and in private, acknowledged the debt of gratitude they owed to their Russian liberators, and although there was a widespread and genuine desire within the SPD for friendly relations with both the Soviet military government and the USSR, Social Democrats were also forthright in their criticism of the territorial changes, of reparations, and of the behaviour of Russian soldiers. This in turn had a significant impact on the popularity of the SPD, for, more than any other organisation in the Soviet Zone, it gave expression to the anger and anxiety produced in the population by the activities of the Russians. By October 1945 the SPD, with 300,000 members, had caught up with the KPD, despite the fact that the latter party had access to massively superior resources. By the end of the year, with 407,000 members, the SPD had overtaken the KPD and was clearly establishing itself as the most vigorous political force in East Germany (Suckut, 2000: 27).

From the point of view of the Soviets, the massive growth of an increasingly self-confident SPD, coupled with the less than dazzling performance of the KPD, posed a serious challenge to their political control. What no doubt further added to Soviet alarm were the miserable results of the Communists in elections in both Hungary and Austria in November 1945, where they achieved just 16.9 per cent and 5.4 per cent of the vote respectively (Klessmann, 1991: 139). In an effort to neutralise the increasing threat posed by Social Democracy, the Soviets, and their underlings in the KPD leadership, suddenly, in the late autumn of 1945, began to push for the most rapid possible merger of the two working-class parties.

The creation of the SED

The unity campaign of November 1945 to April 1946 has been the object of more scholarly attention that any other aspect of the Soviet occupation. The main point at issue has always been whether or not the creation of the SED represented a 'forced union' (*Zwangsvereinigung*). The general consensus since the opening of the archives in 1989 seems to be that it was indeed a *Zwangsvereinigung*, and even the PDS, the reformed Communist party in East Germany, has now apologised to the SPD for the violence and intimidation used against Social Democrats during the unity campaign (Müller, Mrotzek and Köllner, 2002: 248–9). There are still voices, however, who, whilst acknowledging that coercion played a crucial in bringing the SPD to the altar, insist that to depict the marriage of the two parties as nothing more than a shotgun wedding is inadequate (Benser, 1995). Manfred Wilke and Peter Erler, for example, have described the merger in terms of the 'voluntary submission' (*einverständliche Unterwerfung*) of the SPD (Suckut, 2000: 33). So much has been written on this question that it would be inappropriate, in the limited space available here, to rehearse the arguments used by the various factions or to attempt a resolution. However, two points pertaining to the merger of the working-class parties are so important that they deserve at least a brief mention.

First, there can be no question that there was widespread reluctance in the ranks of the SPD to enter the unity party. On 6 January 1946, for example, a packed meeting of Social Democrats in Rostock unanimously passed a motion arguing that a merger in the Soviet Zone alone was likely to lead to a schism in the German working class as a whole, and that the unification of the KPD and SPD could only come about after a referendum of the entire membership of both parties (SAPMO-BArch, DY28 II 2/11). At a joint meeting of Communists and Social Democrats in the small Saxon town of Grossvoigtsberg, a KPD speaker demanded that all those who were against unity should rise from their seats, at which point 'all the SPD comrades present in the room . . . rose up as a bloc' and could only with some difficulty be persuaded from storming out of the meeting *en masse* (SStA Chemnitz, BPA Karl-Marx-Stadt, I-4/18). In Leipzig, it was reported that only a small minority of SPD functionaries 'adopted a clear line in the spirit of the united front', and that at joint SPD-KPD party meetings, those who spoke in favour of unity received little applause from the Social Democrats in the audience (SStA Leipzig, BPA Leipzig, I/3/16). Given this level of opposition, the merger could never have been achieved in such a short space of time without the concerted pressure of the Soviet military authorities. Many thousands of un-cooperative SPD functionaries suffered harassment, or worse, at the hands of the Soviets (Malycha, 1996a: lxxxii–lxxxv). According to Erich Ollenhauer, the leader of the SPD in West Germany from 1952, some 20,000 Social Democrats were imprisoned for longer or shorter periods, or even killed (Fricke, 1964: 29–30).

Second, despite the central role of coercion during the unity campaign, it is insufficient to describe the merger as a '*Zwangsvereinigung*' but to take the analysis no further than that. A significant minority of Social Democrats, for example, were enthusiastically in favour of unity. In the coal-mining town of Freiberg, the local SPD reported that its members supported the merger as 'only unity can ensure for all time the security of the proletarian masses in a united German workers' party and the peace of Europe and the entire world'. The SPD group in Colmnitz, also in Saxony, reported that its members were unanimously in favour of unity, and that it was the local Communists who were insufficiently enthusiastic about the creation of the SED (SStA Chemnitz, BPA Karl-Marx-Stadt, II/3-05). Even amongst Social Democrats who were opposed to the immediate creation of the Unity Party in the Soviet Zone alone, there was a widespread acceptance that the eventual creation of a united working-class party remained a worthy, indeed, essential goal. Thus the very same Social Democrats who, at the mass meeting in Rostock in January 1946, unanimously rejected an immediate merger, also declared in their motion that 'an honest, trusting and close co-operation of both workers' parties, which eventually must be crowned with an organisational merger, is a political necessity' (SAPMO-BArch, DY28 II 2/11). According to a Social Democrat from the town of Klostermansfeld in Saxony-Anhalt, about 10 to 15 per cent of members were totally opposed to merger, whilst a similar percentage was enthusiastically in favour. The majority, however, 'was made up of those who waited on events – we'll see how things turn out, and if needs be we have a majority [in the new party] after all. That was how the majority thought' (Bouvier and Schulz, 1991: 196–7). Many Social Democrats, though they had grave reservations about the speed and the character of the unity campaign, nonetheless believed that it was better to give way to Soviet and Communist pressure rather than risk yet another bitter schism in the German labour movement. At a meeting in Markrandstädt, for instance, a veteran Social Democrat proclaimed 'that he had always been an enemy of the KPD, but that we must now bite into the sour apple in the interests of the working class' (SStA Leipzig, BPA Leipzig, I/3/23). At the last SPD meeting to be held in Leipzig until the revolution of 1989, one SPD speaker declared: 'We are sacrificing our party for the freedom of Germany' (SStA Leipzig, BPA Leipzig, II/2/02).

The destruction of social democracy

Life for former Social Democrats in the new united workers' party was not at first too uncomfortable. Though the SPD had ceased to exist, the new unity party 'presented itself in its programmatic documents more as a Social Democratic party, which professed itself in favour of "consistent Marxism", but which avoided any Leninist terminology and advocated a "democratic road" to Socialism' (Suckut, 2000: 36). The political atmosphere within the SED was, to begin with, fairly relaxed. According to a Social Democrat from Saalfeld: 'The decisive turning point only came with the proclamation of the "party of a new type" [in June 1948]. Up to this point in time it was still possible, for example in speeches, to put forward our own ideas; in meetings and conferences we could still operate

more or less discretely' (Bouvier and Schulz, 1991: 284). Fritz Schenk, an
anti-Communist Social Democrat who later fled to the western zones,
noted that:

> After the merger I perceived at first no striking difference in the life of the
> party. Admittedly propaganda work and schooling was considerably
> strengthened, and one heard ever more Communist vocabulary; but nobody
> minced their words and free rein was given to discussion and party meetings
> were if anything even more interesting than before. One said what one thought.
> (Schenk, 1962: 16–17)

Within the new party, former Communists and Social Democrats continued
to work together in the implementation of the 'antifascist democratic transformation', for example during the campaign to secure a 'yes' vote in the
Saxon referendum on the expropriation of Nazi factory owners. Even at
the higher levels of the party apparatus, there were genuine and occasionally heated arguments, in which the lines of division often crossed the
former party allegiances of the participants (Pritchard, 2000: 149–51). In
the autumn of 1946, the new party went twice to the polls, first of all in
local and then in regional (*Land*) elections. These elections can hardly be
described as fair, for the Soviets intervened vigorously in favour of the SED.
But the fact that they were at least comparatively free is demonstrated
by the SED's relatively poor performance. In the regional elections, for
example, the Communist leadership had expected to gain up to 70 per cent
of the vote, but when the results were announced they had to content themselves with 47.6 per cent (Suckut, 2000: 44). Though these results, from
the point of view of the SED, were disappointing, they nonetheless reveal,
as Herman Weber has pointed out, that the party 'still found support in
the population' (Weber, 1985: 142).

The advent of the Cold War, however, greatly accelerated the authoritarian processes that had been at work in the Soviet Zone from the very
beginning. As international tensions rose, the Soviets began increasingly
to insist that the various satellite states of East-Central Europe move into
a closer orbit around the USSR. As early as 1947, a positive attitude to
the Soviet Union was proclaimed to be a prerequisite for party membership (ThHStA Weimar, BPA Erfurt, AIV/2/5-141). The following year, the
party officially abandoned the doctrine of the 'German road to Socialism'
to be replaced by the doctrine that: 'Learning from the Soviet Union means
learning victory!' (Grieder, 1999: 9–17). In June 1948, a decisive step in
the direction of Stalinism was taken with the announcement by Walter
Ulbricht, the leading former Communist in the SED leadership, that the
party was henceforth to be transformed into a 'party of a new type', closely
modelled on the Communist Party of the Soviet Union. Accordingly, from
the period 1947–48 onwards, a whole series of measures were introduced
that undermined the importance of Social Democratic ideas in the SED

and the influence of former Social Democrats (Malycha, 1996b: 148–92; Grieder, 1999: 17–25). Much more emphasis, for example, was placed on ensuring that SED members regularly attended 'educational' evenings and party schools, at which the standard fare would be 'classic' works of Stalin such as *Foundations of Leninism* and *History of the CPSU (Short Course)*. In January 1949, the principle of parity, which stated that responsible positions in the party should be distributed equally between former Communists and Social Democrats, was abolished. A Soviet-style politburo was introduced, along with the Stalinist doctrine of 'democratic centralism'. Most fatefully of all, in September 1948 the party leadership introduced 'control commissions' at a central, regional and district level, whose task it was to undertake a review of the entire membership of the SED. Individuals who, for whatever reason, were suspected by the party leadership of not being true to the party line (*linientreu*), were summoned to appear before tribunals staffed by trained inquisitors, the vast majority of whom were veteran Communists or younger, neophyte Stalinists only recently hatched from the party schools (Pritchard, 2000: 163–9).

In the ensuing purge, many tens of thousands of members were expelled from the party. As a result, between 1949 and 1954, the membership of the SED shrank by approximately 20 per cent (Lewis, 1994: 83). Though people found themselves on the wrong side of the party commissions for a variety of reasons, including 'immoral behaviour', corruption, or ultra-left sectarianism, the single most important target of the purge was Social Democracy. Thousands of SPD members were expelled from the SED, many of whom were subsequently arrested and imprisoned, on the grounds that they were 'Schumacher agents' engaged in a systematic plot to sabotage the construction of Socialism in East Germany (Malycha, 1996b: 193–227).

The spectre of a giant conspiracy, conceived in Washington but co-ordinated by the 'Ostbüro' of the West German SPD in Berlin, had no basis in reality. As one former Social Democrat in Dresden commented: 'The creation of any kind of illegal cadre organisation was not planned by us. It was quite clear to me that the more the Russians and the SED dug themselves in, the more senseless it was to offer up endless victims' (Bouvier and Schulz, 1991: 242). On the other hand, it is also certainly true that, whilst discontented Social Democrats only rarely joined together to form self-conscious resistance cells, they often belonged to loose oppositional networks not so different from the 'circles of friends' (*Freundschaftskreise*) which had sustained the Social Democratic milieu through the years of Nazi persecution. Particularly amongst higher ranking functionaries, these networks extended across the Soviet Zone and sometimes included contacts with old comrades in the West German SPD. There is some evidence that former Social Democrats in positions of authority used their influence to provide jobs for their political friends, leading to concentrations of former SPD members in particular localities or enterprises. Thus, whilst there was no grand conspiracy against the party, one can speak of an SPD 'resistance' in the sense that there existed an oppositional milieu within the SED. Moreover, many individual Social Democrats, who were deeply committed to their own traditions of democratic Socialism, were becoming increasingly disenchanted, and openly critical, of the changes in party policy and culture. Many Social Democrats found themselves in difficulties because they had publicly denounced Leninist doctrines such as 'democratic centralism', or for denying that a consistent Marxist must also be a Leninist, or for continuing to argue in favour of a German road to Socialism, or for praising old heroes of the Social Democratic movement such as Ferdinand Lassalle, Eduard Bernstein and Karl Kautsky. Other Social Democrats got into trouble for refusing to attend party schools, or for rejecting demands that they publicly recant for having been members of the SPD during the Weimar period (Pritchard, 2000: 174–6).

All such expressions of opposition and resistance proved to be in vain. In the face of an increasingly well organised and pervasive state security police, and in the wake of structural changes to the nature of the working class, it proved impossible in the long term to maintain oppositional networks, or to pass on Social Democratic traditions to the next generation. The final, violent spasm of East German Social Democracy occurred during the workers' uprising of 17 June 1953, when much of the unrest had a strong Social Democratic flavour (Diedrich, 1991: 128–32; Mitter and Wolle, 1993: 67, 116–17, 128; Pritchard, 2002: 123–4). The Red Army tanks that, on the evening of 17 June, crushed the uprising of the East German working class, sealed the fate of a proud political tradition, the roots of which stretched all the way back to the 1860s. Isolated individuals no doubt continued to cherish the faith, but by the mid-1950s Stalinism had accomplished something that the Nazis never had – the smashing of the Social Democratic milieu, and the extirpation of its traditions. When, in the turbulent autumn of 1989, groups of East Germans dissidents began the process of re-establishing the SPD, they were unable to build on any surviving foundations, but instead had to start completely afresh (Müller, Mrotzek and Köllner, 2002: 219–21, 227–38).

Conclusion

In 1945, inspired by the belief that at last, after decades of struggle and suffering, their moment had come, Social Democrats attempted to revive the pre-1914 vision of revolutionary change achieved through democratic means. In the mistaken belief that the Communists had converted to democracy, Social Democrats not only worked closely with the KPD in the implementation of the 'antifascist democratic transformation', but also allowed themselves, with more or less reluctance, to be dragooned into the SED. Much was achieved, and by 1947 many of the main demands of the pre-First World War SPD had been realised on East German soil, albeit at the price of the organisational independence of the party. The heady expectations of 1945, however, proved illusory, and the price demanded by the KPD for the 'fraternal unity' of the working class proved to be too high. The same set of circumstances that presented radical Social Democrats with a unique opportunity to implement their programme also unleashed powerful degenerative tendencies that would lead to the destruction, first of the SPD, and then of the entire Social Democratic milieu in East Germany.

References

Allen, W. S. (1986), 'Die Sozialdemokratische Untergrundbewegung: Zur Kontinuität der subkulturellen Werte', in Schmädeke and Steinbach, 1986: 849–66.

Benser, G. (1995), *Zusammenschluss von KPD und SPD 1946* (Berlin: Hefte zur DDR Geschichte 27).

Bouvier, B. and Schulz, H. (1991), '. . . *die SPD aber aufgehört hat zu existieren*' (Bonn: J. H. W. Dietz Nachf).

Diedrich, T. (1991), *Der 17. Juni in der DDR* (Berlin: Dietz).

Faulenbach, B. and Potthoff, H. (eds) (1998), *Sozialdemokraten und Kommunisten nach Nationalsozialismus und Krieg* (Essen: Klartext).

Fricke, K. W. (1964), *Selbstbehauptung und Widerstand in der sowjetischen Besatzungszone Deutschlands* (Bonn: Bundesministerium für gesamtdeutsche Fragen).

Grieder, P. (1999), *The East German Leadership 1946–73* (Manchester: Manchester University Press).

Jodle, M. (1997), *Amboss oder Hammer? Otto Grotewohl* (Berlin: Aufbau).

Klessmann, C. (1991), *Die doppelte Staatsgründung* (Göttingen: Vandenhoeck & Ruprecht).

Krusch, H.-J. (1991), 'Neuansatz und widersprüchliches Erbe. Zur KPD 1945/46', *Beiträge zur Geschichte der Arbeiterbewegung*, 1991/5: 616–25.

Lewis, P. G. (1994), *Central Europe since 1945* (Harlow: Longman).

Loth, W. (1994), *Stalins ungeliebtes Kind* (Berlin: Rowohlt).

Major, P. and Osmond, J. (eds) (2002), *The Workers' and Peasants' State* (Manchester: Manchester University Press).

Malycha, A. (1996a), *Auf dem Weg zur SED* (Bonn: J. H. W. Dietz Nachf).

Malycha, A. (1996b), *Partei Stalins Gnaden?* (Berlin: Dietz).

Mitter, A. and Wolle, S. (1993), *Untergang auf Raten* (Munich: C. Bertelsmann).

Müller, W., Mrotzek F. and Köllner, J. (2002), *Die Geschichte der SPD in Mecklenburg und Vorpommern* (Bonn: J. H. W. Dietz Nachf).

Naimark, N. (1995), *The Russians in Germany* (Cambridge, MA: Belknap).

Pritchard, G. (2000), *The Making of the GDR* (Manchester: Manchester University Press).

Pritchard, G. (2002), 'Workers and the Socialist Unity Party of Germany in the Summer of 1953', in Major and Osmond, 2002: 112–29.

Ross, C. (2000), *Constructing Socialism at the Grass Roots* (Basingstoke: Macmillan).

Rössler, H. (1965), 'Das Niemandsland: Berichte und Dokumente aus dem Jahre 1945', *Der Heimatfreund*, Stollberg: 1965.

Rudolph, K. (1998), 'Die Ausschaltung der SPD aus der sächsischen Politik (1945/46)', in Faulenbach and Potthoff, 1998: 171–82.

Schenk, F. (1962), *Im Vorzimmer der Diktatur* (Cologne: Kiepenheuer & Witsch).

Schmädeke, J. and Steinbach, P. (eds) (1986), *Der Widerstand gegen den Nationalsozialismus* (Munich: Piper).

Suckut, S. (1982), *Die Betriebsrätebewegung in der Sowjetisch Besetzten Zone Deutschlands (1945–1948)* (Frankfurt am Main: Haag & Herchen).

Sucket, S. (2000), *Parteien in der SBZ/DDR 1945–1952* (Bonn: Bundeszentrale für politische Bildung).

Weber, H. (1985), *Geschichte der DDR* (Munich: Deutscher Taschenbuch Verlag).

Wentker, H. (2001), *Justiz in der SBZ/DDR 1945–1953* (Munich: Oldenbourg Wissenschaftsverlag).

Wilke, M. (1993), 'Die Staatskonzeption der KPD-Führung im Moskauer Exil 1944' (paper given at the International Conference of the Institute of Contemporary History, Academy of Sciences of the Czech Republic, 9–11 September 1993).

Archival sources

Sächsisches Staatsarchiv (SStA) Chemnitz, Bezirksparteiarchiv (BPA) Karl-Marx-Stadt.

Sächsisches Staatsarchiv (SStA) Leipzig, Bezirksparteiarchiv (BPA) Leipzig.

Stiftung Archiv der Parteien und Massenorganisationen der DDR im Bundesarchiv (SAPMO-BArch), Berlin.

Thüringisches Hauptstaatsarchiv (ThHStA) Weimar, Bezirksparteiarchiv (BPA) Erfurt.

7

Social democracy at the turn of the 1960s

Paolo Pombeni

Introduction

At the end of the 1950s the political parties that led post-war stabilisation were firmly in power. This was entirely evident in Germany and in Italy. At the September 1957 German elections, in spite of Adenauer's advanced age of eighty-two, the CDU/CSU alliance obtained 50.2 per cent of the votes (winning with the significant slogan: *Keine Experimente!*). As far as Italy is concerned, despite the constant challenges to the hegemony of Christian democracy raised by both the heirs of the pre-fascist ruling class and important elements of the Vatican hierarchy, who considered the party to be too independent and negligent of the overall defence of papal orthodoxy, in the elections of 25 May 1958 the party obtained fully 43.4 per cent of votes (an increase of 3.3 per cent on the previous elections). The DC thus incontrovertibly confirmed itself as the pivot around which rotated a 'centrist' coalition; that is to say, a political alliance whose underlying rationale was the conviction that social and economic progress did not demand co-participation in the government by the parties of the left (Pombeni, 1997; Lupo, 2004).

The picture is less clear-cut as regards Britain and especially France. As far as Great Britain is concerned, although it is true that post-war stabilisation was the work of Labour governments, Attlee's reconstruction was regarded by many as a 'socialist' experiment in a period seen as 'exceptional' (Morgan, 1984; Jefferys, 1992; Tomlinson, 1997). But stabilisation was also the work of the Conservatives whose governments after 1951 operated in great continuity with the earlier Labour governments (Pinto-Duschinsky, 1970; Jefferys, 1997; Jones H., 1997). Harold Macmillan, Prime Minister in 1957 won the general election of October 1959 with 49.3 per cent of the votes and an increased lead over the Labour Party in terms of constituencies won (365 compared to Labour's 258).

The case of France may appear to be the one most at variance with this trend. The May 1958 crisis led to the inglorious end of the Fourth Republic. However, the man responsible for the Fourth Republic's demise, General De Gaulle, continued the work of post-war stabilisation. Indeed, a 'social' dimension was by no means absent from Gaullism in the first phase of the new regime (Rudelle, 1988; Quagliariello, 2003).

The 1960s' turn: Socialists are back in power

However, five years later the European panorama was to thoroughly change. By the end of 1963 the 'Adenauer era' had come to an end in Germany. This was well reflected in the so-called 'Spiegel affair': for the first time, the CDU was forced to negotiate over the future government with both the Liberals (FDP) – its long-standing allies, but to whom it now had to make concessions – and the Socialists, by now recognised as a component of the new political system in their own right (Schwarz, 1997; Nicholls, 1997).

In the same year, Italy saw the birth of the first 'organic' (i.e. with the direct participation of the Socialist party) centre-left government. This marked the end of an ideological taboo, whose cultural and political weight should not be underestimated (Scoppola, 1991: 342–54).

In the autumn of 1964, the Labour Party returned to power in Britain, after a thirteen-year period of opposition, which had prompted authoritative political scientists of the time to wonder if, in the new context of affluence, the Labour Party was doomed to constant electoral defeat (Rose-Abrams, 1960).

What happened in France was also consistent with this trend. From 1963 onwards it was, in fact, clear that De Gaulle's victory had not spelt the end of the political ethos that had emerged from the Second World War (Berstein, 1989; Quagliariello, 2003). Those who joined the 'Cartel des nons' for the referendum of 28 October and then for the elections of 18 and 25 November 1962 now began the long electoral campaign that would reap significant success in the presidential elections of December 1965. De Gaulle won, but only by a narrow margin: 44.65 per cent of votes in the first round (5 December: his opponent, François Mitterrand, obtained 32 per cent), and 55.2 per cent in the second (19 December: Mitterrand obtained 44.8 per cent).

Explaining Socialists' electoral revival

I think we have to interrogate the reasons for and the roots of this change. Was it simply the result of the 'affluent revolution' that John Kenneth Galbraith described in 1958 in his *Affluent Society*? The latter contains a well-known thesis, often put forward by scholars, that does indeed hold some elements of truth (Pombeni, 2003): there is no doubt that 'affluence' was a conquest which post-war society was beginning to fully appreciate and was loath to forgo. One may add that the signals of economic crisis apparent almost everywhere in Europe at the turn of the 1960s heightened worry, if not outright fear, that what had been gained could so easily be lost. There was consequently a certain willingness among voters to accept political innovation as long as their hard-won affluence was protected.

Scholars have also drawn attention to the 'age' of the politicians who had carried out the stabilisation during the previous decade, what is sometimes known as the 'Kennedy factor'. Just about everywhere public opinion was touched by the image of the youthful American president, smiling and vigorous, as he spoke of the 'New Frontier'. If a super-power like the USA had shown the courage to appeal to a new generation, was this not a lesson to be emulated in Europe? The examples here abound. Just to mention a few, I will cite the 'German Kennedy', or the young burgomaster of Berlin, Willy Brandt – 47 years old in 1960 – (Merseburger, 2004: 343–95), who stood against the octogenarian Adenauer (but also against the corpulent, though significantly younger, father of the German economic miracle, Ludwig Erhard); and Harold Wilson, who at the age of 46 stood in marked contrast to the old and unwell Harold Macmillan and to the latter's temporary replacement: the grey Sir Alec Douglas-Home.

Overall, a much more vigorous wind of youthfulness was blowing through politics. Even in France, a nation which had no traditional sympathy for the 'American model', Lecanuet, the MRP candidate against De Gaulle in the presidential elections of 1965, was a university professor of forty-five who presented himself as the 'French Kennedy' (Chalin, 2000; Philippe, 2001). A certain rejuvenation of the ruling class was also apparent in countries, like Italy, where the Kennedy myth could not be taken on board, both because there was not a pre-eminent executive (indeed, Amintore Fanfani, who had been a 'youthful' alternative to the traditional ruling class already in the mid-1950s, was set aside precisely because he wanted to give greater power to the prime ministership), and because of a lack of personalities who resembled the American president.

Nevertheless, there are also examples that can be cited to disprove the 'Kennedy factor'. Not only was De Gaulle aged 67 when he was returned to power in 1958, but Adenauer's successor in 1963, Ludwig Erhard, was 56. In Italy, the socialist leader Pietro Nenni was 60 years old in 1961, and the communist leader Palmiro Togliatti was not far behind him (58 in 1961). In short, 'youthfulness' is not a valid key of interpretation for the 1960s' political renewal I am referring to.

Affluence, economic growth and the revival of Socialism

In my view, the key factor here to be considered is the extent of the credibility that individual parties had in the eyes of public opinion, more in regard to the management of affluence than the prospects for further growth. If the question was the promotion of affluence, the old ruling class had sufficient credentials to stay in power. As I argued above, the various 'economic miracles' of the post-war period had mostly come about under the aegis of centre and centre-right coalition governments. None of them had adopted policies of 'unregulated capitalism' – as conjured up by the forces of the extreme left; nor did they divert from a social welfare agenda, which not even the fascist dictatorships had abandoned. Fiscal policies were relatively moderate, and the need to defend the greater purchasing power now acquired by the working class was universally accepted.

Why then did the 'conservatives' lose credibility? Was it because the idea of the need for 'more advanced equilibria' (an Italian expression meaning a coalition between the centre and the moderate left) started gaining ground? For me this is the key explanatory factor: during the years in question, it became entirely obvious that economic growth was leading to deep transformations of society. This was a matter of great concern to the conservatives who found it increasingly hard to govern growth in such a way that the status quo ante was not called into question (Giersch, Paqué and Schmieding, 1992; Crainz, 1997; Freeden, 1996: 317–44). They also looked increasingly inept in dealing with the first signs of a faltering economy.

In this regard, Germany and Italy are, indeed, two emblematic cases. In Germany the effects of economic growth began to appear slowly but inexorably. In October 1963 Ludwig Erhard, the father of the economic miracle achieved by the classic mechanisms of the market economy (Kielmanseeg, 2000: 432–50), was elected. His popularity was further reflected in the result of the elections of September 1965, which the CDU/CSU won with the excellent percentage of 47.6 per cent of votes. However, as the signs of recession – already apparent in mid-1964 – grew more alarming, Erhard rapidly lost his grip on public opinion. On 27 November 1966, as a result of the recession of 1966–67, the so-called 'Grand Coalition' was brought to power (Hilldebrandt, 1984; Schmoeckl and Kaiser, 1991). This outcome had been presaged by the results of elections in the North Rhine–Westphalia *Land* (10 July 1966), when the CDU lost 4 percentage points and the SPD obtained almost 50 per cent of the votes – undoubtedly a victory for the new social democracy that had emerged after the famous Congress of Bad Godersberg (November 1959), which proclaimed the SPD no longer a 'class party' but a 'popular party' (Bouvier, 1990). The dictum propounded by the Hamburg economist, and later Social Democrat minister, Karl Schiller – 'as much competition as possible, as much planning as necessary' – became the formula by which the new legitimation was established. This was not, as the extreme left claimed, a surrender by social democracy to capitalism; rather, it was an offer by social democracy to place at the service of the new economic system based on the production of general affluence its own ability to guarantee 'popular participation' at a moment of the economy's temporary difficulty, a moment that could be attenuated by government intervention. This offer, however, was grounded in the belief that only a 'competitive' economy could ensure that the affluence now being enjoyed by the population would continue and expand.

In Italy, the question of a 'broadening to the left' was first raised after the centrist parties' failure to introduce a new majoritarian electoral system in 1953, which would have allowed the survival of the old centrist formula that had been dominating Italian politics since mid-1947 (Piretti, 2003).

The inclusion of Nenni's Socialist Party in the majority was regarded by many as a way to reinforce future coalition governments but also to address – in so far it would lead to the adoption of policies of greater state intervention and planning – the Italian economy's distortions, that now seemed to threaten further economic growth. However, the PSI's entry into a coalition government was anything but easy (Degl'Innocenti, 1993: 269–327; Pombeni, 1997; Craveri, 2002). On the one hand, it was recognised that without this opening up to the left the government coalition would be weak and therefore reliant on surreptitious help from the neo-fascist right. On the other hand, an alliance with the Socialists meant opening the door to a sub-culture that was rather distant from that of Christian democracy; that is, a sub-culture which comprised lay traditions with marked anti-clerical and Masonic sympathies, together with pacifist international attitudes. The Vatican hierarchy was particularly hostile to any development that, by strengthening the DC-led coalition government, might increase lay Catholics' independence in politics from the Vatican (Sani, 2002; Galavotti, 2004; Marchi, 2006). This was the core issue, much more than the officially proclaimed impossibility for Catholics to associate with a party that professed atheist Marxism as its creed.

One must also bear in mind the extent of hostility that existed to this formula within the PSI ranks: the party's culture was inimical to an alliance with a force still regarded by many as 'obscurantist' and 'reactionary'. This gave rise to an impasse from which neither of the two forces was able to extricate itself on its own. Both sides were constrained by external actors: the DC by the Vatican hierarchy; the PSI by organisations within the Left such as the cooperatives and trade unions, all of which practised co-participation in top jobs by communists and socialists (Paggi and D'Angelillo, 1986; Ajello, 1997). Eventually, in December 1963 the first organic centre-left government was formed and the centre-left formula was to dominate Italian politics for the rest of the 1960s.

The new 'scientific revolution', the Labour Party and 'Wilsonism'

In the same years Britain witnessed the return of Labour to power. The context was obviously entirely different, but the British Labour Party too was faced with the choice of simply accepting the 'capitalist' system that had led to the historic defeat of widespread poverty or of somehow preserving a 'socialist identity'. The electorate which could tip the electoral scales in the Labour Party's favour wanted guarantees that the socialists would do nothing to undermine the economic system which had turned Great Britain into an 'affluent society' (Black-Pemberton, 2004).

Hugh Gaitskell died prematurely in January 1963 without achieving any success in his battle to revise the programmatic grounds for the Labour Party's legitimacy. His successor, Harold Wilson, apparently had no difficulty in doing so, given that he managed to win the general election of October 1964. Indeed, it was maliciously opined that he had merely dressed himself in the clothes of his predecessor.

In reality, matters were somewhat different. Wilson showed considerable tactical skill in avoiding the problem of having to pronounce on the nature of socialist power. His celebrated 'science speech' at the Party Conference of October 1963 did not address the problem, but instead was a classic feint. Although he did not say so, Wilson refused to enter a debate which he called 'theological', but which for precisely this reason he recognised as to some extent 'holy'. A masterpiece of political spin was contained in his famous radio interview (February 1964) when he explained that the reaction of a large part of the party leaders and militants to Gaitskell's attempt to amend Clause IV was understandable: as he put it, 'we were being asked to take Genesis out of the Bible; you don't have to be a fundamentalist in your religious approach to say that Genesis is part of the Bible' (Jones T., 1997: 19). On the one hand, the reference to Genesis made it clear that what was being talked about was a myth in whose technical meaning no one believed any longer, just as few Christians believed any longer that man was directly shaped by God out of clay. On the other hand, it highlighted the founding character of myths and the impossibility of dispensing with them without throwing the entire apparatus of 'political faith' into crisis.

In any case, Wilson exploited this climate cleverly. His speech opening the 1964 electoral campaign is, in this respect, highly revealing: 'Those who are satisfied should stay with the Tories. We need men with fire in their bellies and humanity in their hearts. The choice we offer . . . is between standing still, clinging to the tired philosophy of a day that is gone, or moving forward in partnership and unity to a just society, to a dynamic, expanding, confident and, above all, purposive new Britain' (Jefferys, 1997: 128). Once again 'progress', albeit kept within the bounds of 'affluence', was the note behind the call to change tack. And historically, as Wilson knew, the socialists had closer ties with 'scientific progress' than the other political traditions (Coopey, Fielding and Tiratsoo, 1993; Morgan, 1998).

If we now turn our attention to developments in the German SPD, we will find other parallels for the kind of evolution we have been describing. Writing for the party review after the Stuttgart conference (18–23 May, 1958), which many see as the real turning point leading to the Bad Godesberg conference, SPD leader Erich Ollenhauer harked back to the traditional line: 'The 1957 election showed that we must fight to obtain the majority . . . In such a situation a party like ours should not confine itself to mundane affairs, but strive to improve its own line-up, ready for battle every day against the policies of the current majority in parliament, against militarism, nationalism and the selfish propertied classes. It must also fight to create a new spirit of democratic socialism' (Ollenhauer, 1958: 171). However, the younger generation of socialists, like Werner Push, countered with greater insight: 'When we failed to reach the majority of votes on September 15th, 1957, it was not only defeat for the SPD, but a battle lost by the whole people . . . The new [Stuttgart] programme seeks to cling on to the basic ideas of Marxism, claimed to be valid now as in the past. But in the ways and methods of concrete politics today, we see things quite differently from fifty or sixty years ago. The SPD has some-times been described as bearing the stamp of its tradition. But tradition is only one feature, and not even the most important. In other words: this tradition lacks a majority. At Stuttgart, accordingly, we have to choose between the past and the present' (Pusch, 1958: 223). All this was no more than a prelude to the Bad Godesberg watershed, as we all know (Görtemaker, 1999: 159–98).

As recent literature has highlighted, this was a change of direction that was powerfully assisted by the new 'social sciences' – not just economics (as the traditional intellectual history of socialism emphasises), but also the newly fledged sociology and political science, strongly influenced by the American experience. The success of theories like the 'second industrial revolution', connected as it was to ever-greater automation and a new type of working class, or theories on atomisation or even youth studies (the new 'skeptical generation', as Helmuth Schelsky called it), was important in explaining the shifting line of analysis appearing in German political culture (and more widely in Europe).

In some respects, this approach was common to a substantial compon-ent of the political forces which in Europe embodied the turning point of the 1960s, just as the socialism of the 1910s had regarded the *Wege zur Macht* (the way to power), as the natural outcome of a cultural and economic transformation which only required the support of a new ruling class freed from its ties with tradition, because history would do the rest by itself. However paradoxical it may seem, given these are almost in-variably highly 'pragmatic' politicians being discussed, the result of this illusion was a political Utopia, a vision that forcefully arose at the end of the decade and predominated thereafter. Its opposite was the technical dodge of a 'new constitution', as witnessed by the success of the Gaullist experi-ment: by intelligently changing the framework and the rules of the game, one could fashion a new form of crisis resolution, which then became available – as the French example made increasingly evident in the years to come – not only to those who had 'invented' it but also to their adver-saries (Donegani and Sadoun, 1998; Quagliariello, 2003).

Even the intellectual elites became convinced at the watershed of the 1960s that a competitive economy required a political context equally able to foster competition; this aspect had been absent from the political culture of the men who led the stabilisation of the 1950s, men who were on the contrary convinced that the political side should consist of 'continuity' and compliance with the system of traditional values that had previously shaped society (and, in fact, culturally speaking, such a conviction had been broadly shared even by the communists).

Of course, competition brought with it the risk of instability and unknown factors in the selection of the ruling class. This might create problems for political systems still mindful of the crisis between the two wars – a crisis which had been largely blamed on factors of this kind. The onset in France, in parallel with this Europe-wide cultural pattern, of an event like the demise of the Fourth Republic, and the troubled beginnings of the Fifth, made it even more difficult to abandon this stereotype, although with hindsight these events seemed to have worked in the opposite direction. Though the adverse judgement on such patterns began to wane and fade as the 1960s got into their swing, we should not forget that originally Gaullism was commonly seen as the new form of fascism.

I hope it is evident from this argument what political legacy I think the 1960s turning-point represented for the debate on the future of 'social democracy'. Jocularly summarised, one could say it was like an attempt to marry the secularisation of political ideologies – which had been an issue ever since the 1950s (see Aron's well-known last chapter on the opium of the intellectuals in Aron, 1955) – to the resurgence of political utopia, seen as an alternative to allegedly outmoded forms of 'false philosophy'.

One is tempted to see the two horns of this dilemma as somehow united by that naïve faith in the mechanical exactitude of the social sciences, which still lives on with us today. The 1960s were marked by a certain faith in science and technology – not to mention 'technocratic' aspects of economic and social policy. This somewhat allayed the fear (stoked by Marxist analysis) that prolonged affluence was based on a giant speculative bubble, a huge confidence trick that would soon be laid bare. (The Marxist theory of the day was 'neocapitalism', remember.)

While confidence in science was boosted by achievements in various fields (aeronautic and space technology may do service as examples), it could not completely remove the age-old fear that it might be misused. This was still related to anxiety over the atomic threat, though that alarm had been somewhat scaled down by the so-called 'balance of terror' theory (Dunbabin, 1994; Formigoni, 2000). There is undoubtedly ambivalence here; on the one hand, the 1960s left in their wake a sort of benign political utopia, which was merely the romantic reaction to disappointment at the difficulties which beset political reformism (mainly left-wing, except for Gaullism); on the other, the end of the 1960s would see a resurgent mood of apocalyptic dystopia: namely, that regeneration would only come by some 'world's end' scenario, jolting history out of the doldrums that dogged it (we might mention in this connection the third world myth, ranging from South America to China, or the various faces of the pacifist movement). Even the Catholic Church, with two such different pontiffs as John XXIII and Paul VI, seemed steeped in the very contradiction we have just outlined.

One might almost say that European socialism would never find its way out of the quicksand of these dilemmas. Alternately, and as national circumstances dictated, it would be sucked either into the delusion of providing a 'moral' answer to political crisis (whether by 'reformist', utopian or radical recipes) or else into the fog of wishful 'third ways'.

Note

Translated from the Italian by Ralph Nisbet.

References

Ajello, N. (1997) *Il lungo addio: Intellettuali e PCI dal 1958 al 1991* (Rome and Bari: Laterza).

Aron, R. (1955) *L'opium des intellectuels* (Paris: Calman Lévy).

Berstein, S. (1989) *La France de l'expansion*, Vol. 1: *La République gaullienne 1958–1969* (Paris: Seuil).

Black, L. and Pemberton, H. (eds) (2004) *An Affluent Society? Britain's Postwar 'Golden Age' Revisited* (Aldershot: Ashgate).

Bouvier, B. (1990) *Zwischen Godesberg und Grosser Koalition: Der Weg der SPD in die Regierungsverantwortung* (Bonn: Dietz).

Chalin, N. J. (2000) *Jean Lecanuet* (Paris: Beauchesnue).

Coopey, R., Fielding, S. and Tiratsoo, N. (1993) *The Wilson Governments 1964–1970* (London: Pinter).

Crainz, G. (1997) *Storia del miracolo italiano* (Rome: Donzelli).

Craveri, P. (2002) 'Ugo la Malfa dal centrismo al centro sinistra', in *La democrazia incompiuta: Figure del '900 italiano* (Venice: Marsilio).

Degl'Innocenti, M. (1993) *Storia del Psi: Dal dopoguerra ad oggi* (Rome and Bari: Laterza).

Doering Manteuffel, A. (2000) 'Wie westlich sind die Deutschen?', in A. Schildt, D. Siegfried and K. C. Lammers, *Dynamische Zeiten* (Hamburg: Hans Christians Verlag), pp. 311–41.

Donegani, J.-M. and Sadoun, M. (1998) *La Ve Republique: Naissance et Mort* (Paris: Gallimard).

Dunbabin, J. P. D. (1994) *The Cold War: The Great Powers and Their Allies* (London: Longman).

Favretto, I. (2003) *The Long Search for a Third Way: The British Labour Party and the Italian Left since 1945* (Basingstoke: Palgrave).

Formigoni, G. (2000) *Storia della politica internazionale nell'età contemporanea* (Bologna: Il Mulino).

Freeden, M. (1996) *Ideologies and Political Theory* (Oxford: Oxford University Press).

Galavotti, E. (2004) 'Dell'Acqua sostituto e la politica italiana (1953–1967)', in A. Melloni (ed.), *Angelo Dell'Acqua Prete, Diplomatico e Cardinale al cuore della politica vaticana* (Bologna: Il Mulino), pp. 119–60.

Giersch, H., Paqué, K. H. and Schmieding, H. (1992) *The Fading Miracle: Four Decades of Market Economy in Germany* (Cambridge: Cambridge University Press).

Görtemaker, M. (1999) *Geschichte der Bundesrepublik Deutschland* (Munich: Klett).

Hilldebrandt, K. (1984) *Von Erhard zur Grossen Koalition 1963–1969* (Stuttgart: Deutsche Verlags-Anstalt).

Jefferys, K. (1992) *The Attlee Governments 1945–1951* (London: Longman).

Jefferys, K. (1997) *Retreat from New Jerusalem: British Politics, 1951–64* (London: Macmillan).

Jones, H. (1997) *The Welfare Game: Conservative Politics and the Welfare State 1942–1957* (Oxford: Oxford University Press).

Jones, T. (1997) ' "Taking Genesis out of the Bible": Hugh Gaitskell, Clause IV and the Socialist Myth', *Contemporary Records*, Vol. 11.

Kielmanseeg, P. (2000) *Nach der Katastrophe: Eine Geschichte des geteilten Deutschland* (Berlin: Siedler).

Kirchheimer, O. (1954) 'Notes on the Political Scene in Western Germany', *World Politics*, April, pp. 346–21.

Lupo, S. (2004) *Partito e antipartito: Una storia politica della prima Repubblica (1946–78)* (Rome: Donzelli).

Marchi, M. 'Moro, La Chiesa e l'apertura a sinistra La "politica ecclesiastica" di un leader post-dossettiano', in *Ricerche di Storia Politica*, 9 (2006), pp. 147–79.

Merseburger, P. (2004) *Willy Brandt 1913–1992* (Munich: dtv).

Morgan, K. (1984) *Labour in Power 1945–1951* (Oxford: Clarendon).

Morgan, K. (1998) 'The Wilson Years', in N. Tiratsoo (ed.), *From Blitz to Blair: A New History of Britain since 1939* (London: Phoenix), pp. 132–62.

Nicholls, A. (1994) *Freedom with Responsibility: The Social Market Economy in Germany 1918–1963* (Oxford: Clarendon).

Nicholls, A. (1997) *The Bonn Republic* (London: Longman).

Ollenhauer, E. (1958) 'Um Sinn und Zweck der Organisation', *Neue Gesellschaft*, May–June.

Paggi, L. and D'Angelillo, M. (1986) *I comunisti italiani e il riformismo* (Turin: Einaudi).

Philippe, P. (2001) *Jean Lecanuet: le vol de l'albatros* (Caen: Maitr Jacques).

Pinto-Duschinsky, M. (1970) 'Bread and Circuses? The Conservatives in Office 1951–1964', in V. Bogdanor and R. Skidelsky (eds), *The Age of Affluence 1951–1964* (London: Macmillan), pp. 5–77.

Piretti, M. S. (2003) *La Legge Truffa* (Bologna: Il Mulino).

Pombeni, P. (1997) *I partiti e la politica dal 1948 al 1963*, in G. Sabbatucci and V. Vidotto (eds), *Storia d'Italia*, Vol. V.: *La Repubblica* (Rome and Bari: Laterza), pp. 127–251.

Pombeni, P. (2003) 'La legittimazione del benessere: nuovi parametri di legittimazione in Europa dopo la Seconda Guerra Mondiale', in P. Pombeni (ed.), *Crisi, legittimazione, consenso* (Bologna: Il Mulino), pp. 357–417.

Pusch, W. (1958) 'Fragen an Stuttgart', *Neue Gesellschaft*, May–June.

Quagliariello, G. (2003) *De Gaulle e il gollismo* (Bologna: Il Mulino).

Rose, R. and Abrams, M. (1960) *Must Labour Lose?* (London: Penguin).

Rudelle, O. (1988) *Mai 58, De Gaulle et la République* (Paris: Plon).

Sani, R. (2002) *Da De Gasperi a Fanfani: La Civiltà Cattolica e il mondo cattolico italiano nel secondo dopoguerra, 1945–1962* (Milan: Vita e Pensiero).

Schmoeckl, R. and Kaiser, B. (1991) *Die Vergessene Regierung* (Bonn: Bouvier).

Schwarz, P. (1997) *Konrad Adenauer*, Vol. 2: *The Statesman, 1952–1967* (Providence and Oxford: Berghann Books).

Scoppola, P. (1991) *La repubblica dei partiti* (Bologna: Il Mulino).

Tomlinson, J. (1997) *Democratic Socialism and Economic Policy: The Attlee Years 1945–1951* (Cambridge: Cambridge University Press).

8

Growth and security: Swedish reformism in the post-war period

Jenny Andersson

Introduction

This chapter discusses the ideological development in Swedish social democracy in the post-war period and the shifting relationship between the concepts 'growth' (*tillväxt*) and 'security' (*trygghet*) in the ideology of the SAP. The point of departure is that a core notion in the ideology of Swedish social democracy was the articulation of 'growth' and 'security' as coherent and mutually supportive ideological objectives. This was expressed, from the 1930s onwards, in a conceptualisation of social policy as 'productive'; as a means not only for security but also for growth and economic efficiency (Esping-Andersen, 1990; Esping-Andersen, 1985; Tilton, 1990).

In this manner, security was articulated not only as compatible with, but also as a prerequisite for, growth, and as an integral element in the creation of an efficient society, whereas, on the other hand, *in*security (*otrygghet*) was articulated as something fundamentally inefficient and costly. Furthermore, the growth-orientation of Swedish social democracy and its focus on the supply-side stemmed from an articulation of economic growth as something socially desirable and, ultimately, as the fundamental means for security. This articulation of growth and security as ends in harmony was a central element in the hegemonic position of social democratic ideology in the post-war period. On the one hand, the expansion of social policy could be defended as an economic investment against the right, and, on the other hand, by articulating growth as a social force social democracy could meet rival articulations from the left with references to its capacity to create individual security within the capitalist economy. This discursive linkage of 'growth' and 'security' underpinned the development of the Swedish welfare state.

The SAP's rise to hegemony in the period from the 1930s was based on this ability to represent both 'growth' and 'security' as coherent ends. However, the period from the mid-1960s was characterised by an increasing discursive struggle around this very relationship, as the meaning of both 'growth' and 'security' became more and more contested and the relationship between them came to be seen as deeply antagonistic. Social democracy's increasingly vulnerable position in the post-war period can be traced to this rising struggle over key ideological articulations, and in the following I suggest that from within the Swedish context, the much-discussed 'crisis' of social democracy can be understood as a succession of historical moments of struggle over the relationship between 'growth' and 'security', struggles that eventually lead to social democratic rearticulation and ideological change (Laclau and Mouffe, 1985).

This interpretation of crisis as a gradual process of increasing antagonism is different from how the rise of Third Way policies, particularly from within the British context, has been described as a historic break with old, golden age articulations because of the influence of hegemonic neoliberalism (Driver and Martell, 1998; Hall, 1988; Hay, 1998; Ryner, 2002). Ultimately, I make an argument for continuity, not in the sense of stasis, but in the sense of a gradual transfer of meaning between different periods of critique, and between social democratic reaction and rearticulation. The chapter provides an historical narrative of the dynamic relationship between the concepts of 'security' and 'growth' in the post-war ideology of the SAP, and particularly, it addresses the party's relationship to two periods of critique and radicalisation: the late 1960s and its (social) critique of growth, and the 1980s (economic) critique of security. I argue that the interdependency between these two periods is central to our understanding of the multiple origins and trajectories of Third Way policies in both radical critique and reformism. In the chapter, both the critique of the late 1960s and the critique of the early 1980s are discussed as *radical,* in the sense that in both periods ideological struggle focuses on perceived discrepancies between social democratic ideology and a changed social or economic reality, but also as inherently *reformist,* in the sense that struggle, in both cases, takes place within or in the near vicinity of the labour movement itself. The actors discussed in the chapter, social workers in the first case, and economists in the second, are groups that exist in the borderland between social democratic ideology and the knowledge production in social and economic policy-making. They exist between what may be called the ontological and the ideological – in the sphere between description of what is, to prescription of what should be, and in this position they are powerful critics of social democracy. The chapter focuses in particular on the way that concepts and metaphors put forward by these groups *in critique* of social democratic ideology gradually become integrated elements *in* social democratic ideology and structure processes of ideological change.

A strong society

In the electoral campaigns of the mid-1950s, the SAP under party leader Tage Erlander and the young Olof Palme coined the concept of the strong society. The ideology of the strong society was inherently optimistic. It drew on a notion of progress that can be described as linear, as progress was understood as an evolutionary process in which economic expansion and growth lead to increasing security and the fulfilment of ever more sophisticated social needs. Poverty and other social problems were regarded as belonging to less developed societies and to a past of uncontrolled capitalist markets. This conception of the historical character of social problems lay behind the deeply symbolic social democratic rhetoric employed around the introduction of a modern social services act in 1956 which finally abolished the term 'poor law' in Sweden, and it echoes in social democratic descriptions of social problems through metaphors like *silverputs* (silver polish), or *restnöd* ('left-over needs') (Erlander, 1956, 1962, 1954).

Within the ideology of the strong society, then, 'growth' and 'security' were concepts in harmony. Growth, under the control of democratic socialism, was identified as the primary means for social development and increased security, and as a means that would, in the near future, overcome the evils of capitalism and spread affluence to all groups in society. But security was also given a clear role for encouraging growth. According to the SAP, 'modern' social policies differed from old poor relief policies in their link to growth and their productivist orientation, aiming at the rehabilitation of socially problematic groups and individuals. As the Rehn-Meidner model was drawn up in the economic policy programmes of the SAP and the trade union federation, the LO, in the mid-1960s, social policy was given a specific role, alongside active labour market policies, to include 'remaining groups' outside of the labour market in production (LO-SAP, 1964). This productivist attitude towards social policy was expressed in social democratic rhetoric through the use of metaphors such as 'productive consumption' and 'social investment', metaphors that described the productive character of the resources put into the public sector. It also coloured the SAP's outlook on the objects of social policy, as groups such as the remaining poor, the disabled, the elderly, women and the 'asocial' were regarded as potential production factors and central labour market reserves.

Social exclusion and the critique of growth

The SAP's belief that social and economic development were processes hand-in-hand came to an abrupt end in the late 1960s, with the production of social statistics and reports that pointed to the rise of inequality in the heart of the strong society.

In the early 1970s, the results produced by the Committee on Low Income, *Låginkomstutredningen*, a government committee appointed in 1965 to discuss the persistence of pockets of poverty in the country of full employment and solidary wage bargaining, convincingly showed that almost a million people suffered from low income levels and related risks of health problems, work injuries, and long-term social exclusion. The discrepancy between the SAP's optimistic worldview and what now seemed like a dramatically different social reality triggered an increasingly radical critique of its social policies. Influenced by critical developments in sociology and Marxism, actors previously deeply involved in social policy reform – social workers in the social administration and economists within the Trade Union Federation, the LO – turned against policy and accused social democracy of failure in the reformist project. The results of the Committee on Low Income were soon dispersed in polemics and pamphlets, issued by the trade union federation as well as by the Social Democratic Youth Party (SSU) (Burstedt, 1971; LO, 1971; SSU, 1967). The Föreningen Sveriges Socialchefer (FSS), an association consisting of the chairmen of Sweden's local social councils, closely associated with the professional organisations of Sweden's social workers, became one of the most outspoken critics of the strong society. Having led a peaceful existence since the early 1930s, in the years from the late 1960s to the early 1970s the FSS held heated meetings at which its members disputed the subdued role of social policy in the capitalist economy. The main problem was quickly identified as the growth orientation of the Swedish model. Its productivism had not solved the problem of inequality, rather, by inducing 'vulnerable' individuals to take part in the competitive production structures of the 1950s and 1960s, social policy had contributed to the alienation of society's weakest. In 1971, a report issued by a group of young economists within the Economic Bureau of the LO, the very centre of post-war economic policymaking, argued that social democracy's preoccupation with the production sphere had failed to control capitalism's tendencies towards social destruction. A new kind of capitalism had been created in Sweden, 'social democratic capitalism', with new patterns of poverty and inequality. Under historical capitalist conditions, the labouring masses had suffered under the privileged few. But under social democratic capitalism, inequality was the result of the systematic exclusion of a small minority of socially vulnerable individuals in the interest of the big majority of the working class. These new poor were not a class. Born into social exclusion and rendered passive over the course of their lives by the production discipline of the welfare state, they would never mobilise. They lacked all political resources and were an underclass in the true sense of the word. Modern social policies, from this perspective, did not amount to emancipation from capitalist structures, but rather a recreated poor relief system, designed by the labour movement to provide the system of production with a new *Lumpenproletariat*.

This outlook on the nature of social problems went against the strong society's idea of social policy as a central means of social progress and its conception of inequality and insecurity as a temporary problem, to be solved in the immediate future. In glaring contrast to the SAP's description of social needs as the left-over problems of done-away-with capitalist structures, this discourse of social exclusion saw social problems as the direct effects of the growth orientation of the strong society, indeed as the effects of growth. Thus growth was articulated as the source, not of security, but of *in*security (*otrygghet*) and social exclusion. Within this articulation, growth and security became irreconcilable elements. As social workers and LO economists fundamentally questioned the link between social policy and growth, they also turned against the SAP's conceptualisation of social policy as a productive investment. The LO-economist Per Holmberg explicitly dismissed this postulated link as a theoretical absurdity. Rather, the continual subordination of social policy to economic policy was the source of social problems and led to a deeply inefficient and unproductive society. The resources put into social policy were thus not productive investments, but costs for the destruction of social resources, 'the social costs for growth'.

The solution, then, was to be found in a new and radical – 'genuinely socialist' – social policy that intervened in production and was directed at the economic structures behind social exclusion, and ultimately at growth itself. In its most radical form, the critique demanded that growth be replaced, as the dominant ideological objective of the Swedish 'market economy', by the social objective of security (FSS, 1970, 1971, 1969; LO, 1971). By the early 1970s, growth had become a deeply antagonistic concept and the critique had created a deep fissure in the ideology of the strong society. Confronted with the prospect of social problems arising as unexpected consequences of the very policies meant to eradicate them, the SAP's optimistic idea of social progress was replaced by a rather defeatist conception of social problems as a constant; as something that was constantly recreated with economic and social transformations. In her speech to the party conference of 1968, Alva Myrdal, chair of the party's Equality group, illustrated this new fundamentally pessimistic outlook on change: 'our naïve faith in progress has been replaced by the insight that change itself constantly recreates social risk' (SAP, 1969:15).

The social costs of growth: social democratic rearticulation

The SAP's instinctive response to the critique of the late 1960s was to reject it. The new party leader Olof Palme, in particular, went to great lengths to defend the value of growth by stressing its link to security. At a public meeting of the FSS in 1972, Olof Palme dismissed the social workers' critique as misconceived and dangerously revolutionary. Growth was not an end in itself, but merely an instrumental value as the primary means for security, but as such it was indispensable. He included a warning: by setting growth and security against each other, the critique of the radical left risked opening up a space for familiar right-wing arguments that saw social policy as a drag on the economy. Growth and social policy were not enemies; on the contrary, 'they should be joined together as friends', and social policy was productive 'in the true sense of the word'. Only with this conceptualisation of growth as a social force and social policy as productive could social democracy defend the welfare state (FSS, 1971:189). Similarly dismissive reactions met Alva Myrdal's Equality group and its attempts at ideological renewal. The party ignored Alva Myrdal's suggestions for radical social policy reforms such as a citizen's wage.

The initial unwillingness of the SAP to take the critique seriously is probably symptomatic of the extent to which the images of social reality put forward by it clashed with the SAP's own worldview. From within the ideology of the strong society, the phenomenon of social exclusion was simply unthinkable. But behind these defensive reactions a process of ideological rearticulation began that gradually incorporated the critique and its metaphors. Olof Palme's rhetoric underwent a significant change from his defensive reactions and his aggressive attacks on the revolutionary sympathies of young social workers to expressions of deep concern. In the early 1970s, Palme returned again and again to the ideological problem of growth. Growth, the hope of the old generation of social democracy was now the origin of social conflict, ideological polarisation, and human suffering. In his writings and speeches Palme now incorporated the definition of social exclusion as the social costs for growth; the 'price' to pay for the gains of the post-war production.

> Growth has social limits. It is no longer created by putting social resources and labour reserves to work . . . It is created through the destruction of social resources. It is not strange from this perspective that our social workers attack growth. This is how they see the problems in the reality they work in . . . For 30 years we believed in the harmony between growth and social development while the social price of growth was rising. A tension has been created between our culture's faith in growth, and the fear of its social consequences. (Palme, 1971:39)

Palme saw the problem of growth as social democracy's big dilemma for the 1970s. Social democracy had to break with the post-war idea of growth as unlimited expansion and find new articulations for the role of growth in the modern society; articulations that incorporated the critique from the left and accommodated the demands of a young and post-material generation. The 1970s challenge to social democracy was to find a new definition of growth that gave it a social face; a new articulation that defended growth as an ideological objective, but strengthened its social side. To Palme this was the essence of a Third Way, between the 'failed' systems of Soviet communism and American capitalism, both 'obsessed with the myth of growth' (Palme, 1975:19; 1972:392).

A socialist social policy

So the SAP embarked on a fundamental rethinking of the concept of growth. In 1972 the party's Economic policy committee redefined growth as 'economic development leading to welfare – not to social exclusion'. In this manner, social exclusion was explicitly contrasted to *welfare (välfärd)*. The concept of 'welfare' rose in importance in reports and programmes in the 1970s, and took on a very specific meaning. 'Welfare' drew on the idea that growth had historically led not only to benefits, but also to costs, and that growth should consequently be assessed by its positive and negative effects in terms of increased or decreased individual security (LO-SAP, 1972:31; SAP, 1972:21).

'Growth' redefined as 'welfare' was suddenly again an ideological objective consistent with security. 'Welfare', however, contained a much broader notion of 'security' than the notion that informed the strong society. 'Welfare' was not a question of material standard, but, rather, of the totality of factors controlling the social situation of individuals, including their work environment, their access to green areas and clean air, and general levels of stress and psychological pressure. Importantly, 'welfare' made claims on economic policy. The 1970s saw a reversal of the power structure between 'growth' and 'security', as individual security and welfare took the upper hand in the party's economic discourse. In a clear break with the growth-orientation of the social policy ideology of the strong society, social policy was no longer articulated as a means *for* growth, but rather as a means *against* growth, as its role was redefined so as to prevent and balance the effects of capitalism. A party report in 1972 stated that social policy had finally caught up with the socialist agenda of other policy areas, such as active labour market policies, and become a genuinely socialist or 'structural' means of reform, aiming at greater welfare, equality, and security.

This radicalisation of the social policy ideology took place parallel to the general radicalisation of the SAP's ideology in many other areas in the 1970s, for instance in the debate over wage-earner funds (Pontusson, 1992). But while the party's dreams of economic democracy and its advanced plans for investment policies went up in smoke towards the end of the decade, culminating in the breakdown of corporatism and the Swedish Employers Federation's march against the wage-earner funds, the social policy ambitions of the 1970s simply evaporated into thin air, leaving little trace. The so-called socialist or structural role of social policy was codified in the new Social Services Act (*Socialtjänstlagen*) in 1982, when economic developments and the turn of the ideological tide had caught up with the social ambitions of the late 1960s. The final results in terms of policy change were marginal.

The waste of the industrial society

The enduring result of the critique of the late 1960s was a break with the SAP's definition of social policy as a productive investment. Social policy became deeply associated with the cost-side of the economy, seen as a cost for social problems and ultimately identified more with consumption than with production. Moreover, the deeply contradictory discourses of social exclusion of the 1960s and 1970s meant a break with the party's idea of the groups identified by social policy as a potentially productive labour reserve. The 1970s party rhetoric described the objects of social policy as 'the weak', 'the disabled', and 'those who can't keep up'. In 1969 Alva Myrdal pleaded for radical social reform by insisting that 'we can *afford* a generous attitude towards those who cannot make it in our competitive society', an interesting turn of words. The socially excluded were, fundamentally, not an economic resource but a cost – a cost that could be 'afforded' in an advanced welfare society – but still a cost that put pressure on the solidarity of the labour movement (SAP, 1969:112). Olof Palme voiced this cost metaphor in a more brutal way in a speech to the party conference in 1978. In a highly emotionally charged speech, Palme spoke of social exclusion as the 'waste' of the industrial society (Palme, 1987:162–74). 'Waste', of course, is a metaphorical description of used-up and exhausted resources that no longer have a productive function.

The cost of social policy

In spite of the attempts to suture the relationship between growth and security in the 1970s through the redefinition of 'growth' as 'welfare', it remained a deeply problematic link. As the central concern of Swedish economic policies from the late 1970s onwards was to actively (re)create growth and economic efficiency, social policy was no longer part of growth policies, but what was socially desirable seemed to be in direct conflict with the economically necessary. 'Growth' and 'security' were fundamentally incompatible goals, and as the dominant position of the concept of 'growth' was gradually re-established in the wake of the oil crises, security lost in importance. The problem of social exclusion and the discussion of the social costs of growth gave way to a dominant discourse on the costs for security – and the cost of social policy.

The economic stagnation of the late 1970s lead to a growing obsession with productivity in western societies, which took the form of persuasive narratives of falling productivity levels in service production and the cost explosion of public consumption, an economic disease later diagnosed as 'swedosclerosis'. In Sweden, as in many other countries, new planning models based on micro-economic cost–benefit analyses were introduced into the administration of social policy, and in the late 1970s programme budgeting was imported from the American administration in an attempt to increase the cost-efficiency of the resources used in the public sector. The introduction of programme budgeting and planning models based on cost efficiency and micro-economic cost–benefit analysis went silently by for most of the decade, perhaps because the intention was not initially to identify areas of saving, but rather to increase cost efficiency in order to maintain and even expand social ambitions in a time of shrinking financial resources. But at the end of the decade, both concepts of productivity and efficiency became the subject of intense discursive struggle, following the introduction of a crisis bill by the liberal government and an increasingly aggressive critique of the welfare state from the Swedish right, that also found an echo within the labour movement.

Social democracy faced the critique from the right by bringing out its historical defences of the economic efficiency of the welfare state and its articulations of the link between growth and security. The liberal government's crisis policy was represented as a bourgeois plot to first destroy public finances and create a narrative of crisis, and then dismantle the welfare state. The writings of Milton Friedman and Friedrich von Hayek, published in Swedish by the right-wing publishing house Timbro in 1979 and 1980, were dismissed as 'bourgeois propaganda' and contrasted to the economic theories of social democratic classics such as Wigforss (see speeches in Ingvar Carlsson's and Olof Palme's archives). But while Olof Palme and Ingvar Carlsson defended the welfare state's role for economic growth in the electoral campaigns of 1979 and 1982, the critique of welfare grew within the ranks of the social democratic movement. In 1979, in reaction to the failure of the SAP to regain a parliamentary majority in the elections, a social democratic discussion group on economic policy was formed, the Social Democratic Economists (*Socialdemokratiska ekonomgruppen*). The nucleus of this group was a group of young economists connected to the Stockholm School of Economics, and what eventually became known as the *Kanslihushögern*, a group of modernisers that took over economic policymaking after the return to power in 1982 (Ryner, 2002). Just as '1968' in the Swedish context took the form of a radical left *within* social democracy, advocating ideological change in response to what they saw as a new social reality, this 'neoliberal' critique of the 1980s was also a radical social democracy of sorts, advocating renewal in order to create a better fit between social democratic ideology and a dramatically different economic world. Influenced by the so-called 'new economic ideas', they argued that the postwar ideology and the party's economic policies were outdated, outrun by the changes in the international economy and no longer able to provide a coherent defence of social democratic values. In contrast to how the party's official rhetoric demonised Pinochet, Reagan and Thatcher, in 1981 the Social Democratic Economists commissioned field studies of economic and social policy reform in Chile, the US and the UK, with the hope of finding out what was really liberal propaganda, and what could possibly be used as elements in a new and radical politics for the Swedish welfare state (Socialdemokratiska ekonomgruppen, 1982). The phrase 'new economic ideas' was an obvious play of words, referring to the influence of Keynesian ideas and the Stockholm school in the crisis policies of the

SAP in the 1930s. Indeed, Olof Palme wrote in a forward-looking party report in 1977 of 'a new generation of radical social democratic economists', whose economic knowledge he claimed gave him new faith in the future of the Swedish welfare state (SAP, 1977:13).

In fact, the Social Democratic Economists was a group that incorporated two radically different worldviews. One, represented by the trade union economists in the group, sternly defended the 'old' ideology and the historical outlooks of the SAP on public-sector provisions and social services as productive means for growth. The other, represented by the group of younger economists led by Klas Eklund, later the director of the Swedish central bank, called for ideological renewal, and advocated saving and cost-cutting as the radical means of reform. The meetings of the group consequently became the arena of a discursive struggle that took the form of a clash between old and new, over the correct interpretation of the crisis and the role of the public sector in creating it.

The central metaphor underpinning the critique of the latter, rapidly gaining in influence, was 'efficiency'. But efficiency was given a meaning radically different from its 1970s connotations of welfare and the minimisation of social costs. 'Efficiency' was not 'social efficiency' (*samhällsekonomisk effektivitet*) but 'cost efficiency' (*kostnadseffektivitet*). 'Cost efficiency' in the interpretation of the advocates of renewal relied heavily on the theorem of marginal utility. In frequent use in the Swedish social policy administration from the late 1970s the notion of marginal utility conveyed a clear picture of the constantly increasing costs for social policy, as the resources put into social policy had increased exponentially throughout the post-war period, and the constantly decreasing productivity of these resources (see the reports of the Expert Group for Studies in Public Finance, ESO (*Expertgruppen för studier i offentlig ekonomi*)). To the Social Democratic Economists, the solution to this problem was clear: efficiency could only be achieved by cutting the costs of social policy and forcing 'new solutions' on social policy making, solutions that were not dependent on extra resources (Socialdemokratiska ekonomgruppen, 1981).

Can we afford security? The SAP and the Third Way

While the SAP continued to contest similar ideas when they came from the Swedish right, within the party, this critique gained in authority. The party discussions of the 1980s were a far cry from the optimism of the 1950s. Change itself was no longer associated with progress, but with crisis. Moreover, the balance of power between the process of change and ideology had been turned on its head. The strong society's conception of change as something that needed to be steered and controlled by increased social democratic intervention had been transformed into a discourse of adaptation that constantly referred to the limits set by the process of change to the political project. As the SAP embarked on its Third Way after its return to governmental power in 1982, the critique of the Social Democratic Economists became the cornerstone of a new radical ideology.

The crisis programme of 1981, *A Future for Sweden* (*Framtid för Sverige*), internalised much of the economic critique of the 1980s. Its key message was the need for a thorough reform of the policies underlying the welfare state: a 'Third Way', at the core of which was the need to recreate growth. In contrast to Olof Palme's 1970s notion of finding a Third Way in a redefined concept of growth as 'welfare', the Third Way of the 1980s departed from a narrow concept of economic growth. The crisis programme made this clear. It was a programme of economic restructuring, a programme concerned with the need to 'take on' the serious issues of economic efficiency. The party's previous understanding of social exclusion as the effect of growth was dismissed as a 'misinterpretation'. During the period of economic crisis, the social situation had clearly deteriorated. This, the programme stated, was clear proof that social exclusion and insecurity was not the result of growth. In fact, all problems associated with growth – ecological and social – were dependent on the recreation of growth for their solution (SAP, 1981:32). In this manner, the programme firmly established that growth was indispensable for future security. But the role of security for growth was much more problematic. The circumstances for the creation of security were dramatically different from the post-war period. 'We have never believed that insecurity and inequality are necessary components of economic development . . . but we must realise the seriousness of the situation' (SAP, 1981:31). There was no room for social reform, rather, the central means of social reform had to be to find a way out of crisis, a way which lay in saving and cost cutting.

The programme insisted that this was not a question of ideological change, but, rather, a question of a pragmatic reconsideration of the means with which ideological postulates could be defended in a radically different reality. In a careful rhetorical move, the programme contrasted the social democratic interpretation of the political role of saving against 'bourgeois' conceptions of saving. Saving, in the hands of the social democratic party, was only a means to an end, not part of a big scheme for the rolling back of the welfare state. Anticipating the reactions of the labour movement to what seemed like a complete break with the ideology of the post-war period, the programme garnered ideological legitimacy through a reinterpretation of its own past ideology, and particularly, through what stands out as a bold rereading of one of the party's main economic theorists, Ernst Wigforss, and his pamphlet from 1932, *Can We Afford to Work?* (*Ha vi råd att arbeta?*). Wigforss' pamphlet pleaded for expansionary economic policies and investments in public expenditure in the crisis policies of the 1930s and contained a fuming critique of those 'bourgeois' concepts of saving that the crisis programme had referred to just a few paragraphs earlier. However, Wigforss' critique of saving was now read as a justification of saving as a social democratic means of reform, 'part of a radical strategy for welfare' (SAP, 1981:24; compare Wigforss, 1932:7).

This reinvention of past ideology continued throughout the 1980s, as social democracy tried to give social content to the economic project of the Third Way. In 1984, the crisis programme was followed up by a manifesto, *The Future in the Hands of the People* (*Framtiden i hela folkets händer*), directed primarily at the public sector and social services (SAP, 1984). The programme was constructed as a break with the ideas of the strong society. When Olof Palme presented the programme to the party conference he described it as social democracy's new utopia, 'a utopia of people, not of institutions', and both Palme and the programme's principal author, Ingvar Carlsson, compared it to the party programmes that had set out the direction of social policy in the 1950s and early 1960s (SAP conference protocol, 1984: 262–3). Under the slogan 'Renew the People's home!' (*förnya folkhemmet*), *The Future in the Hands of the People* contained an ambitious attempt to construct a new social policy ideology. The core of this, as stated in the presentations of the programme to the congress, was the need to recreate public trust in social democracy's capability of combining economic growth with social welfare, through a process of rearticulation that fundamentally broke with the articulations of the post-war period and managed to recreate a coherent outlook on the relationship between growth and security in adaptation to a new economic world. In this new articulation, it was clear that social policy was not a means for growth, but a cost that needed to be cut. In the mid-1980s social democracy used slogans such as 'not more money for reform – but more reform for our money', and 'we have the world's best – and most expensive – welfare state' (LO, 1986). Social policy was an area that had to be subordinated to the limits of sound finances. New forms of social policy discussed in the course of the 1980s, and in many cases introduced into reform in the 1990s; community work, home care, privatisation, and large-scale decentralisation, were ideologically justified with reference to their double capacity of providing a degree of individual security, and maintaining cost efficiency.

Conclusion

I have argued that in many ways the critique of growth of the late 1960s led the way for the critique of security in the 1980s. With the late 1960s critique of growth, the belief in growth as a social force was replaced, also in social democratic ideology, by an idea of growth as a threat to social progress. As the party accepted the critique's definition of social exclusion as a consequence of growth, the coherence between economic and social objectives that was the basis of its historical outlooks on active labour market policies or productivist social policies was lost, as economic and social objectives were fundamentally separated and ultimately in conflict. Social policy became an area in opposition to economic policy. This divorce between economic and social policy, growth and security, led the way for the economic critique of security in the 1980s. The critique of the SDE was based on the presumption, that social objectives were fundamentally social, and inherently a question of redistribution and spending. This dichotomous outlook on the economic and the social mirrored in the SAP's rejection, in the Third Way, of historic conceptualisations of the effect of social policy on the economy as a whole in favour of micro-economic approaches to social policy, and its redefinition of efficiency from 'social efficiency' to 'cost-efficiency'.

Both these two periods of critique emanated from groups close to the party, and from groups within the knowledge production in economic and social policymaking and planning. Their critique, in both cases, stemmed from the successful claim that a gap had opened between a dramatically changed reality and party ideology. The reactions of the SAP to these two periods of critique can be read as processes of ideological rearticulation in attempts to make sense of a new reality, but also as a reflection of the historical need of social democracy to defend the relationship between 'growth' and 'security' as key ideological elements. The processes of ideological rearticulation in the 1970s and in the 1980s were attempts to re-establish coherence and harmony and move away from apparent conflict through redefinitions of the meaning of each concept and new articulations of their relationships of causality and hierarchy. Ultimately, in Third Way ideology this was resolved through a break with the party's historic articulations and the introduction of an articulation where 'security' was fundamentally subordinated to 'growth'.

References

Burstedt, Åke, ed. (1971) *Sociala mål i samhällsplaneringen*. Stockholm.
Driver, Steven and Martell, Luke (1998) *New Labour: Politics after Thatcherism*. Cambridge: Polity.
Erlander, Tage (1956) *Framstegens politik*. Stockholm.
—— (1954) *Människor i samverkan*. Stockholm.
—— (1962) *Valfrihetens samhälle*. Stockholm.
Esping-Andersen, Gösta (1985) *Politics Against Markets*. Princeton: Princeton University Press.
—— (1990) *The Three Worlds of Welfare Capitalism*. Cambridge: Polity.
FSS, Föreningen Sveriges Socialchefer (1969) *Socialvården söker nya vägar*.
—— (1970) *Alternativ socialvård*.
—— (1971) *Socialvård i framtiden*.
Hall, Stuart (1988) *Thatcherism and the Crisis of the Left*. London: Verso.
Hay, C. (1998) *The Political Economy of New Labour*. Manchester: Manchester University Press.

Laclau, Ernesto and Mouffe, Chantal (1985) *Hegemony and Socialist Strategy: Towards a Radical Democratic Politics*. London: Verso.

LO (1971) *Låglön och välfärd*. Stockholm.

—— (1986) *Fackföreningsrörelsen Och Välfärdsstaten*. Stockholm.

LO-SAP (1964) *Resultat Och Reformer*. Stockholm.

—— (1977) *Näringspolitisk rapport*.

Palme, Olof (1972) 'Socialdemokratin i Europa, starkare än någonsin'. *Tiden*, 7–8.

—— (1971) 'Tillväxt, Balans, Jämlikhet'. *Vårt ekonomiska läge*.

Palme, Olof, W. Brandt and B. Kreisky (1975) *Briefe und Gespräche*. Frankfurt.

—— (1987) 'Den sociala utslagningen', Tiden.

Pontusson, Jonas (1992) *The Limits of Social Democracy: Investment Politics in Sweden*. Ithaca: Cornell University Press.

Ryner, J. Magnus (2002) *Capitalist Restructuring, Globalisation and the Third Way: Lessons from the Swedish Model*. London: Routledge.

SAP, Socialdemokratiska Arbetarpartiet (1969) *Jämlikhet*.

—— (1972) *Jämlikhet, allas deltagande i politik och arbetsliv*.

—— (1977) *Ekonomisk politik för 1980-talet*. Stockholm.

—— (1981) *Framtid för Sverige*. Stockholm.

—— (1984) *Framtiden i hela folkets händer*. Stockholm: Tiden.

Socialdemokratiska ekonomgruppen (1982) 'Nyliberalismen i praktiken', Ekonomgruppens arkiv, ARAB, F 11 A 19–20.

—— (1981) 'Solidaritet i de små och stora kollektiven: Bommersviks seminarium om den offentliga sektorn'.

SSU (1967) *Inkomst och standardhöjning*. Stockholm.

Tilton, Tim (1990) *The Political Theory of Swedish Social Democracy: Through the Welfare State to Revolution*. New York: Clarendon Press.

Wigforss, Ernst (1932) *Ha vi råd att arbeta?* Stockholm: Tiden.

Part III
Problems of social democracy: in the golden age

9

The British Labour Party and 'participation' in the 1960s

Steven Fielding

Introduction

Harold Wilson's time as Prime Minister between 1964 and 1970 has long been seen, on the British left at least, as yet another instance of the Labour Party leadership's reluctance to take advantage of circumstances to try and build 'socialism' (Miliband, 1972; Saville, 1988). For the 1960s is generally considered to have been a uniquely 'radical' moment. Eric Hobsbawm believes the decade falls within 'a sort of Golden Age', a time of 'extraordinary economic growth and social transformation', which, 'probably changed human society more profoundly than any other period of comparable brevity' (Hobsbawm, 1995: 6, 258). That which Arthur Marwick called a 'cultural revolution' affected the 'material conditions, lifestyles, family relationships, and personal freedoms' of 'the vast majority of ordinary people' (Marwick, 1998: 15). Indeed, according to Ronald Inglehart, those in advanced industrial societies embraced 'post-material values' and demanded a direct say in decision-making (Inglehart, 1977). Wilson's government is seen as preoccupied with defending the established order against the political consequences of these developments.

This chapter forms part of a more general attempt to recast our understanding of politics during the 1960s, its main purpose being to question dominant characterisations of the Labour government (Fielding, 2003; Tomlinson, 2003; Young, 2003). For, while an invigorating moment for those few who attacked the status quo, the vast majority of Britons were left mostly untouched by events. Many actually embraced quite reactionary positions, if the popularity of Enoch Powell after his infamous 'rivers of blood' speech is any guide. The radical minority has nonetheless attracted most historical attention – just as it did at the time. Some recent studies of the period have however taken a more balanced view. One recent collection for example suggested that the entire post-war period was composed of numerous 'extraordinarily contradictory impulses towards the modern' rather than a simple, single moment of revolutionary rupture (Conekin, Mort and Waters, 1999: 1–3). As Henry Pelling remarked in 1968, the 1960s marked no decisive break with the past but enjoyed an essential continuity with the late nineteenth century (Pelling, 1968).

This more sober interpretation does not mean Britain during the 1960s was a country of universal calm and contentment: it *did* experience significant cultural changes with important political consequences. It *does* imply however that these changes and consequences were more uneven and less dramatic than usually supposed. It is undoubted, for example, that Britain's civic culture was not destroyed – as some have claimed – but was instead reconfigured and put on a more 'modern' or, as Anthony Giddens has it, 'post-traditional' basis, one bereft of deference and defined by a stronger sense of individuality (Giddens, 1994: 5–7). When talking of post-war 'invidualism' and the Labour party, historians usually focus on the social impact of popular 'affluence' and the extent to which this provoked disagreement over nationalisation. This chapter will instead concentrate on the party's response to demands for 'participation'. It will put the subject into historical context and outline how ministers responded to its emergence as an issue and then look closely at planning and local government, areas where different forms of 'participation' were tentatively broached.

Most contemporaries criticised Labour's attitude to promoting access to decision-making and this opinion still informs historical perspectives. Most notably, the New Left presumed Wilson's ministers opposed change due to their devotion to the parliamentary system (Williams, 1968: 143–50; Miliband, 1972: 13). Censure was not however restricted to the far left. The backbench Labour MP John Mackintosh was one of an increasing number of younger revisionists unhappy with the government's apparent lack of interest in redistributing power from Whitehall. This was because, he believed, the cabinet was captive to the Fabian tradition, one underpinned by the 'conviction that well-educated well-disposed people' working in London were 'more likely to be right and impartial than the more remote and backward inhabitants of the provinces' (Mackintosh, n.d., but late 1960s).

It is certainly true that most leading Labour figures saw their party's main purpose as improving voters' *material* conditions. The number of individuals involved in deciding how to achieve that outcome and the means by which they did so were considered second-order matters. Thus, in the 1964 and 1966 general elections consideration of how to enhance popular influence on decision-making was brief, vague and placed towards the end of the party's manifestos. Yet, there was still talk of 'humanising' government and establishing a 'true partnership' between people and parliament (Labour Party, 1964: 22–3; Labour Party, 1966: 18–19). By the end of the decade these thoughts had been given greater salience. The National Executive Committee (NEC) had also issued two strategic statements, which emphasised the need to make Britain's institutions more accountable (Labour Party, 1968: 340–2). Ministers had also fostered an impressive collection of reports and Royal Commissions whose ostensible purpose was to augment people's influence over decisions that most affected their lives. It will be argued here, therefore, that Labour's response to calls for 'participation' does not vindicate those narratives that stress the leadership's apparently insatiable desire to betray the British people's radical potential.

Participation

For a variety of reasons, the 1960s undoubtedly saw demands for popular participation in decision-making reach unprecedented levels. The proliferation of unofficial strikes and violent demonstrations as well as the emergence of single-issue pressure groups suggested that an increasing number of people were questioning the pre-eminence of established representative institutions and wanted a direct say in determining their fates. If most prominently embraced by the young, in particular students, 'participation' denoted a disparate set of new and old concerns that appeared to challenge the basis of the post-war political order.

Established academic opinion suggested that too much participation, beyond voting in elections, threatened the stability of democracy (Pateman, 1970: 1–21). Many also doubted how typical were those who wanted to participate. Even enthusiasts conceded they only formed a minority, albeit, they claimed, a significant one (Arblaster, 1972: 47–8). Most manual workers for example still appeared happy to vote for Labour candidates promising to advance their material interests and were reluctant to assume a direct role in achieving that outcome. The extent to which such seeming indifference was the result of social change is open to doubt although some commentators figured 'affluence' encouraged workers to retreat further into their private domains. Others however argued the majority only appeared apathetic. People, they said did not believe meaningful participation was currently possible but would respond positively if conditions changed – as they were assumed to have done by the late 1960s (Arblaster, 1972: 50).

Yet, according to Des Wilson, Director of the pressure group Shelter, while 'participation' achieved the status of a radical cliché by 1968, most advocates remained unclear as to what it meant in practice (*Guardian*, 8 November 1968). Those with experience in promoting popular engagement certainly appreciated how difficult it was to achieve. In particular, increasing numbers involved in decision-making required a set of careful balancing acts. The most prominent of these was ensuring elected representatives promoted participation while maintaining their legitimate leadership role. It also required opening up decisions to scrutiny while preventing the process being monopolised by those dedicated to 'negative' protest (Hill, 1970). More than a few of those insisting on the right to participate refused to take such complications seriously as some wanted not to reform the established order, but to destroy it. Yet, most saw participation as a means of ensuring liberal democracy finally lived up to its full potential and reforms inspired from this quarter were relatively modest, locally focused and designed to improve the political order.

Labour, the individual and the state

From its inception, as the political wing of the trade union movement, Labour was committed to making the established political system work to the advantage of its supporters. Even so, not everyone was an uncritical devotee of parliamentarism and Labour's history reveals a consistent if fitful interest in constitutional reform and direct forms of representation (Taylor, 2000). Before 1914 the party was host to debates about the merits of referenda, proportional representation, abolition of the Lords and Home Rule for Wales and Scotland. Advocates wanted to promote participation because they thought it was inherent to the building of socialism. They lost out, however, to the view, that it was safer for an elite to manipulate the existing system towards progressive ends (Barrow and Bullock, 1996). When Labour became an active enthusiast of extensive state ownership of the economy in the 1930s there was, then, little sense that new forms of accountability were required. Aware that the state might encroach on liberty, Labour thinkers still believed, as the future member of Wilson's Cabinet Douglas Jay famously wrote, that usually 'the gentleman in Whitehall really does know better what is good for the people than the people know themselves' (Jay, 1947: 258).

The Second World War confirmed Labour's faith in extending the state while maintaining the political status quo and the ease with which Attlee's government implemented its programme reinforced that view. Even the doyen of the Labour left, Aneuran Bevan, praised the unwritten nature of the constitution because it allowed legislators to define the limits of their own authority (Bevan, 1952: 100–2). Like their predecessors Attlee's ministers believed the enlightened few could achieve progressive ends by manipulating the established political system. Not all however thought this would be sufficient if the party was to fully transform society: to achieve that, they believed, the people had to become more involved. As the supposed arch-pragmatist Herbert Morrsion declared in 1948:

> Ballot box democracy, where people go and vote – if they can be bothered and persuaded and shoved around to go and vote – every few years and do nothing in between, is out of date. We must have an active, living democracy in our country and we must whip up our citizens to their responsibilities.

This vision nonetheless assumed that 'responsible' citizens would become Labour members and conform to the party's outlook (Fielding, 1992: 145–7). In this regard at least Labour seemed at one: left-inclined bodies such as Victory for Socialism also took it for granted that radical change should only occur through the party (Jenkins and Wolfgang, 1956).

The party's emergent revisionist wing ensured that after the mid-1950s Labour at least nodded towards pluralism, although the likes of Hugh Gaitskell were not especially innovative, reflecting as they did long-standing concerns about the dangers posed by unaccountable public bureaucracies (Gwyn, 1971). Reflecting their perspective the 1956 policy document *Personal Freedom* claimed that while Labour believed certain forms of individualism harmed the collective interest, it did not seek to create 'an all-powerful State or excessive centralisation'. Instead, Labour believed 'many important decisions and activities should be left to voluntary and local effort'. Given the expansion of the welfare state, contact with any number of public authorities had however become commonplace. The document declared Labour's determination that these should never 'degenerate into irresponsible bureaucracies'. Yet, the proposed remedies were superficial, something that was probably inevitable given its assertion that Britain had 'the most efficient, incorruptible and "non-political" Civil Service in the world' (Labour Party, 1956: 7–9, 11–12).

Attitudes to 'participation'

Some in the leadership did reject out of hand demands for greater participation. One of Wilson's favoured conversational themes at the time of the 1966 election was, for example, that the public was 'bored' with politics and wanted him to be their 'doctor who looked after the difficulties so that [they] could go on playing tennis' (Benn, 1988a: 422). Others, if sceptical, were not wholly dismissive. Despite being a leading revisionist Anthony Crosland considered 'participation' a 'hideously abused word' and believed only a small minority wanted to influence decision-making – and most of these, being middle-class, were hostile to Labour. The rest, he claimed,

> prefer to lead a full family life and cultivate their gardens. And a good thing too. For if we believe in socialism as a means of increasing personal freedom and the range of choice, we do not necessarily want a busy bustling society in which everyone is politically active, and fussing around in an interfering and responsible manner, and herding us all into participating groups. The threat to privacy and freedom would be intolerable.

Despite this, Crosland drafted his 1970 Local Government White Paper to encourage manual workers to become more active in local affairs (Crosland, 1970: 12–15; *The Times*, 25 September 1970).

Yet, if Crosland was more positive than he sometimes appeared, even those revisionists who looked on the subject with more obvious sympathy agreed that only a few wanted to participate. Nor did they imagine that accommodating such demands required the authorities to fundamentally transform themselves. Mackintosh for example considered most simply wanted recourse to a 'clear system of accountability' (Mackintosh, late 1960s).

On the other hand, while the NEC advocated individuals' 'right to be consulted about, and to influence, particular decisions which affect their daily lives', it also claimed some decisions still had to be taken centrally and free from local influence (Labour Party, 1969: 388–9). There were, then, thought to be practical limits to participation: those of popular interest, technical knowledge and ability as well as the need to ensure decision-making was not unduly delayed and efficiency compromised (Editorial, *Socialist Commentary*, December 1968). This meant most Labour reformers – like many of those who called for more participation in fact – focused on the immediate and local rather than national matters.

Despite not being responsible for the matter it was the Minister for Technology, Tony Benn, who made the issue his own, through a series of speeches thought to have laid the foundation for his later role as leader of the Labour left. Benn had long been interested in the issue: during the early 1960s he helped establish an early example of participation, the New Bristol Group, to promote public debate in the city. Significantly, however, it was in 1968, the year of Parisian student unrest and massive Labour unpopularity that Benn systematically considered the challenge posed by participation. He believed the electorate was better educated and more self-confident than ever before: this meant they embraced a 'political individualism' that could not be accommodated by conventional organisations, such as the Labour Party (Benn, 1988b: 59, 67–8, 73, 81, 107–13, 122; *The Times*, 19 April and 13 May 1968; *Guardian*, 23 March, 10 June and 6 November 1968; *Observer*, 26 May 1968; *Daily Telegraph*, 6 November 1968). People, he claimed, were no longer 'prepared to have policy handed down from on high'; instead they sought 'a greater say and greater voice' than allowed by the parliamentary system. The perception was that people were being 'kicked around' by authority and it was this alienation that gave rise to Welsh and Scottish nationalism, student radicalism and union militancy. Yet, such forces were hostile to government only because they had been denied direct political expression: most merely wanted to 'participate constructively' and win 'responsibility'.

Benn's proposals were, all things considered, remarkably modest. First, ministers needed to recognise the electorate's intelligence and so foster a 'higher level of argument'. Politicians should tell the truth and present the full complexity of the choices to be made. Election campaigns therefore had to stop being 'vast marketing operations, with the voters cast in the role of consumers looking for bargain offers that give the most for the least' and should be the occasion for 'solemn choices'. Moreover, while the parties had to give leadership, they needed to involve voters in decision-making. As he explained to the Prime Minister, he should not be 'Dr Wilson' but become a teacher, encouraging the people to achieve things by themselves.

Benn secondly proposed Labour needed to find new ways of allowing voters to influence policymaking. For example, he invited his Bristol constituents to write about selected issues so he could assess opinion – although he refused to be bound by it. More ambitiously, Benn anticipated the time when people could press a button in their homes and vote in referendums. Thirdly, he wanted voters to enjoy better access to information and to this end supported televising the Commons. Finally, Benn supported ceding power to the regions: prior to 'the Troubles' he believed Northern Ireland proved that the devolution of industrial policy could be economically advantageous given local politicians knew how to deploy resources better than Whitehall.

Benn's intervention generated a largely negative response. Some MPs resented his 'thinking out loud' while Wilson claimed he compromised collective responsibility. Others, like Michael Stewart, claimed their Cabinet colleague had just 'dressed up a lot of old ideas as if they were new' while Judith Hart thought Benn's proposals 'too safe and dull'. Still more, like the junior minister John Stonehouse, looked on his notions as irresponsible, deprecating 'the current vogue of attacking institutions as though they were mainly to blame for the maladies that we suffer'. Yet, in their irritation, critics failed to notice Benn's proposals were meant to help Labour 'lead back into the system of peaceful political change', those he supposed were operating outside it. In other words, he wanted to alter the established political system in a variety of modest ways to domesticate the supposed threat posed by strikers, students, nationalists and the like.

Hart's Green Paper

Wilson gave Judith Hart responsibility for co-ordinating the government's response to calls for participation when he promoted her to Paymaster General in October 1968. With mounting by-election and municipal losses, the autumn of 1968 was perhaps not the best time for a Labour Cabinet minister to show faith in the people. As Hart stated immediately prior to her elevation, a Labour government was 'by its nature, a two-way process' in which 'we demand ideals and sense of purpose both from ourselves and from the community'. Given that, she believed ministers were 'entitled to a little more of both from the people than we are getting at this moment' (Hart, 1968).

Despite this, Hart set about drafting proposals (Hart, 1968b, 1969a, 1969b, 1969c). For, reformers were, she claimed, presented with 'the most exciting opportunity open to us for 20 years to inject whatever new patterns and institutions we believe best to meet individual and community needs into a democratic system suffering, perhaps, from a little hardening of the arteries'. Echoing the earlier Seebohm Report on the social services, Hart believed the welfare state had created a novel situation. Once income had determined the quality of an individual's health care and education but the expansion of welfare provision meant this was now determined by the state. Unfortunately, she claimed, public institutions had 'failed to satisfy many of the people for whom they existed' and were 'totally inadequate' in their 'provision for user-participation'. Thus, pressure groups had grown up to represent consumers who were now better educated, more affluent and increasingly willing to achieve 'direct involvement'. Conveniently perhaps Hart stated that as parliament was currently reforming itself she would focus on the 'peripheral area of our democratic structure' by which she meant 'town halls, education committees, nationalised industries, [and] local offices of government bodies'. What Hart termed the 'built-in unresponsiveness of outdated and inadequate institutions' had to be overcome and new patterns discovered 'which not merely permit but invite and encourage effective participation'.

Informed by this analysis, during the spring of 1969 Hart drafted a Green Paper (Jardine, 1969a and 1969b). Like many others, she believed few craved more involvement in decision-making but thought a greater number wanted to participate in working out the implications of agreed policies for their own communities. To that end, Hart proposed creating 'neighbourhood councils' that would operate below established representative bodies. These would be less extensive than the local councils proposed by Redcliffe-Maud's contemporaneous investigation into local government, as they would fit into areas smaller than existing municipal wards. Such bodies would enjoy the right to be consulted by council officials who could be called to attend meetings; would have access to relevant information; and be able to nominate representatives to sit on a variety of public bodies.

Hart's draft contained many grey areas. In particular the exact nature of the relationship between a neighbourhood council and higher bodies was not spelt out. Moreover, while wanting neighbourhood councils to represent an 'organic community', defining such an entity proved hard. Hart nonetheless passed her document to the Prime Minister for comment with a mind to publishing a final version in the autumn. Wilson however had already told Hart the time was not ripe for concrete proposals and was unenthusiastic about her work (Jardine, 1969b). In fact the Prime Minister was generally unimpressed by his Postmaster' General's overall performance, describing her as 'just a prattling woman who had done absolutely nothing' (Benn, 1988b: 193), moving her sideways to the Ministry of Overseas Development in October 1969.

Planning

One criticism of the demand for more participation was that it was too vague. Labour's proposals to enhance the public's ability to influence planning promised to give it a practical application. For the 1968 Town and Country Planning Act gave the public the chance to make representations that authorities were obliged to take into account at a much earlier stage than hitherto. With no little hyperbole, this stipulation was described by Arthur Skeffington, junior minister at Housing and Local Government as 'a new Magna Carta in planning' (Skeffington, 1969).

The Committee on Public Participation in Planning, chaired by Skeffington, was established to determine how authorities should facilitate the public's new voice and published its recommendations in July 1969. While Skeffington underlined how important it was that the public enjoyed adequate means of influencing planning, he still believed responsible authorities should retain the final voice. His proposals aimed at directing the people's talents into 'constructive channels' so planning could be 'collaborative and friendly' allowing people and planners to realise they were on the same side (Skeffington, 1968, 1969). Skeffington's proposals nonetheless proved contentious, in particular those relating to the creation of 'community forums' and the appointment of 'community development officers'. The object of the former was to gather together local voluntary associations to help them better represent their views; the role of the latter was to mobilise the opinions of individuals belonging to no formal organisation – which in practice meant helping working-class residents articulate their views.

The Skeffington Report was written to win over those many local authorities, be they Labour or Conservative, that were deeply sceptical of the need for greater participation (Sub-committee on public participation, 1968). Despite this, most of those who spoke for municipal representatives opposed Skeffington's proposals: while not all were against forums, the majority rejected development officers. Ministers were reluctant to go against such views and prevaricated when they were obliged to formulate a circular to be issued to local planning authorities. In fact they were still grappling with the task when Labour lost power in June 1970. Civil servants had however prepared a draft that ceded most ground to Skeffington's critics, as neither forums nor development officers were made obligatory. Authorities were instead expected to take steps to ensure they merely consulted a cross-section of the public about any proposal: how that was to be achieved was left to them. This was undoubtedly a step back from what had been promised. If this draft represented a new Magna Carta, it was one in which King John had regained most of his powers.

Local government

The Redcliffe–Maud Commission was established in 1965 as Wilson's response to concerns about the relevance of local government. For when Attlee nationalised utilities such as gas and water, then created the National Health Service he stole many of the municipal authorities' responsibilities. Introducing the Redcliffe–Maud report in June 1969, the Prime Minister rightly described it as recommending the 'most far-reaching reorganisation of local government the country has ever seen'. Wilson particularly welcomed its proposals to rationalise a confusing array of bodies, something he hoped would create more effective authorities. He also correctly predicted that some of the report's proposals would be contentious, although he did not say much opposition would come from his own party (*Hansard, 5th Series, Vol. 784, Session 1968–9,* cols 1461–4). For while it raised the possibility of regional government and suggested new means by which people might participate at the grass roots Redcliffe–Maud was seen as further centralising power and interested only in efficient rather than democratic administration (Regan, 1969).

The report's main recommendation was to create three tiers of responsibility. It proposed that England (excluding London) should have its current 1,200 elected bodies replaced by just 61, all but three of which would have exclusive responsibility for local services. Given their size, Birmingham, Manchester and Liverpool were granted metropolitan status, which meant they would share service provision with a number of smaller councils. These 61 bodies were to each appoint some members – and co-opt a smaller number of outside experts – to eight provincial councils. Building on the Department of Economic Affair's regional economic councils, their main role was to lie in economic planning and development. Below these two layers Redcliffe–Maud suggested a third, composed of local councils of various sizes with limited and mostly undefined responsibilities.

Labour was divided over the report. Wilson was attracted to the creation of newer, fewer and (he presumed) more competent authorities. However, George Thomson, who the Prime Minister charged with assessing party opinion, detected a 'depressingly conservative response' among councillors and activists. Not only did they fear for their own prospects as a result of boundary changes required by reform, they had become attached to administrative units with venerable traditions. Crosland similarly noted that the proposed reduction of councillors – numbers were set to drop from 32,000 to 7,000 – caused 'dismay' within the ranks. Given their influence in constituency Labour parties, Thomson warned the Prime Minister that he needed to take full account of councillors' views when drafting legislation. Transport House, Labour's headquarters, was consequently persuaded to arrange a series of regional conferences designed to win over critics (Crosland, 1969; Thomson, 1969).

Such was the concern in Bristol West, its General Management Committee devoted two meetings to the subject, which confirmed Labour activists' largely critical response. The future MP Michael Cocks feared rural areas would enjoy undue weight in the provincial councils and so loosen Labour's already precarious grip on local government in the south west. He also believed the report 'had an air of Civil Service thinking about it' inasmuch as it gave too much power to chief executives and appointed members over elected representatives. Some of those present called for municipal authorities to be reshaped to allow people to actively participate, believing it was better to have more democracy even at the cost of efficiency. Paradoxically however Cocks did not want Whitehall to give up too much power to the provincial councils, as he feared the quality of services would then vary across the country – an understandable worry in a region where the Conservatives were likely to dominate. In the end Bristol West supported a motion rejecting the report because it would concentrate power in too few hands (Bristol West, 1969: 31 July and 25 September).

Labour's 1969 annual conference revealed that other activists believed Redcliffe–Maud sacrificed democracy 'on the altar of efficiency'. If applied, many feared the 'apathy and feeling of cynicism felt by many people, the feeling of remoteness that the elector has to even his town or civic hall' would only get worse. The provincial councils would be undemocratic, the unitary authorities too big and local councils toothless (Labour Party, 1969: 152–4). Those 1,000 or so members who attended Labour's eight regional conferences held on the subject during October generally supported that view. Those especially in the north east and west Midlands called for provincial councils to be directly elected and exert legislative powers. Members were also sceptical about local councils and regarded them as functionless sounding boards (Regional and Local Government Advisory Committee, 1969a, 1969b; Labour Party, 1969: 149–64).

As the minister responsible for local government, and latterly participation, Crosland had his own doubts about Redcliffe–Maud. His White Paper, published in February 1970, reflected those misgivings. Possibly influenced by Hart's abortive Green Paper, he nonetheless made proposals in regard to local councils, suggesting they be created throughout all unitary areas – although in metropolitan districts these should come into being only if demanded by residents. If unwilling to give them responsibility for providing services, Crosland ensured they could play a part in their administration. More generally, he presented the White Paper as giving authorities greater freedom from central government. If having to conform to certain national policies – like the introduction of comprehensive education of which he was a keen advocate – they would be free of detailed supervision in a variety of areas and enjoy unprecedented financial autonomy (Crosland, 1974: 173–89).

Conclusion

Labour's 1970 manifesto devoted five pages to policies designed to make Britain an 'active democracy' and announced how seriously the party took the need to 'infuse a democratic element into the increasingly complex institutions which dominate our lives' (Labour Party, 1970: 20–5). While normally unwise to place too much credence on the contents of a manifesto, it would be churlish to dismiss out of hand this shift of focus since

1964. For, while Labour's response to demands for greater participation was more ambivalent and limited than some wanted, its engagement was more positive than is often supposed.

It would still be fair however to stress how far the party had *not* moved. Despite Labour ministers' 'pious words', Mackintosh considered that Britain in 1970 remained one of the most centralised of industrial societies (Mackintosh, 1966, n.d.). Labour's was however an open-ended legacy, one consisting of a generous number of royal commissions, reports, experimental projects and White Papers but comparatively little substantive change. At least some of this was deliberate. Wilson was most definitely uninterested in changing the process, being preoccupied with manipulating the established mechanics of decision-making. Even so the Prime Minister still gave colleagues some scope to develop ideas that echoed radical opinion outside the government. Defeat in June 1970 meant their developing intentions could not be tested in office.

Change in this matter, above all others, was protracted and Labour in office had obviously taken but a few faltering footsteps. As Hart warned in relation to the Skeffington report, even after some reform, the people 'will continue to show the irrationality and ingratitude which is their right as citizens'. Moreover, 'for a long time all that will be possible to demonstrate as a result of the whole effort will be a little more understanding and give and take here and there'. However, at least there might be 'a willingness on the part of the authorities to take the public into their confidence rather more fully and at an earlier stage than hitherto' (Hart, 1969d). Hart was an enthusiast for modest innovation. It is perhaps little wonder that others more sceptical about change preferred to cling to familiar ways of doing politics rather than take even one short step into the dark.

References

Arblaster, A. (1972), 'Participation: Context and Conflict' in G. Parry (ed.), *Participation in Politics* (Manchester: Manchester University Press).

Barrow, L. and Bullock, I. (1996), *Democratic Ideas and the British Labour Movement, 1880–1914* (Cambridge: Cambridge University Press).

Benn, T. (1988a), *Out of the Wilderness: Diaries, 1963–67* (London: Arrow).

Benn, T. (1988b), *Office Without Power: Diaries, 1968–72* (London: Arrow).

Bevan, A. (1952), *In Place of Fear* (London: Heinemann).

Bristol West Constituency Labour Party (1969), General Management Committee Minutes, 38598/1/g, Bristol Record Office.

Conekin, B., Mort, F. and C. Waters (1999), 'Introduction' in B. Conekin, F. Mort and C. Waters (eds), *Moments of Modernity. Reconstructing Britain, 1945–1964* (London: Rivers Oram).

Crosland A. (1969), Redcliffe–Maude: The Options, PREM 13/2763, Public Record Office (PRO).

Crosland, A. (1970), *A Social Democratic Britain* (London: Fabian Society).

Crosland, A. (1974), *Socialism Now* (London: Cape).

Fielding, S. (1992), 'Labourism in the 1940s', *Twentieth Century British History* 3:2.

Fielding, S. (2003), *The Labour Governments, 1964–70. Volume One: Labour and Cultural Change* (Manchester: Manchester University Press).

Giddens, A. (1994), *Beyond Left and Right* (Cambridge: Polity).

Gwyn, W. B. (1971), 'The Labour Party and the Threat of Bureaucracy', *Political Studies*, 29.

Hart, J. (1968a), Speech to rally of Sudbury and Woodbridge CLP, Judith Hart papers, File Hart 10/4, Section 10, Labour Party Archive (LPA).

Hart, J. (1968b), Speech to London conference, Hart papers, File Hart 10/4, Section 10, LPA.

Hart, J. (1969a), Speech to the Council of Social Services, CAB 151/57, PRO.

Hart, J. (1969b), Notes on participation, February 1969, CAB 151/57, PRO.

Hart, J. (1969c), Notes for speech to the Council of Social Services, CAB 151/58, PRO.

Hart, J. (1969d), Letter to A. Greenwood, 10 July, CAB 151/63, PRO.

Hill, D. M. (1970), *Participating in Local Affairs* (Harmondsworth: Penguin).

Hobsbawm, E. (1995), *Age of Extremes: The Short Twentieth Century 1914–1991* (London: Joseph).

Inglehart, R. (1977), *The Silent Revolution: Changing Values and Political Styles among Western Publics* (Princeton: Princeton University Press).

Jardine, R. (1969a), Note for record. Local councils, CAB 151/57, PRO.

Jardine, R. (1969b), Outline of Green Paper on Participation, CAB 151/57, PRO.

Jay, D. (1947), *The Socialist Case* (London: Faber).

Jenkins, H. and Wolfgang, W. (1956), *Tho' Cowards Flinch*, Victory for Socialism.

Labour Party (1956), *Personal Freedom*, Labour Party.

Labour Party (1964), *Let's Go with Labour*, Labour Party.

Labour Party (1966), *Time for Decision*, Labour Party.

Labour Party (1968), *Report of the Sixty-seventh Annual Conference*, Labour Party.

Labour Party (1969), *Report of the Sixty-eighth Annual Conference*, Labour Party.

Labour Party (1970), *Now Britain's Strong Let's Make It a Great Place to Live In*, Labour Party.

Mackintosh, J. (1966), 'Democratic Reform and Economic Planning', Dep 323/44/1, John P. Mackintosh papers, National Library of Scotland (NLS).

Mackintosh, J. (n.d. but late 1960s), 'Democracy and the Devolution of Power', Dep. 323/231 Mackintosh papers, NLS.

Mackintosh, J. (n.d.), Evidence for the Crowther Commission, HO 221/84, Mackintosh papers, NLS.

Marwick, A. (1998), *The Sixties* (Oxford: Oxford University Press).

Miliband, R. (1972), *Parliamentary Socialism* (London: Merlin).

Pateman, C. (1970), *Participation and Democratic Theory* (Cambridge: Cambridge University Press).

Pelling, H. (1968), 'Then and Now: Popular Attitudes since 1945' in his *Popular Politics and Society in Late Victorian Britain* (London: Macmillan).

Regan, D. (1969), 'Start Not End of a Debate', *Socialist Commentary*, August.

Regional and Local Government Advisory Committee (1969a), Report of Regional Conferences on Local Government Reform in England, LPA.

Regional and Local Government Advisory Committee (1969b), Principles for Local Government Reform in England, LPA.
Saville, J. (1988), *The Labour Movement in Britain* (London: Faber).
Skeffington, A. (1968), Press release for speech, HLG 120/1045, PRO.
Skeffington, A. (1969), Press release for speech, CAB 151/63, PRO.
Sub-committee on public participation (1968), Note of first meeting, HLG 136/274, PRO.
Taylor, M. (2000), 'Labour and the Constitution' in D. Tanner, P. Thane and N. Tiratsoo (eds), *Labour's First Century* (Cambridge: Cambridge University Press).
Thomson, G. (1969), Letters to H. Wilson, 23 June, 30 July and 4 August, PREM 13/2763, PRO.
Tomlinson, J. (2003), *The Labour Governments 1964–70. Volume 3: Economic Policy* (Manchester: Manchester University Press).
Williams, R. (ed.) (1968), *May Day Manifesto 1968* (Harmondsworth: Penguin).
Young, J. W. (2003), *The Labour Governments 1964–70. Volume 2: International Policy* (Manchester: Manchester University Press).

10

Arts and crafts: social democracy's cultural resources and repertoire in 1960s Britain

Lawrence Black

Introduction

A long-standing critique of British Labourism has centred on its failure to cultivate a fuller presence in civil society. For the New Left's Perry Anderson (1965: 235–8, 244–5, 260, 279), Labour's miscalculation was in equating power with the parliamentary legislature. Power resided far more diffusely in a heteronomy of institutions and ideologies of business, education, media, professions, culture, sport, family, moral values and the 'myriad micro-social formations' constituting civil society. Anderson observed that 'diminishing scarcity tends to diversify and dilate the whole fabric of society'. And whilst contemporary theorists of civil society debate whether this constituted a rich pluralism of identities or fragmented individualism and difference, Anderson anticipated the political relevance of what Inglehart (1990) has described as post-material values. Anderson's strategy was to extend Labour's 'arc of action' to the 'whole complex landscape of civil society', to make this a more conducive terrain and make Labour politics more than just an alternative executive, but a whole way of life. This meant 'inhabiting civil society at every possible point', not by imposing party discipline on these arenas, but acquiring for Labour 'an authentic universality by linking it to the whole social life of the community'.

European social democracy by comparison seemed – through festivals, subsidies and sponsorship – a more all-embracing political culture, more embedded in national and working-class cultural life. Many commentators noted how Conservatism seemed more at one with civil society. The 'apolitical sociability' McKibbin (1998: 96–8, 204–5) argues was a norm in inter-war England – the (in practice, highly political) deflection of politically charged conflict and discourse outside elections, cultivated in Conservatism's associational networks and detached style, that contrived to mark Labour out as more 'political' – was remarked upon by political scientists and anthropologists in the post-war period too (Stacey, 1960). And in the Young Conservatives, extensive social networks were retained within civil society.

Variants on Anderson's theme remain current. Eley (2002: 8–9) argues its narrow remit, its parliamentary–industrial–male complex, was a self-imposed constraint and one reason why 'socialists lost their hegemony in the left after the 1960s and other radicalisms entered the left's political space.' McKibbin (1998: 534–5) has critiqued the Attlee government's 'all-too-limited social democracy' and its choice 'not to enter the sphere of civil society, except in the most modest way'. It operated 'deeply, but on a narrow front', leaving spheres of entrenched (invariably conservative) interest like sport or education, safe from incursion, beyond its reforming remit. From this perspective, the Wilson governments appear bolder – engaging education, sexuality, culture and aiding a tranche of permissive legislation. In a New Labour spin-off of this thinking, Mulgan (1996: 212–13) has argued that rooted in the workplace much more than its European counterparts, 'old' Labour was (unduly) wedded to the state, to tradition and high culture rather than modernity or popular culture and thus to 'balance and sobriety, not pleasure and risk'. So were conceived the rather British peculiarities of 'old' Labour.

This chapter proposes a mild rejoinder to such accounts through a description of three left cultural initiatives – the 1962 Festival of Labour, Arnold Wesker's Centre Fortytwo project (1960–70) and Jennie Lee's tenure as Minister of Arts (1964–70). They demonstrate the mainstream left was keenly aware of cultural matters, had resources to draw on and an agenda to press. It can then be properly regarded as social democracy rather than labelled 'labourist'. A mild rejoinder because it cannot be said they dramatically raised the left's influence within civil society. In short, Anderson and others' theory of the left's shortcomings is sustainable, but not for the reasons of ideological deficiency alleged. Historians need other explanations for the limits to the left's presence in civil society.

For starters, the New Left cannot be taken as holy writ on matters cultural. It was self-congratulatory about its (admittedly vibrant) London social and cultural life at its own Soho Partisan café or the Whitechapel Gallery. It was as if taking popular culture seriously (defining culture less as a select activity and more inclusive of everyday life, as Raymond Williams did), was sufficient to establish its cultural authority on the (otherwise dull) left. Whilst mixing more easily with the cutting edge of metropolitan artistes, it was hardly at one with the 1960s' counter-culture, peopled (in a large minority) by the fallout from CND and formal politics. As 1960s counter-cultural journalist Jonathon Green (1998: 239–44) put it, 'if the hippies found the left boring, then the left found them trivial' and for all the New Left 'claimed to back libertarian attitudes to sex and drugs', it could be 'po-faced when actually indulging'. Anderson himself, once at the helm of *New Left Review* from 1962, trimmed its cultural dalliances with high-falutin, continental Marxist theory. Not that the first generation of the New Left was that culturally conscious. The original *May Day Manifesto* of 1967 and the expanded 1968 version, a revival of this older New Left by Williams (1968), E. P. Thompson and Stuart Hall, rationed 'culture' to a few lines about the means of communication. Janey Buchan, an actress and cultural beacon of the Edinburgh left, married to MP Norman Buchan and herself later a Labour MEP, wrote to Arnold Wesker (August 1960, AW 136/9) despairing of the New Left's Londo-centrism. Having 'prodded Stuart Hall and NLR until I'm sick' to participate in the burgeoning fringe of the Edinburgh International Festival she felt, 'NLR need their heads looking at because they could have the most tremendous stage ready-made for them'.

Pessimism pervaded the left-wing cultural guidebooks most likely to be on bookshelves. Less Williams' *Culture and Society*, but the bigger selling (both feature in Sutherland's (2002) account of British bestsellers) Hoggart's (1957) *The Uses of Literacy* which aired anxieties at the Americanisation of British popular culture and Marcuse's (1964) *One-Dimensional Man*, a critique of the 'repressive tolerance' of mass culture in modern Western society from the Californian-based Frankfurt School Marxist.

There was a broader 'cultural turn' in later 1950s politics – interest in matters of leisure and culture being less the New Left's preserve than contingent upon prosperity and akin to Inglehart's shift from the standard of living to the quality of life (Shafer and Stears, 1999). Labour looked to section 132 of the 1948 Local Government Act permitting local councils to tax and spend on cultural provision and the 1951 Festival of Britain that Conekin (2003) argues projected a social democratic vision for the nation. This was a platform for other state initiatives, like the Council of Industrial Design. With its deference to the Arnold–Leavis tradition of cultural thought that saw enlightening potential in elite culture, Labour's state-mindedness helped fashion a notion of public culture as more virtuous than the private sphere. Crosland (1956: 515–29) took issue with this earnest temper, urging upon the left an agenda of culture, leisure and happiness to avoid getting trapped in a Webb-like sobriety. By the 1960s such thinking was more common.

Festival of Labour

The Festival of Labour offers historians an audit of Labour's cultural and leisure repertoire and, because more partisan than the Festival of Britain, better captures its vision for these spheres. The Festival's neglect evinces contemporary historians' disinterest (compared with earlier periods) in the more theatrical, carnival (literally in this instance) aspect of politics, something that with the professionalisation of political communication and movements like CND (to take two prominent examples) was salient. This neglect might be due to the Festival's limited impact and legacy, but not its scale or ambition. Some 150,000 party people visited London over the weekend 16–17 June. Labour spent £12,000 on the event. Festival

Director Merlyn Rees (speech, 10 March 1962, FOL1) explained its chief aim was to link Labour with modernity and 'show that socialism is not only concerned with material welfare'.

The centrepiece public displays were regional Labour, trade union and Co-op floats. These took seven hours to parade from East India Dock to Islington, along the Embankment, to Battersea Park (the main site), ending in Camberwell. London visitors were also offered a concert of Stravinsky, Tchaikovsky, Mozart and Haydn at the Royal Festival Hall with the Philharmonia Orchestra. A jazz concert at the Festival Hall featured Johnnie Dankworth and Chris Barber. The Musicians' Union floats bore Harry Gold and his Pieces of Eight and Terry Lightfoot's band (featured in the recent film *It's Trad Dad*), competitors to the popular trad players Acker Bilk and Kenny Ball. Their trad version of the Red Flag was a hit with crowds en route (*South London Press*, 19 June 1962). The jazz note resounded better with the Union's 'Keep Music Live' slogans ('no bands anywhere make a living from making gramophone records alone'), than with the Rolling Stones' first Marquee gig a month later. Film-goers were enticed to the National Film Theatre by *The Stars Look Down* (a 1939 version of A. J. Cronin's Durham mining disaster novel); the Peter Sellers industrial relations satire *I'm Alright Jack* and versions of John Osborne's play *Look Back in Anger* and John Steinbeck's US depression novel *The Grapes of Wrath*. A British Film Institute advert appealed to the festival-goers as 'the sort of cinemagoer who prefers *La Notte* to *Carry On?*' (Labour Party, 1962a).

Ted Willis commissioned a play from 'Labour sympathiser' Elaine Morgan. A leading TV writer himself who served on Labour's 1959 Youth Commission and was elevated to the Lords by Wilson, Willis (to Rees 2 January 1961, FOL4) rated Morgan 'one of the top . . . TV writers in the country', though her play *Nothing Personal* was completed too late to be performed. Key was that there would be 'no difficulty in asking her to keep off the more controversial topics'. Willis meant the unilateralism he also aimed to avoid in funding the Young Socialists' essay competition (in which Paul Foot of Glasgow Woodside YS won second prize). There were scuffles with CND supporters. On the other hand the Eastern Labour region float depicted the Sizewell and Bradwell nuclear plants and the rocket on the West Midlands Labour float was of the space not nuclear sort, embracing the modern rather than generating protest. Further relief came in the resolution of the West Lothian question, with Tam Dalyell's by-election triumph on the Festival's eve (File 'YS essay prize', FOL1; Dunn, 1962).

There were two art exhibitions. At the South London Art gallery in Camberwell 'Prints of the World' displayed art from 18 nations including Thai, Argentinean and Eskimo prints. Modern art was at Congress House. This was itself one of London's most notable modernist constructions, designed by David de Rieu Aberdeen, with sculptures by Bernard Meadows and Jacob Epstein, opened in 1958 and a listed building within thirty years (TUC, 2004). The festival exhibition used the glass-fronted ground floor and memorial hall, facing Epstein's sculpture (Gaitskell to George Woodcock (TUC General Secretary) 15 February 1962, TUC). TUC support was hesitant, preferring for cost and commitment reasons to introduce trade unionists to existing art centers (Woodcock to A. L. Williams, 2 June 1961, FOL1). Nevertheless, the exhibition included: a Frank Auerbach oil painting; Peter Blake collage, 'Elvis Presley wall'; two Patrick Heron oils; three David Hockney paintings; and Henry Moore and Eduardo Paolozzi sculptures. Sir Kenneth Clark, art historian and TV broadcaster, opened it, making contemporary references to 'the twist' and Blake's pop art (Labour Party, 1962b; *Times*, 14 June 1962).

In Battersea Park, Labour's Women's Advisory Committee displayed handicrafts (knitting, preserves, dress-making). A town-planning exhibit showed post-war urban redevelopment, alongside Socialist Medical Association, Labour College, Coal Board and Fabian stalls. The Woodcraft Folk put on country dancing and the Flying Cobinas, acrobatics. Peter Knight's TV orchestra, Captain Strelsky's Cossack Orchestra and the Cresswell Colliery Band supplied 'easy listening' music. The Co-op (after a spat with the Musicians' Union over its preference for using pre-recorded music) mounted a fashion show. For youngsters there were Punch and Judy shows. A variety concert produced by impresario Jack Hylton was hosted by BBC *Tonight* presenters Robin Hall and Jimmy McGregor and included the Morlais Glee Welsh singers. Sports included keep-fit, British Amateur Gymnastics Association displays and YS Soccer and Netball tournaments. The Athletics meeting featured the European shot put champion and a UK high jump record by Gordon Miller (Labour Party, 1962a).

Whilst the focus was in London, a host of regional events were undertaken. The bill at Belle Vue stadium in Manchester featured Harold Wilson, three *Coronation Street* stars (the actors who played Harry and Concepta Hewitt, judges of the Festival Princess competition and Elsie Tanner, guest at a dinner dance) and comedian Ken Dodd (press release, 30 April 1962, FOL1).

Labour was not without experience or support in organising this jamboree. Reg Underhill in the Agents office drew on experience of Labour League of Youth events at Butlins Skegness. MP Dennis Howell's (1968) refereeing expertise aided the soccer tournament. Phillip Noel-Baker MP, twice an Olympic athlete (at 1,500 yards in 1912 and 1920), was president of the Athletics meeting. This was organised by Dave Curtis, secretary of the British Workers' Sports Association until its demise in 1960. The BWSA long advocated a Sports Minister, a post Howell would occupy in the Wilson government (Rees, 'Report on the Festival of Labour' (August 1962), FOL1; Bird, 1985). Tom Driberg was behind the art exhibitions and Michael Ayrton (artist, TV presenter and son of Labour MP Barbara Ayrton

Gould) also proffered counsel. Misha Black, architect and designer (most famously of the Festival of Britain's Regatta restaurant) advised and judged the 'Brighter Premises' contest held in conjunction with the Festival. Float and tableaux designs were provided by the Co-op Wholesale Society's shopfitting department and a professional socialist design company, Mountain and Molehill (1959), run by ex-Communists Ray Bernard and Ken Sprague. Sprague and Bernard's politics were raised, but Rees reported that whatever their past they now had 'impeccable clients on their books' (Bernard to Rees, 4 July 1961 and 22 June 1962, FOL1. Rees to A. L. Williams, 3 January 1962, FOL5).

Equally a number of problems were encountered. Most were internal party conflicts or organisational: such as Frank Cousins' invite going missing or LCC regulations hampering the art sale on the Sunday and likewise a collection at the Christian Socialist service taken by Donald Soper and Tony Greenwood. Others had a more political subtext. Rees noted 'political problems . . . concerning the hiring of vehicles from British Road Services'. Road haulage having been privatised by the Conservatives, BRS were not keen to deal with Labour – a problem for transporting tableaux to London and around its streets. (Memo 'Festival of Labour' (n.d), LLP; Rees to Willie Marshall (Scottish Regional Organiser) 28 February 1961, FOL2).

Others suggested the limits rather than extent of Labour's reach and networks in civil society. Some of the more ambitious touring theatre plans – with Theatre Workshop or Unity Theatre – were deemed financially unviable. Rees' middling tastes did for A. L. Lloyd's expansive plans for folk music recording. Equally, in convening the variety concert, Hylton reported '"sympathetic" stars were conspicuous by their absence' (Rees 'Report on the Festival of Labour' (August 1962), FOL1). Several institutions spurned Labour on the basis they might suffer through association. The National School of Opera feared imperilling its LCC funding. Its Principal, Anne Wood (to Rees, 25 August 1961, FOL1), regretted this and was 'impressed [Labour] should have offered us assistance to commission a new ballet and new opera'. Though a popular venue with the New Left, the Whitechapel Gallery Director Bryan Robertson told Rees (10 January 1961, FOL2) it was, 'impossible for us to hold an exhibition of any kind with political sponsorship'. The British Film Institute, *Daily Mirror* and Caravan Club (touted as an accommodation solution for the influx of Labour members) expressed similar anxieties about participation. Some distinction might be drawn between association with party and politics per se. But that as Rees (to Marshall, 26 January 1962, FOL2) put it, 'we have to avoid being too aggressively political', said much about the comparatively cold climate in which (against which, in some respects) politics was practised and by which it was delimited.

The Festival also reproduced the spatial divide between the more educational, uplifting, formal offerings (at the Royal Festival Hall or art exhibitions) and the less demanding, more leisurely (epitomised by TV orchestras), entertainment in Battersea Park that had characterised the Festival of Britain. This suggests that Labour's mind retained a worthy, necessary or sustainable distinction between high and popular arts – if one it (theoretically) aspired to bridge – and one in many ways the 1960s would quash.

Wesker's Centre Fortytwo

Playwright Arnold Wesker's initiative to create a people's artistic hub generally prompts discussion of how the project became consumed by the Roundhouse in North London and was abandoned by 1970. Why did it prove so fruitless (in the title of Clifford Odetts' play) waiting for.lefty? Wesker's talent for alienating financial, cultural and political support more than matched his (Wilson-esque) ability to schmooze luminaries and celebrities – from Lord Harewood (the Queen's cousin and Edinburgh Festival Director) to Beatle John Lennon. Centre Fortytwo passed in and out of favour with, amongst others, Jennie Lee, Vic Feather, Jack Hylton, Arnold Goodman and Robert Maxwell. Others like Ted Willis, who suggested a merger with cash-strapped Unity Theatre (*Railway Review*, 10 May 1963), were consistent critics. The TUC remained at arm's length – for reasons of cost and resistance to novel projects, as with the Festival of Labour (Wesker, 1960b) – though trades councils were keener. Labour and the Arts Council received Fortytwo coolly after 1964. Other than local club visits and use of Williams' college office (*Cambridge News*, 17 May 1963), so did the New Left. This was despite the congruence between Wesker's analysis and its own (Anderson's and Williams'); his international agenda (plans for the Roundhouse were drafted by architect Paul Chemetov, who worked on the PCF HQ in Paris) and reputation in Cuba, America, Sweden and Japan and CND ties (Wesker, 1970: 103–27). By 1967, ricocheting around the left, Wesker was treated to a fund-raising party at Downing Street by Wilson and was a signatory to the *May Day Manifesto*.

Wesker's kitchen-sink political trilogy of plays *Roots, Chicken Soup with Barley* and *I'm Talking about Jerusalem* (1958–60) were critically acclaimed. But Wesker was frustrated that they did not reach a wider audience. In *O, Mother, Is It worth It?*, sent to trade union leaders in 1960, Wesker (1960a: 2, 5–11) pondered 'is anybody listening?' given so few were theatre-goers and so many cinema-goers, bingo-players or TV-viewers. Having convinced workers to contest habits of low pay and long hours, the struggle now was how to use this time and money. The Labour movement needed to address cultural habits, Wesker adduced, since 'if we are not to be materially exploited neither should we be culturally exploited'. 'Economic barriers of class maybe less definable, but the cultural ones are still there' and if the Labour movement continued to neglect this it could only expect more films like *I'm Alright Jack* (and later *The Angry Silence*), mocking trade unionism. Cultural exemplars for Wesker were 'the Gorkis, Chekovs, Millers . . . Steinbecks . . . Zolas . . . Beethovens . . . de Sicas . . . Van Goghs and yes, the Louis Armstrongs'. As this canon suggests, Wesker took a dim view of contemporary popular culture and was not shy of value judgements. Wesker (*Nottingham Evening Post*, 20 April 1963) was in no doubt 'that the music of Bach is superior to the music of Elvis Presley'.

At the 1960 TUC (1960: 435–8) motion 42 (thus the project's moniker) asked the General Council to 'make proposals . . . to ensure a greater participation by the trade union movement in all cultural activities'. Moved by Ralph Bond of the Association of Cinematograph, Television and Allied Technicians, its case was that 'a measure of our civilization' was how military spending was a thousand times that on the Arts Council. He lamented how 'our spiritual heritage, its culture, its songs, its living drama, its poetry is dying away . . . vulgarized by the purveyors of mass-production entertainment'. But its neglect by the Labour movement was also indicted. At the International Confederation of Free Trade Unions' recent Stockholm Film Festival, Bond witnessed West German, Belgian, US, Canadian and Scandanavian work, but was 'sad to say not a single film made by a British Trade Union'. William Whitehead, South Wales NUM seconder of the motion, bemoaned anyone 'satisfied that culture and art mean rock 'n' roll . . . *Yogi Bear* and *Rawhide* . . . Our heritage is William Morris, Shakespeare, Shaw . . . Vaughan Williams . . . Benjamin Britten'. This was carried against the General Council's case stressing the higher rate of European Union's subs. In an example of the attitude towards culture the motion refuted, the Congress President interrupted one of its backers to urge, 'I hope delegates will be brief as I want to take the economic section after this'!

Festivals in Wellingborough in 1961 and Hayes and Southall, Nottingham, Birmingham, Leicester and Bristol in 1962 aimed to enact the motion. At local trades councils' behest, Centre Fortytwo put on pub and workplace poetry readings by Dannie Abse, Christopher Logue ('Poet at the Canteen table', *Times*, 27 July 1963), Dominic Behan and Laurie Lee. Plays came in form of Bernard Kops' *Enter Solly Gold* and Wesker's *The Nottingham Captain* based on the 1817 Pentrich Luddite rising and set to classical and jazz scores. Music included Stravinsky's *A Soldier's Tale* and generally, Ewan MacColl, Peggy Seeger and folk revivalists like AL Lloyd would perform. Jazz came courtesy of the FortyTwo big band, a sixteen-piece led by Tommy Watts whose repertoire included 'TUC twist' and 'Wesker jumps in' and was well regarded enough to record an album with Columbia Records in 1964. Charles Parker's Theatre Folk Ballad, *The Maker and the Tool* recorded workplace sounds and transformed them into songs. Michael Croft's National Youth Theatre put on *Hamlet*, 'Shakespeare's Jimmy Porter' it was claimed. (Centre Fortytwo, 1962a, 1962b: 13–16; press release, 4 May 1964, AW 134/7).

The festivals prompted comparisons with William Morris – a lodestar Wesker would readily follow – 'A Victorian Wesker' the *Western Daily Press* (17 September 1962) reckoned, reviewing the Bristol festival and from Jennie Lee, one of Wesker's early champions (*Encounter*, August 1962: 95–6). But saddled with debt and amateurish in organisation, Centre Fortytwo did not take up the forty-five requests they received for festivals in 1963, turning attention to the Roundhouse. This derelict Victorian railway shed-cum-warehouse meant legal and financial squabbles prevailed over creative output. By the late 1960s it was hosting commercial (BBC TV ice-shows, an early Campaign for Real Ale festival) and counter-cultural (the psychedelic launch-rave for *International Times* and 1967 Dialectics of Liberation conference) events, far from Wesker's preferred blend of 'authentic' proletarian / folk cultures and the best high arts.

The cultural *Zeitgeist* bypassed Centre Fortytwo and its conception of class-based cultural life. Confined to London after 1962, its thunder was stolen by the likes of Jim Haynes' Arts Lab. But asking if Centre Fortytwo was betrayed (Coppieters, 1975) is a language that by-and-large ignores its legacy for radical theatre and the stage it offered others (John McGrath, founder of 7:84 in 1971, was amongst its early supporters), its post-industrial vision of the Roundhouse (now a norm for Arts Centres) and origins (Itzin, 1979: 4–5, 90, 103–15).

Jennie Lee, Arts Minister

This filtered through to the Wilson government after 1964, particularly to Jennie Lee, Britain's first Arts Minister. Wilson sensed lucrative political and economic dividends in associating with popular culture and leisure (Black: 2006). As British popular culture flourished in the 1960s, so did public subsidies for the arts under Lee and Goodman (Arts Council chair 1965–72). Lee secured a threefold increase – not huge in itself (0.15 per cent of government spending), but achieved in the face of spending restraint. Paradoxically, Lee's financial battles were with Crosland and Jenkins, the revisionists who in the later 1950s had urged the left to pay greater interest to culture.

Lee's 1965 White Paper, *A Policy for the Arts* (Cmnd 2601: paras 5, 7, 88) resounded with Wilson's modernity in its desire to sweep away the 'atmosphere of old-fashioned gloom and undue solemnity' surrounding the arts. It was alert to youth culture and how the 1960s' generation 'more self-confident than their elders and beginning to be given some feeling for drama, music and visual arts in their school years . . . will want gaiety . . . informality and experimentation'. The creative outpouring and expectations of this generation called for subsidies to allay public squalor in the arts, since private sources were scarce. Lee aimed to move arts funding beyond mere survival to extend provision. The state should not produce or guide output, but enable it by fostering 'a larger and more appreciative public'. Like other liberal legislation under Wilson, the state conceived its role as permissive not prescriptive – Lee contrasted the *dirigisme* of her French counterpart André Malraux – supporting voluntary initiative like the 1948 Act. Besides this atmosphere, there were tangible aspects to Lee's policy: rejuvenating the National Theatre project; increasing the British Film Institute's funding; creating the National Film Institute; rescuing the National Youth Orchestra; creating local arts centers and regional civic theatres; enabling access to museums and galleries; and supporting better cafés to brighten the more forbidding establishments and entice audiences.

More than an addendum of material progress, culture and the fine arts were conceived as a social good – making Britons better citizens. Much as Lee and Wilson gestured towards popular culture, the virtues of 'high' culture remained. The language of civilisation was recurrent in Labour's vocabulary. 'The test of a civilized society is diversity, people should have choice', Lee insisted, by which was meant choice from the best since, 'you cannot build a civilization on beer and bingo' (BBC, 2004). Goodman's Arts Council funded mainly the Londo-centric worlds of orchestra, opera, museums, ballet and galleries. Labour can be cast then (Mulgan, 1996) as defender of the faith in orthodox 'high' culture. But Lee's was hardly an easy option, neither pandering to popular taste nor as much to establishment predilections as Mulgan supposes. Indeed rather than being socialised by the elitism of such institutions it was attempting to recast their status. The Arts Council's metropolitan propensities under Keynes were contested – its elitist maxim of 'few but roses' became 'the best for the most' and the (pejorative) 'provinces' became 'regions'. Thus the Scottish Arts Council created in 1967 saw investment in Scotland quintuple, doubling its proportion of national spending (DES, 1968). The metropole's command was diminishing, but in other ways Lee was determined to export its professional standards to the regions, telling the 1969 Musicians' Union May Day concert (JL 2/2/2/1), 'that we should be trying to bring the best within reach of all, but . . . a broadening of opportunities should not lead to a lowering of standards'.

More reactive to voluntary efforts than proactive (like Wesker), regional best practice came from the North Eastern Association for the Arts (Northern Arts Association from 1967). It was the model for English regional associations – two-thirds of which were created between 1964 and 1970. Founded in 1961, its first secretary was Arthur Blenkinsop, Labour MP for South Shields from 1964. It awarded grants, subsidised transport and backed new building like the Billingham Forum Theatre and the modernisation of Sunderland Empire, international exchanges and larger initiatives such as the recently established Northern Sinfonia. Arts spending in the region tripled between 1963 and 1967. Of the total £0.75 million it received in 1961–69, more than half came from the region – 44 per cent from local authorities (some giving more than the 6d rate the 1948 Act permitted), 15 per cent from the private and business sector (of which Tyne-Tees TV were the largest contributor) and 41 per cent from the Arts Council. Its definition of 'culture' was not audacious – 'music, ballet, opera, drama, painting, sculpture, film, literature' *Arts North* explained – jazz, blues and folk being the fringes of its musical ear. More consonant with a strategy for civil society, was the association's sponsoring in 1965 of a pilot project to use post offices as art galleries initiated by Postmaster General Tony Benn (1988: 237, 309). Political tinges were apparent: MacColl, Seeger and Wesker were regular visitors. So too was Vic Feather (later a Vice-President), who as TUC General Secretary warned the Association (at its 1970 AGM) off a specific 'workers art' (of Wesker's sort) in favour of increasing general access and participation (*Arts North*, January 1968, September and December 1970).

The Association (Vall, 2001) echoed the nostrums of Lee and Wesker and the latter's post-industrial ethos. It stressed: 'revitalizing the North East is not merely a matter of more or better factories, jobs, houses, roads, schools and hospitals, it means developing the arts as well' and that 'artists are not a class apart . . . audiences are ordinary people'. There were portents here of the language of 'cultural regeneration' cultivated by the Greater London Council in the 1980s as a means to circumvent the Thatcherite state (and market) and foster community-based ingenuity – later evident in New Labour's professed penchant for the cultural industries and creative economy. In this incarnation a diversity of high and popular and (*pace* Mulgan) traditional and modern were fused, if the tone was less consciously improving (Black, 2006).

Conclusions

Full analysis of these three initiatives must assess their reception (outside the closeted world of the left), appraise their interaction and differences and compare other political traditions. But even with just a description of their scale and content, historians can deduce that it was not for lack of trying that British social democracy made limited inroads into civil society. Indeed inroads were made – Britons were not entirely unreceptive. Wesker and Lee's imprint, as much as the New Left, helped politicise 'culture' (if less dramatically than in other 1960s spheres, from feminism to humour). But negligible as these were, candidates for explaining the left's limited presence become: its specific tastes, ways of conveying these, or popular cultural tastes / attitudes themselves.

Certain common tastes were evident – differences were of strategy and ambition. Most clear was an appreciation of the best of the high Arts and belief in their salutary value – 'are *you* not prepared to spend the price of a packet of cigarettes once a year on the visual arts?' as a Festival of Labour slogan put it ('Middleton memo' (1961), FOL 2). Another was jazz, almost the only a palatable form of US culture and seemingly resistant to mass forces of commercialisation. Centre Fortytwo believed it was the 'last of the authentic folk musics' and even recognised (a key 'pop' appeal) that it was 'meant to be danced to' (Centre Fortytwo 1962b). Anderson's New Left retained a little of its early jazz passions (evident in 1961's documentary, *Living Jazz*) through Alan Beckett. Eligible for Arts Council funding from 1967, Lee's White Paper (Cmnd 2601: para. 71) saw a paradigm in jazz, since it was a form where 'highbrow and lowbrow have met'. Whatever the veracity of this, jazz was hardly 'popular' – no more than Lee's classical leanings. The left's cultural repertoire invariably attempted to influence cultural taste (in something of its own ideal image) more than reflect it – discordant with popular choice, struggling to persuade and unwilling to coerce it.

In terms of conveying, when David Widgery (1989: 115) helped found Rock against Racism in 1976, he was still berating the left's narrow definition of the cultural and political and how by failing to address 'emotional as well as economic' needs it was 'boring a generation to political death.' Wesker's despair (a frustration incorporated into his plays) was of the philistine attitudes he encountered – both a cause for and a barrier to the left's efforts.

What the left considered lacking in popular cultural attitudes – what historians would more judiciously identify as Britons' changing aspirations – were as accountable as any lack of idealism or ambition on the left's part for cultural patterns. As a youth in Wellingborough's Phoebe's café told the *Sunday Times* (17 September 1962) as he stood by the jukebox, with his 'Tony Curtis haircut' during Centre Fortytwo's Festival: 'doesn't appeal . . . that kind of stuff. We got all we want. Cinemas, dancing . . . six caffs, 12 pubs. Anything else you want you go to Northampton, only ten mile'. This put limits on politics, but also implied politics' limits as a mobilising force – surely as impressive as any self-inflicted shortcomings of social democracy. Cultural change (counter-cultural and more popularly), took place all around the left, it was hardly its chief lever as either a repertoire or source of authority from which people wished to take cultural cues. The cultural change of the 1960s itself blurred and levelled divisions of high and popular, not by creating a common culture, but one marked by trends towards diversity and plurality. If this achieved something of the left's aims – making a more conducive environment for social democracy – the left deserves as little credit as it does the criticism that it lacked a strategy for civil society.

Note

Thanks for feedback from the Political Studies Association, Labour Movements conference, Bristol University (2002) and Western Social Science Association Conference, Las Vegas (2003).

References

Festival of Labour (FOL, Boxes 1–6), Labour Party Archives, John Rylands University Library, Manchester

Jennie Lee Papers, (JL), Open University (GB/2315/JL)

London Labour Party Papers (LLP), London Metropolitan Archives (Acc.2417/g/98)

TUC Papers, (TUC), Modern Records Centre, Warwick University (MSS.292B/750.1/3)

Arnold Wesker Papers (AW), Humanities Research Center, University of Texas at Austin

Interviews: Lord Merlyn-Rees (January 2002), Arnold Wesker (August 2003)

Anderson, Perry (1965), 'Problems of Socialist Strategy' in Perry Anderson and Robin Blackburn, (eds), *Towards Socialism* (Ithaca, NY: Cornell University Press)

BBC (2004), *The Cultural State* (Radio 4, 20 September)

Benn, Tony (1988), *Out of the Wilderness: Diaries 1963–67* (London: Hutchinson)

Bird, Stephen (1985), 'The British Workers' Sports Association, 1930–60', *Bulletin of the Society for the Study of Labour History* vol. 50

Black, Lawrence (2006), ' "Making Britain a gayer and more cultivated country": Jennie Lee and the Creative Industries in the 1960s' in Glen O'Hara, and Helen Parr (eds), *Contemporary British History* vol. 20, no. 3

Centre Fortytwo (1962a), *Hayes and Southall Trade Union Festival: Programme* (London)

—— (1962b), *Annual Report, 1961–62* (London)

Cmnd 2601 (February 1965), *A Policy for the Arts: The First Steps* (HMSO)

Conekin, Becky (2003), *Autobiography of a Nation* (Manchester: Manchester University Press)

Coppieters, Frank (1975), 'Arnold Wesker's Centre Fortytwo: A Cultural Revolution Betrayed', *Theatre Quarterly* vol. 5, no. 18

Crosland, C. A. R. (1956), *The Future of Socialism* (London: Jonathan Cape)

Department of Education and Science (September 1968), *Report on the Arts: A Going Concern* (HMSO)

Dunn, Nell (1962), 'Trip to Battersea', *New Statesman* (22 June)

Eley, Geoff (2002), *Forging Democracy* (Oxford: Oxford University Press)

Green, Jonathon (1998), *All Dressed Up: The Sixties and the Counterculture* (London: Pimlico)

Hoggart, R. (1957), *The Uses of Literacy* (London: Chatto and Windus)

Howell, Dennis (1968), *Soccer Refereeing* (London: Pelham)

Inglehart, Ronald (1990), *Culture Shift in Advanced Industrial Society* (Princeton, NJ: Princeton University Press)

Itzin, Catherine (1979), *Stages in the Revolution: Political Theatre in Britain since 1968* (London: Methuen)

Labour Party (1962a), *Festival of Labour* (London)

—— (1962b), *Programme for Exhibition of Modern Art* (London)

Marcuse, Herbert (1964), *One-Dimensional Man: Studies in the Ideology of Advanced Industrial Society* (Boston: Beacon Press)

McKibbin, Ross (1998), *Classes and Cultures: England 1918–51* (Oxford: Oxford University Press)

Mountain and Molehill (1959), *The Next Five Years* (London)

Mulgan, Geoff (1996), 'Culture: The Problem with Being Public' in David Marquand and Anthony Seldon (eds), *The Ideas That Shaped Post-war Britain* (London: Fontana)

North Eastern Association for the Arts (1966), *Annual Report 1965–6* (Newcastle)

—— (1968–70), *Arts North* (Newcastle)

Sinclair, Andrew (1995), *Arts and Cultures: The History of the Arts Council of Great Britain* (London: Sinclair-Stevenson)

Shafer, Byron and Stears, Marc (1999), 'From Social Welfare to Cultural Values', *Journal of Policy History* vol. 11, no. 4

Stacey, Margaret (1960), *Tradition and Change* (Oxford: Oxford University Press)

Sutherland, John (2002), *Reading the Decades* (London: BBC Books)

TUC (1960), *Annual Conference Report* (London)

—— (2004), *Congress House at Fifty* (London)

Vall, Natasha (2001), 'The Emergence of the Post-industrial Economy in Newcastle 1914–2000' in Robert Colls and Bill Lancaster (eds), *Newcastle: A Modern History* (Chichester: Phillimore)

Wesker, Arnold (1960a), *The Modern Playwright or O, Mother, Is It Worth It?* (Oxford: Gemini)

—— (1960b), 'Vision! Vision! Mr. Woodcock', *New Statesman* (30 July)

—— (1970), *Fears of Fragmentation* (London: Jonathan Cape)

Widgery, David (1989), *Preserving Disorder: Selected Essays, 1968–88* (London: Pluto Press)

Williams, Raymond (ed.) (1968), *May Day Manifesto 1968* (Harmondsworth: Penguin)

Wollheim, Richard (1961, reprinted 1969), *Socialism and Culture* (Fabian Tract 331, London)

11

Resisting the 'pervasiveness of capitalist ideals'? The Italian left and the challenge of affluent society since 1945

Ilaria Favretto

Introduction

The aim of this chapter is to explore the efforts made since 1945 by the Italian Socialist Party (Partito Socialista Italiano, hereafter PSI) and the Italian Communist Party (Partito Comunista Italiano, hereafter PCI) to forge 'new men' out of their grassroots and militants; the two parties' struggle to resist the pervasive ideological influence of affluence and the consumerist ethos up to the mid-1960s; and their later gradual adaptation. Attention will first be focused on the Italian socialists, particularly in the years after 1956. In this crucial year, the party distanced itself from the PCI and embarked upon what is conventionally referred to as a process of 'social-democratisation' that brought Nenni's party into line with other Western European socialist parties. The second part of the chapter will then deal with the Italian Communist Party. The analysis will be taken up to the 1980s and 1990s – to the period when the PCI formally broke with its communist past, moved closer to European socialism and transformed itself into a fully fledged social democratic party. By this time the heirs of Gramsci had lost their cultural battle for a 'working-class counterhegemony'. However, they lost a battle that, following the party's rupture with its Marxist past and ideological legacy, they were not interested in fighting any more. Consistently with the party's abandonment of class politics, they have also now long relinquished their past vocation as explicit political and ideological organisers of the working class and dropped the notion of the party as an instrument of cultural guidance and direction.

'Constructing' the working class

A united working class was long regarded by Marxism-inspired parties as the precondition for a socialist revolution: workers should be provided with the self-awareness of belonging to a specific social category sharing identical interests and encouraged to think of themselves as a historical 'subject'. To this end, since their birth in the last quarter of the nineteenth century, socialist parties, most prominently the SPD in Germany, organised in such a way to act as veritable 'counter-societies', that is, communities that catered for the social needs of their members but also, if not foremost, their cultural and political education. As Gerassimos Moschonas put it, historically the left never conceived itself as simply 'a force for the representation of socio-economic interests'. Social democracy and the left in general also established itself as 'a central, strategic force of civilization', 'bearer of an ethical project and universalist, egalitarian, values'. The latter were, in other words, first and foremost 'parties of propaganda'; parties that played a crucial role in 'constructing' an identity for the working-class people and in value orienteering it (Moschonas, 2002: 28).

Nevertheless, increasing affluence and the profound transformations that Western European society underwent in the post-war years, were to undermine, in the period since the mid-1950s, the notion of the party of 'social integration'. Against the context of working-class decline, middle-classisation of society and embourgeoisment of the working class, socialist and social democratic parties began gradually to dilute their working-class appeal and increasingly to transform themselves into electoralist, catch-all parties. As soon as the working class stopped being considered as 'the historical subject', socialist parties' efforts to mould it for that purpose came to a close. This is a trend that, with some variations, applied to all social-democratic and socialist parties. The case of the Italian socialists is in this respect quite exemplary.

The Italian socialists and the rise of 'working-class aristocracies'

From 1956 Italian socialists abandoned their strategy of unity with the Communists and embarked upon an overall reassessment of the party's policies and strategies, which brought them into line with other Western European socialist parties. Together with a thorough revision of the party's agenda, the PSI also underwent a profound organisational transformation, acquiring an increasingly pronounced electoral and inter-classist orientation.

Several factors account for the latter development. First, far reaching transformations in the social environment, namely the expansion of the middle class, suggested the need for a broadening of the party's electoral appeal, if the PSI were to survive under the new economic and social circumstances produced by the 'golden years' of capitalism. The Italian socialists scored fairly poor results among the petit and middle bourgeoisie. The latter represented only 12% of the socialist electorate at the 1963 elections (Dogan, 1963: 454). In the light of the rapid expansion under way of public administration and the tertiary sector, greater inroads into these occupational strata would be crucial for the future expansion of the party. Furthermore, Nenni's party was conscious that it had to cope with a new development usually referred to as the 'embourgeoisement' of the working class.

The decline of class consciousness which social mobility entailed, combined with the self-assignment of a considerable number of manual workers to the middle-class due to the greater prosperity they enjoyed, constituted a real electoral challenge to all socialist parties and called for an overall reconsideration of their image and appeal. The 'embourgeoisement of the working class' was, for example, a long-enduring obsession of the British Labour Party throughout the post-war period.

The phenomenon of 'embourgeoised' working-class defection was in the 1950s certainly much more limited in Italy than in Great Britain. To start with, social mobility and the widening of prosperity were much less pronounced than in the UK. In a study of upward mobility from the occupational categories of manual workers, farm workers, and routine non-manual employees into those of farm-ownership and high level non-manual positions, Denmark and Great Britain scored respectively 22% and 20%, while Italy did not exceed 8% (Lipset and Bendix, 1959: 23). As far as private consumption was concerned, suffice it to say that only 1% of workers owned a washing machine in 1957; 2% owned refrigerators and 1% owned a car (Momigliano and Pizzorno, 1959: 198).

Furthermore, it should not be forgotten that both Italian socialists and communists were well used to seeing a considerable proportion of the working class vote for other 'bourgeois' parties. In contrast with Great Britain where at this time political attitudes seemed to be primarily correlated with social class position, different divisions cutting across classes operated in Italy, viz. religion: in the post-war years, deeply rooted religious traditions and the organisational machine of Catholic Action meant that the DC and the Catholic trade unions managed to make great inroads into the working-class vote, especially among women. Western European socialist parties tended to be adversely affected by the voting behaviour of women. Yet, it was demonstrated that in Catholic countries the difference between electoral behaviour of men and women was much greater than in Protestant countries such as Great Britain. (Lipset and Rokkan, 1967: 159; Dogan, 1963: 94).

Nevertheless, despite the above qualifications, in the 1950s the Italian socialists were also confronted with transformations in the working class and the problem of 'working-class aristocracies'. Although as we have seen above, if calculated on a national level, mass consumption was still relatively very low, differences between the various regions were marked: at the end of 1958 in the northern region of Piedmont there were 48 cars for every 1,000 inhabitants, while there were only 7 in Basilicata – one of the poorest southern areas (Pizzorno, 1964: 219). Since the achievement of full employment in the late 1950s, manual workers of the advanced sector, mainly in the north, achieved a substantial increase in their wages, resulting in a small proportion of manual workers considerably improving their living conditions. In an interview (Rome, 1995), Vittorio Foa, a leading PSI and CGIL member at that time, recalled the revolutionary effects that TV and cars had on Italian workers' lives and deeply rooted habits. The rapid diffusion of television in individual households resulted in the decline of collective television viewing in bars and clubs and a revival of forms of family privacy. John Foot calculates that in the new public housing estate of the Comasina in Milan (the biggest public housing estate in Italy, completed in 1958–60), which was densely populated by the working class, nearly 90% of families possessed a TV (Foot, 1995: 30). In the new neighbourhoods like the Comasina, which were built in response to the wave of immigration from the south to the industrial north of the 1950s, social isolation became a defining feature of working-class life. As opposed to the typical *case a ringhiera* (long balconies with a number of flats close together) – the form of working-class housing previously prevailing which entailed an 'enforced intimacy' with neighbours (Foot, 1995: 33), the new estates created a far more class-mixed and atomised life for their inhabitants.

New lifestyle patterns were combined with considerable differentiations along the lines of skill and sector. Automation meant the growth of the so-called 'non-productive' workers, that is technical experts and administrative staff, who rose from an average of 5% of the total of employees, at the beginning of the century, to an average in the mid-1950s of 25–30% (Leonardi, 1956: 55).

Many other factors were said to be at work in the weakening of class consciousness. The increasing spread of consumer durables and leisure pastimes such as TV, radio, cinema and sport created a fertile ground for the 'integration' of the worker into the social order, now that they were no longer segregated from bourgeois society and opposed to it as an 'enemy in a land to be conquered'. As Giuseppe Tamburrano wrote in *Mondo Operaio*, the leading Italian Socialist political cultural magazine at that time, the workers now aspired to the comforts which had hitherto been the monopoly of the bourgeoisie – the car, the scooter, TV, cinema, radio and holidays – and ended up mingling with it (Tamburrano, 1959: 22–3).

Action, it was argued, had to be taken immediately to catch up with the social changes described above. In the 1950s skilled workers tended to vote for moderate parties. The ratio of skilled workers to unqualified workers had always been higher in parties such as the DC and, above all, the PSDI. This was also reflected in the high percentage of votes obtained by the UIL (Unione Italiana del Lavoro – the social democrat/republican union) and the CISL (Confederazione Italiana dei Sindacati dei Lavoratori – the Catholic union) in those industries where a high proportion of skilled workers were employed. As opposed to the weakness demonstrated by the PCI among these strata, socialists did quite well, coming third after the DC and the PSDI (Dogan, 1963: 422). However, in view of the losses to the communists among unskilled workers which their shift towards the centre was likely to provoke, as discussions in *Mondo Operaio* on this question in the years from 1957 show, it appeared even more urgent to increase the Socialist appeal to this sector of the working population. As a start, as it was argued, socialists should tone down their hostility to affluence and consumerism.

Coming to terms with the 'candy-floss' word

On the wave of the 'economic miracle', as soon as signs of prosperity appeared, the attitude of many sections of the party was one of moral reproach. The so-called 'artificial wants' and private prosperity were throughout the 1950s the object of severe criticism and moral condemnation. Consumerism was regarded as a new and subtle form of alienation. An article which appeared in *Mondo Operaio* in 1958 argued that alienation, as described by Marx, had given way, in neo-capitalist societies, to far more subtle forms of alienation such as 'the alienation of consumption', that is the subjection of the collectivity to the hegemony of big businesses in determining the nature of needs: 'it is no longer the needs which determine supply but *vice versa*' (Bonazzi, 1958: 17–18).

From the late 1950s in Italy, as in the case in other Western European countries, a marked contrast emerged between private prosperity and 'public squalor'. By the time private versus social consumption became a central issue in the political debate, Italian socialists were talking a different language, with the old moral approach fading away: private consumption was still criticised but almost exclusively because of its pernicious effects on the economy.

In this respect, the publication of the much-quoted *The Affluent Society* (1958) by John Kenneth Galbraith provided European left-wing parties with new and far more powerful arguments against private consumption than those previously used. As is well known, the main argument advanced by the Harvard economist was that Western, affluent, mixed economies had not only long displayed their inability to achieve a balanced allocation of resources but were also doomed to sacrifice communal welfare and the requirements of future growth. In spite of the increasingly apparent affluence and prosperity their citizens had experienced in the last ten years, capitalist countries, were, in fact, jeopardising their long-term expansion and productivity rates.

It should not be forgotten that these were also the years in which the 'Soviet challenge' argument made its appearance: the Cold War, it was argued, had moved from the military to the economic sphere. It was believed that in the face of a thriving Soviet economy, whose strength and growth could only be explained by its adoption of planning and its ability to allocate national resources according to a system of priorities (e.g. promoting technological innovation at the expense of consumer goods), it would not take long for the capitalist world to capitulate under the weight of its own contradictions.

Galbraith's thesis, otherwise referred to in Italy as 'Galbraith's paradox' (Ruffolo, 1971: 174) also made considerable headway in the Italian social-ists' debate; and helped to shift the party's condemnation of consumerism from moral and ideological criteria to far more pragmatic considerations. This becomes evident from considering the party's press in the years from 1960 up to the PSI's return to government in December 1963 when Nenni's party joined a centre-left coalition government led by the Christian Demo-crats. The hidden persuasion of advertising came, for example, from the early 1960s onwards, to be no longer criticised for its corrupting effects on working class minds, but rather condemned as a waste of money and an irrational use of resources. As stated in Fua' and Sylos Labini's *Idee per la Programmazione Economica*, the money spent in advertising in the struggle by individual companies to attract as many consumers as was possible meant an increase in production costs which, in turn, pushed up the costs of distribution (Fuà and Sylos Labini, 1963: 97).

Electoral considerations also played an important role, in toning down the condemnation of consumerism. As Antonio Giolitti wrote in 1968, 'crit-icism of the affluent society is not an adequate answer; on the contrary it is a wrong answer since it takes for granted what still has to be verified, namely that the working class agrees with the critique of affluence and is prepared to renounce it' (Giolitti, 1968: 44). As one reads in *La grande Impresa* by Giorgio Ruffolo (1971: 208), another leading party figure at that time, an intellectual 'luddite attitude' towards fridges, TVs and vacuum clean-ers was hence rather inadvisable: not only was it apt to alienate traditional working-class constituencies but it would also conflict with the efforts which parties like the Italian socialists were making in those years to expand their constituency among the middle classes and transform themselves, in the words of the famous German political scientist Otto Kircheimer, into 'catch-all' parties. This was a process that was to be brought to its final completion after Bettino Craxi's takeover of the PSI's leadership in 1976.

The Italian communists and the construction of a working-class counter-hegemony

A trend similar to the one described above also applied to the Communist Party over the same years. Since Togliatti's return from Moscow to Italy in 1944, the PCI discarded armed insurrection and embraced an 'Italian road to socialism', that is a parliamentary and democratic strategy designed to gradually and peacefully shift by means of 'structural reforms' the balance of economic and political power towards the working class and its allies (Sassoon, 1980). The notion of the dictatorship of proletariat was put aside and replaced with Gramsci's notion of hegemony: the struggle for socialism was to entail the construction of a working-class counter-hegemony to that of the political, economic, and religious forces which dominated post-war Italian society. Cultural dominance would eventually pave the way to political dominance (Vittoria, 1992).

This new strategy entailed a thorough change in the notion of the party. The PCI transformed itself in a few years time from a vanguard party with a very tiny membership to a great mass party with over two million members. Particularly after 1947 and the outbreak of the Cold War that ruled out its participation in government, the promotion of the party's values and ideology, not just among members but among Italian society as a whole, was regarded as the cornerstone of the party's pacific road to socialism.

Consistently, the PCI built up a real 'counter-society' where all kinds of social, recreational and educational needs were catered for. Alongside territorial sections and the *Case del Popolo* (Communist social and cultural centres), affiliated organisations were set up for women, the young, peasants, former partisans, etc. The party created its own press, publishing houses, libraries, film clubs, sporting competitions; a party beauty contest in competition with the annual national Miss Italia was also established in which the moral and political qualities of the participants would be taken into account together with beauty (Gundle, 2000: 55, 67). As was the case with the parish-based Roman Catholic network, which the Christian Democrats contemporaneously mobilised, what was at stake was members' very identity (Kertzer, 1980: 248). Crucial to the accomplishment of socialism was the construction of a counter-hegemony promoting workers' self-awareness of their 'historical' mission and together with it an alternative worldview and value system that were distinct from those reproduced by the capitalist mode of production.

Sharing the 'people's minds' with the Catholic Church

Communists' aspirations met, however, a number of obstacles – the first being the strongly rooted and pervasive social and ideological influence of the Catholic Church. Consistently with Marx's notion of religion as opium of the people, Gramsci's notion of working-class hegemony was first if not foremost supposed to supplant the hegemony of the Church (Kertzer, 1980: 255). Nevertheless, the strong hold of Catholicism over the working class and the peasants, combined with the pursuit of a political strategy that after 1956 envisaged an alliance with the DC, meant that the PCI's leadership could never adopt a fully fledged anti-Catholic stance. The opposite is true. The PCI was always very careful not to face the masses with the choice between their Catholic faith and their communist affiliation (Kertzer, 1980: 115). As Togliatti wrote, an 'atheistic campaign' would be highly counter-productive if the Catholic masses were to be won over (Togliatti, 1964:

38; and Sassoon, 1995). Communists' conciliatory attitude towards religion and Catholicism, was well reflected in the hesitations shown by the PCI in putting its full weight behind the two referendums on divorce and abortion, held respectively in 1974 and 1978 (Sassoon, 1996: 681).

The challenge of consumerism

Catholicism apart, the PCI had, since the late 1950s, to come to terms with far more powerful and pervasive influences on the mental horizons of the workers than those exerted by the Vatican: that is, consumerism. As was the case with the PSI the initial attitude towards affluence and mass culture was one of hostility and rejection. In so far as they were regarded as a threat to the integrity of the workers' consciousness, the party did its best to contest them. The capitalist consumerist ethos with its emphasis on the individual, on the privatisation of leisure, and the pursuit of the comfortable collided with the communists' emphasis on the collective dimension of life, and the virtues of self-sacrifice and commitment.

The escapist and superficial nature of mass culture was attacked for its alienating and conservative influences and the powerful threat they constituted to political commitment and participation (Gundle, 2000; and Forgacs, 1990: 159ff). Party's activists were throughout the 1950s and 1960s expected to show conformity and dedication. An interest in fashion or anything else derived from mass culture was damned as 'petit bourgeoise' (Leonesi, 1992: 71). Hollywood movies were banned as corruptive of people minds and a device used by Capital to soften workers' consciousness. This was a time when party functionaries sent from Rome imposed an agenda of neo-realist movies, films from Eastern Europe, and documentaries of everyday life in the Soviet Union on local cine clubs (Bianciardi, 1957).

However, the gap between the model of social and cultural relations promoted by the party and the reality of everyday life was by the mid-1960s too large to be ignored and more conciliatory tones began to be adopted. The party ended up pursuing a double standard policy. Intellectuals and the party's elites carried on warning the working class not to sell their souls for – as Giorgio Amendola put it – a 'modern plate of lentils' (Gundle, 2000: 90). The affluent working class – that is a working class which seemed ambitious, devoid of socialist values, corrupted by materialist sirens – was at the centre of very harsh attacks by Italian authors such as Volponi, Mastronardi, Arbasino, Pasolini or the 'angry (*arrabbiato*)' one *par excellence* Luciano Bianciardi, with his famous *L'Integrazione* (1962) and *La Vita Agra* (1960) (the title – 'the bitter life', was deliberately opposed to Fellini's *La Dolce Vita*). In all of them the common theme was the anger against any form of 'integration' or embourgeoisement and the emptiness of lives devoid of 'great causes' left to fight for. One should also mention here the 'austerity' rhetoric and the criticism of hedonism and individual consumption that pervaded the political discourse of Enrico Berlinguer, the PCI leader from 1972 to 1984. However, at the grassroots level, the party increasingly diluted its ideological purity and showed a great measure of adaptation to mass culture and entertainment. The Communist popular press, i.e. the weekly magazine *Vie Nuove*, dropped its critical attitude towards Hollywood movies; the daily *l'Unità* expanded its coverage of sport news. The *Unità* festival – a massive party rally held annually – was redesigned in such a way as to strike a better balance between the activities of 'political guidance and education' and more popular leisure activities such as dancing, games, etc. (Leonesi, 1992). The PCI was, in other words, to pursue a multi-levelled cultural policy which, although inconsistent, managed to keep together sophisticated intellectuals, urban youth and popular strata. The PCI also stopped championing a return to the pre-1976 public-service monopoly in television and came to accept the existence of a mixed system in which the state-run RAI competed with commercial television (Gundle, 2000).

The PCI abdicates its 'civilising' mission

By the mid-1980s it was clear that the PCI, while maintaining a relatively good electoral share, had lost its cultural 'civilisation' battle. As Stephen Gundle put it, "The festivals, the press and other features of the culture of the left did not disappear but they were no longer bearers of alternative values; rather they were consumed in much the same way as their commercial equivalents' (Gundle, 2000: 10). What, however, should be noted is that communists lost a battle that they were not interested in fighting any more – particularly following the party's 1991 rupture with its Marxist past, ideological legacy, rituals and symbols.

In the wake of the collapse of really existing socialism, the Italian Communist Party underwent a thorough process of reappraisal of its policies and identity. The heirs of Gramsci formally broke with their communist past, changed their name to the Democratic Party of the Left (Partito Democratico della Sinistra, PDS) in 1991; re-named themselves Democrats of the Left (Democratici di Sinistra, DS), in 1998; and transformed themselves into a fully fledged social democratic party. Following the demise of the PSI at the 1994 elections, the DS is now the main social-democratic force in the Italian political landscape.

In line with the transformations that other European socialist and social democratic parties have been undergoing since the 1990s, the DS renounced the goal of an alternative system – that is, a socialist society – and has now fully embraced the principles of the market economy. Furthermore, it has loosened its link with the trade unions and made significant progress towards its transformation into a catch-all party.

The party's de-proletarianisation and embrace of the middle class was to many a matter of electoral survival. As a result of the crisis of Fordism and the rapid ascendancy of the so-called New Economy, trends that have long been under way – notably the growth of the tertiary sector and the shrinking of the traditional working class – have accelerated since the 1980s. In Italy the percentage of those employed in both industry and agriculture declined consistently throughout the 1980s and 1990s with the tertiary sector accounting for over 50 per cent the active population. A traditional working class that included 45.9 per cent of total employment in 1976 decreased to 35.4 per cent in 1989, and 32.7 per cent in 1994 (Paci, 1992: 278–9). As Achille Occhetto, the PCI leader from 1988 to 1994, put it, in making his case for 'change or die', communist bastions such as Sesto San Giovanni (an industrial area in Milan's periphery) which boasted 24,000 workers concentrated in four or five big factories, now have no more than 2,500 units, all of which are dispersed into hundreds of small factories (Occhetto, 1994: 84; Ginsborg, 1998: 60ff).

Consistently with the party's abandonment of class politics, the DS has also now long relinquished its vocation as explicit political and ideological organiser of the working class and dropped the notion of the party as an instrument of cultural guidance and direction. The party's press has been closed down. The daily *l'Unità*, after going bust was bought by private share-holders and is now being run as an independent newspaper. As for the festival dell'Unità, as Luciano Leonesi an old militant and theatre director remembers, it has now long lost its early rationale as a rally 'which was there to show the party's strength and distinctiveness and point its people the road to follow' and turned instead into a venue where people 'go to listen to David Bowie' (Leonesi, 1992).

The relationship between the party and intellectuals also reflects the extent to which the party has now long given up any aspiration to effect, in Moschonas words, 'the encadrement of the masses' (Moschonas, 2002: 36). 'Organic intellectuals' have now long been supplanted by 'area' intellectuals with far greater autonomy and independence from the party. Moreover, within a context where 'Big vision' politics has now run its course, the wide-ranging intellectual has now fallen into disgrace. A greater importance is now attached to specialised knowledge, practical reasoning and solutions rather than big ideas, with political philosophers making the way for sociologists, political scientists or economists as the new 'Gurus' from whom Italian left-wing politicians seek guidance.

The acceptance of the free market has gone hand in hand with full accept-ance of its underlying system of values. The party's new generation has been displaying since the mid-1980s a far less puritanical approach towards consumerism and mass culture. Walter Veltroni the DS leader from 1998 to 2001, is the epitome of a new leadership that – having grown up in the swinging 1960s – not only seems far more comfortable than their parents ever were in appreciating popular and mass culture but has long advocated its reconciliation with a progressive political discourse. Individualism, long an anathema within traditional Left discourse, has now become one of the most cherished words in the 'new' Left lexicon (Giddens, 1998: 36–7; and Beck, 1992: 127ff).

As we saw earlier, when faced with the challenge of consumerism and growing individualism, socialist parties adopted a more compromising and softer attitude out of electoral calculations. No spin doctors were needed in order to understand that electoral messages aimed at convincing people to dispose of their newly purchased cars for the sake of their soul would be suicidal. This is something that even Christian democratic parties, which shared the socialists' uneasiness towards the consumer society, accepted. However, the accommodation to 'hedonism' and the individualist ethos remained pragmatic and instrumental. No theoretical justification or fully fledged endorsement was ever attempted.

Marketing politics

Consistent with the abandonment of the old socialist idea of socialist parties as agenda-setting vanguards (Sassoon, 1996: 673), the heirs of Gramsci 'market' their policies today as any other political party.

Although with some delay in comparison to countries like the UK, electioneering has been going through a process of increasing professionalisation in Italy. The relatively stable electorate that characterised Italian politics during the so-called First Republic meant that up to the early 1990s parties showed only a modest interest in opinion polls and communication techniques (Venturino, 2000). It was only following the post-Cold War collapse of the old party system after 1992 that a greater concern began to be reflected in electoral behaviour studies and opinion polls. The monopoly of the vote that was once held by the DC-PCI-PSI, which in 1976 was 82.7 per cent, fell in 1992 to 59.4 per cent, proving that the electorate is increasingly mobile (Mannheimer and Sani, 1994: 64). The growth of the Northern League, the demise of the Italian Socialist Party (whose electoral share fell from 13.6 per cent in 1992 to 1.5 per cent at the local election just one year later) were all illustrations of the extent of the electoral volatility which now characterised the Italian political system. This was further exemplified by the 21 per cent result gained in 1994 by Forza Italia, a party that had been founded just a few months before the elections. A careful analysis of voting patterns in two recent elections (1996 and 2001) shows the extent to which mobility tends in fact to occur more within the two main centre-left and centre-right coalitions than between the coalitions themselves (Diamanti, 2001). However, this does not make the competition between individual parties within the same coalition less urgent.

The entry into politics of media tycoon Silvio Berlusconi, who founded his party from a market research and focus group firm, paved the way to a new era in Italian politics in which communication methods became increasingly important (Poli, 2002). The centre-left Progressisti coalition was caught in 1994 fully unprepared and contested the elections in a very amateurish way (Venturino, 2000). However, later electoral campaigns would show that the lesson had been learned. For their electoral campaign in 2001 election, the centre-left Olive Tree electoral alliance hired well-known political communication experts such as Tal Silberstein, who was one of the closest advisers to the electoral team of Al Gore during the American presidential elections.

The DS has also accelerated its transformation into a 'lighter' party. Since the eighteenth congress of 1989, the neo-revisionist group of the '*quarantenni*' addressed the issue of the need for internal reforms conducive to the replacement of Togliatti's mass party by a new more flexible and competent type of 'cadre' party; the final goal being the construction of a 'flexible party' (Baccetti, 1997: 64). This new type of party was eventually created at the Rimini congress in 1991; the party's apparatus was reduced by two-thirds and the local branches were halved in size (Ariemma, 2000: 190). Throughout the 1980s the PCI lost almost one-quarter of its membership. In 1989 there were 1,424,000 members. When the PDS was founded in 1991, only one-quarter of that number adhered to the new party, and the gradual decline of its membership continued. When Occhetto resigned from the party's leadership in 1994, the PDS had 698,212 members, a figure further shrank to 600,000 by 1998 (Baccetti, 1997: 121 and Pamini, 1998).

Conclusions

The Italian left has now long abdicated its struggle for hegemony either in its pre-1989 anti-capitalist or post-1989 capitalist-friendly versions. Far from disrupting the 'pervasive influences of capitalism', like its European counterparts it has now fully embraced the value systems and attitudes of what used to be its eternal enemy. As Moschonas puts it, 'the diffusion and inculcation of social values and norms (the elevation of the collective and collective action, diffusion of an egalitarian culture, etc.) no longer form part of the modern social-democratic discourse' (Moschonas, 2002: 237). Under the severe diktat of focus groups' results, left-wing parties, far from 'shaping' public opinion, seem to be lagging behind it.

This might sound fairly obvious to many. After all, the function of political parties should not be that of providing citizens with 'visions', but instead with finding responses to concrete and practical problems. As one reads in politics textbooks, parties are there to capture political demands emerging within society and offer them political representation. However, left-wing parties long held the aspiration of not just meeting people's material needs but rather – often quite paternalistically – of guiding those very people to understand better what their needs should be. This applies to socialism in all its variants. Utopian socialists, Marxists and Fabians, all believed that not only should socialist policies contribute to the creation of a more just society but they should also facilitate the transition to a more ethically oriented society in which people were made more aware of where, in fact, their 'true' interests lay. This was what 'organic' intellectuals, in Gramsci's words, were supposed to do.

Gone are the days when both the PCI and the PSI conceived their struggle for socialism as leading not just to an economic and political overhaul but also, if not primarily, to a spiritual revolution. Today, both parties' heirs are into intercepting the electoral market's demands as much as their right and centre-right opponents. A 'must do' that has, indeed, turned a far greater challenge for the Italian Left when compared to other European socialist parties, by the competition with the media tycoon and spin-master Silvio Berlusconi.

References

Ariemma, I. (2000) *La casa brucia: I democratici di sinistra* (Venice: Marsilio).

Baccetti, C. (1997) *Il PDS: Verso un nuovo modello di partito* (Bologna: Il Mulino).

Beck, U. (1992) *The Risk Society: Towards a New Modernity* (London: Sage Publications).

Bianciardi, L. (1957) *Il lavoro culturale* (Milan: Feltrinelli).

Bianciardi, L. (1960) *L'Integrazione* (Milan: Bompiani).

Bianciardi, L. (1962) *La Vita Agra* (Milan: Bompiani).

Bonazzi, G. (1958) 'Neo-Capitalismo e alienazione', *Mondo Operaio*, vol. 11, no. 8, pp. 9–18.

Diamanti, I. (2001) *Perché ha vinto il centro-destra* (Bologna: Il Mulino).

Dogan, M. (1963) 'La stratificazione sociale dei suffragi', in A. Spreafico and J. La Palombara, *Elezioni e Comportamento Politico in Italia* (Milan: Edizioni di Comunità).

Foa, V. (1995) (Interview: Rome, December).

Foot, J. (1995) 'The Family and the "Economic Miracle": Social Transformation, Work, Leisure and Development at Bovisa and Comasina (Milan), 1950–1970', *Contemporary European History*, no. 4, pp. 327–38.

Forgacs, D. (1990) *Italian Culture in the Industrial Era: Cultural Industries, Politics and the Public* (Manchester: Manchester University Press).

Fuà, G. and Sylos Labini, P. (1963) *Idee per la programmazione economica* (Rome and Bari: Laterza).

Galbraith, J. K. (1959) *The Affluent Society* (London: Hamish Hamilton) (Italian trans.: *Economia e benessere*, Milan: Ed. di Comunità, 1959; or *La società opulenta*, Milan: Etas Kompass, 1967).

Giddens, A. (1998) *The Third Way: The Renewal of Social Democracy* (Cambridge: Polity Press).

Ginsborg, P. (1998) *L'Italia del tempo presente: Famiglia, società civile, Stato 1980–1996* (Turin: Einaudi).

Giolitti, A. (1968) *Un socialismo possibile* (Turin: Einaudi).

Gundle, S. (2000) *Between Hollywood and Moscow: The Italian Communists and the Challenge of Mass Culture, 1943–1991* (Durham: Duke University Press).

Kertzer, D. (1980) *Religion and Political Struggle in Communist Italy* (Cambridge: Cambridge University Press).

Leonardi, S. (1956) *Progresso Tecnico e Rapporti di Lavoro* (Turin: Einaudi).

Leonesi, L. (1992) *Così cominciò la Festa dell'Unità: Memorie di donne, uomini e cose dal 1945 al 1991* (Milan: Synergon).

Lipset, S. and Bendix, R. (1959) *Social Mobility in Industrial Society* (London: Heinemann).

Lipset, S. and Rokkan, S. (eds) (1967) *Party Systems and Voter Alignments* (London: Collier Macmillan).

Mannheimer, R. and Sani, G. (1994) *La rivoluzione elettorale: Tra la prima e la seconda repubblica* (Milan: Anabasi, 1994).

Momigliano, F. and Pizzorno, A. (1959) 'Consumi in Italia', in F. Momigliano and A. Pizzorno, *Aspetti e problemi sociali dello sviluppo economico in Italia* (Rome and Bari: Laterza).

Moschonas, G. (2002), *In the Name of Social Democracy: The Great Transformation: 1945 to the Present* (London, Verso).

Occhetto, A. (1994) *Il sentimento e la ragione: Un'intervista di Teresa Bartoli* (Milan: Rizzoli).

Paci, M. (1992) *Il mutamento della struttura sociale italiana in Italia* (Bologna: Il Mulino).

Pamini, M. (1998) 'From Militants to Voters: From the Pci to the PDS', in P. Ignazi and C. Ysmal (eds), *The Organisation of Political Parties in Southern Europe* (Westport, CN: Praeger).

Pizzorno, A. (1964) 'The Individualistic Mobilization of Europe', *Daedalus. Journal of the American Academy of Arts and Sciences*, vol. 93, no. 1, special issue 'A New Europe?', pp. 199–224.

Poli, E. (2002) *Forza Italia* (Bologna: Il Mulino).

Ruffolo, G. (1971, 1st edn 1965) *La grande impresa* (Turin: Einaudi).

Sassoon, D. (1980) *La via italiana al socialismo: Il PCI dal 1944 al 1964* (Turin: Einaudi).

Sassoon, D. (1995) 'Italian Images of Russia, 1945–1956', in C. Duggan and C. Wagstaff (eds), *Italy in the Cold War: Politics, Culture and Society 1948–1958* (Oxford: Berg), pp. 189–202.

Sassoon, D. (1996) *One Hundred Years of Socialism* (London: I. B. Tauris).

Tamburrano, G. (1959) 'Per un programma socialista di governo', *Mondo Operaio*, vol. 12, nos 4–5, pp. 21–4.

Togliatti, P. (1988, 1st edn 1964) *Il memoriale di Yalta* (Palermo: Sellerio editore).

Venturino, F. (2000) *Partiti, Leader, Tematiche: La formazione dell'opinione pubblica nelle elezioni del 1996* (Milan: Franco Angeli).

Vittoria, A. (1992) *Togliatti e gli intellettuali: storia dell'Istituto Gramsci negli anni 50 e 60* (Rome: Editori Riuniti).

12

Old social democracy, new social movements and social democratic programmatic renewal, 1968–2000

John Callaghan

Introduction

In this chapter I propose to examine an aspect of the programmatic renewal of social democracy during the 1980s and 1990s and in doing so shed some light on the relationship of social democracy to the new social movements and the overlapping question of the post-materialist values which commentators analysed from the late 1960s. The nature of post-materialist values has since been interrogated in a variety of ways – with reference, for example, to affluence, age, education, voting behaviour, civic order and stability, together with various cultural mediators and subjective perceptions of changes in the economic situation of voters and the individual's place in the social hierarchy. Here, however, I am only concerned with a limited number of influential propositions. First, that the post-materialist agenda of the new social movements posed a fundamental ideological challenge to social democracy. Second, that the Third Way embraced by New Labour in Britain, equipped that party to better meet the challenge than parties rooted in old social democratic values. These contentions, I shall argue, rest on a caricature of social democracy, an underestimation of the permeability of ideologies, and a mistaken analysis of the New Labour phenomenon. I shall take environmental politics to illustrate the points I have to make about these two issues.

It is certainly true that in Britain programmatic renewal in the Labour party since 1983 has been associated with the defeat and marginalisation of the left. This local experience has rendered British analysts of social democracy particularly receptive to theories which connect the eclipse of socialist and social democratic values with modernising secular forces of social and economic change working at national, European or even global level. The conviction took hold in the 1980s that 'modernisation' was synonymous with the defeat of the left. I will suggest here – with special reference to environmental politics – that this local experience fuelled misleading theories. In some social democratic parties programmatic renewal actually bears the imprint of the left – both of the 'old' social democratic left and of the 'new left' which emerged in the late 1960s. Indeed, I will show that the latter was in some ways the engine of both programmatic renewal and the revitalisation of social democracy in the 1980s and 1990s.

It was Ronald Inglehart who announced in the 1970s that a transition from materialist to post-materialist values was taking place in the most affluent societies as generations brought up in the relatively gilded era after the war shifted their political concerns to 'quality of life' issues, while conventional preoccupations with economic growth, class and state-centred politics became less salient. Sustained affluence had seemingly promoted an individualistic concern for self-actualisation and the growth of expressive values at the expense of the old left's collectivism and materialism. This, at any rate, was how Inglehart theorised survey evidence initially gathered in 1970 and 1971 – evidence that was apparently buttressed by later trawls of opinion conducted in 1979, 1981 and 1983 (Inglehart, 1977, 1987). The visible fracturing of the left during these years added credence to Inglehart's analysis.

By the late 1950s it had become a commonplace in Britain that socialist fervour and conventional political activism had both entered long-term decline. In other countries too the attempt to bring an array of social activities and associations within the fold of labour movements had clearly lost momentum and centre-left parties of 'social integration' were in decay (see Favretto in this volume). If anything a reverse process had begun, fragmenting the left and producing a growing number of single-issue campaigns, many of them outside the social democratic parties. Meanwhile, electoral theorists found that the voters were becoming more instrumental. Since the mid-1950s social commentators had been increasingly interested in the cultural aspects of the affluent society. They had noticed that workers were becoming consumers. They worried that lives were increasingly privatised, while solidarity was subject to decay. The working class was shrinking and becoming more heterogeneous, while the middle class was growing. One-third of the working class already voted for the Conservative Party in Britain and the only question for some people was whether affluence and social change would increase the proportion. There was certainly little evidence of a public thirst for radical socialist alternatives and it became fashionable, following Daniel Bell, to talk of the end of ideology. The public was dissolving. The established working-class communities and traditions of solidarity were being broken up, the old values were threatened by everything that was new, from television to social and geographical mobility. Europe was becoming Americanised in the process and the working class was becoming addicted to consumption as one of its effects. Electorates increasingly demonstrated their short-termism by voting for economic growth and throwing out governments which failed to deliver enough of it.

The insularity and lack of history of this largely Anglo-American debate is evident, despite the sweeping generalisations it contained concerning advanced capitalist societies. In many countries working-class affiliation to parties of the left had never been as dominant as the debate implied, not to mention pre-war Britain itself. Furthermore centres of social democratic strength such as Sweden, where working-class affiliation to social democracy was strong, were little affected by the transition to a largely post-manufacturing economy, a process well underway in the 1960s. In any case, out of this seemingly permanent order, this culture of contentment as depicted by some of the prophets of post-industrial society, radical social movements arose across the advanced capitalist world from the 1960s, promoting ideas which challenged the apparent consensus, moving beyond the typical preoccupations of social democracy. These social democratic preoccupations were now closely associated with economic growth, full employment, state-supplied welfare and a measure of egalitarianism in fiscal policy. They also entailed an addiction to bureaucratic centralism and conformity, rather than innovation, in the activity of politics itself. Naturally there were national variations and particularities in accordance with the different histories, institutions and policies of the various countries concerned; for example the West Germany of the Grand Coalition and the Britain of 'Butskellite' ideological convergence displayed different forms of conformity in the politics of the Cold War, which sections of the new left railed against in different ways. But in all the advanced capitalist countries the new social movements raised issues that (increasingly ritualistic) appeals to economic growth and planning could not solve. In a sense they were issues of the cultural superstructure; neglected issues of gender, family, ethnicity, north–south inequalities, sexuality, political participation, direct democracy, devolution, the nature of power and citizenship, quality of life and quality of work problems, and even problems of the broader environment. Politics was also reconceptualised, particularly within the feminist movement and the New Left, in ways that were critical of social democratic centralism, its patriarchy and paternalism, its focus on material advancement, the work ethic and the mobilisations of class.

Class was often deemed insufficient to encompass the range of cultural issues which now demanded attention – including a new libertarian emphasis on pleasure, anti-authoritarianism and personal autonomy. Progress, in this view, was no longer reducible to material advancement. By the late 1960s it was recognised that middle-class intellectuals were prominent in foregrounding these often post-materialist concerns. A younger generation was visibly taking the lead. Some theorists claimed that the new social movements represented a new class vanguard, perhaps with different objectives than the anti-capitalist aims of the traditional socialist left (Touraine, 1991). They noticed that beneath the language of Marxism, which temporarily held sway, a wide variety of positions jostled for attention, not all of them congenial to the left. The new stress on 'identity politics', for example, held its appeals for sectarian and separatist reactionaries alike; even the fascists would belatedly jump on the 'identity' bandwagon. But, as little noticed at the time, the organised working class was also discovering 'post-material' values as evidenced by the rediscovery of industrial democracy and workers' control in countries as diverse as Sweden, France, Italy and Great Britain. It was nevertheless the elements of generational, gender, and ethnic conflict which captured attention. In 1968 the language of Marxism provided a superficial unity to this movement of opinion but it rapidly dissolved in the early 1970s as a further intellectual differentiation took place. Soon a fragmentation and even sectarianism came to dominate the new identity politics whether in France, Germany, Britain or the USA. The rhetoric and policies of multiculturalism helped to reinforce these trends and secure the position of religious and cultural conservatives as spokesmen of their 'communities'. But this is far from being the whole story.

Far from representing a transient, infantile disorder the new concerns of the left showed durability and a capacity for political maturity. The themes of the new social movements were taken up in the 1970s and 1980s within the social democratic parties and the trade unions as well as by the Green parties. The emphasis on *autogestion* in the rhetoric and programme of the French left – particularly the Socialist Party and CFDT in the decade after 1972 – is a case in point. So were the measures of devolution and industrial democracy taken under the Auroux laws by the Mitterrand government in 1981. The Bennite left within the British Labour Party provides another example. Tony Benn's own Fabian pamphlet, *The New Politics*, identified some of the changes as early as 1970. During the rest of that decade the agenda of the Labour left included industrial democracy and democratic reform of the British state, as well as constitutional change of the Labour Party itself, designed to permit the mass organisations greater control of the parliamentary leadership. Democratic, feminist, anti-racist, pacifist and community politics also marked the municipal leftism of the late 1980s in Britain. The new social movements were equally visible in the campaigns against nuclear energy and nuclear missiles which animated the activist left in West Germany in the 1970s and early 1980s, as well as in the politics of *Die Grunen*. The reforms of the Swedish social democrats in the early 1970s, with their emphasis on industrial democracy and equality are another example, so is the programmatic transformation and membership upheaval of the Dutch Labour Party (PvdA) in the 1970s. The feminisation of parliaments and political parties – most advanced in some of the Scandinavian social democracies – can also be traced back to the initiatives and ideas of the new social movements. So too, more broadly, can the acceptance of multicultural definitions of the nation.

In Britain during the 1980s, however, the political influence of the new social movements was stifled both by the governmental hegemony of Thatcherite Conservatism and by the Labour Party's response to it. There was also no new left political formation challenging the Labour Party for votes, a force that might have given the parliamentary leadership the incentive to take new left ideas seriously in a period when programmatic renewal was a matter of political survival. The first-past-the-post electoral system ensured this protection from the left for Labour, as was illustrated in 1989 when the Green Party secured 14.8 per cent of the votes in the European elections – the highest anywhere in the European Community – but failed to elect a single candidate. New social movement ideas could nevertheless be found on the Labour left wing where they coexisted in uneasy alliance with old left ideas. But by the end of the decade both old and new left ideas were increasingly seen as electoral liabilities by the parliamentary Labour party. The sense that old Labour was out of kilter with the age was strongly implied by the Conservative Party's electoral dominance since 1979, all the more so given the corrosion of class voting alignments at a time when the Conservative Party embraced a neo-liberal ideology utterly repugnant to Labour activists. This sense of old Labour's obsolescence was reinforced intellectually in many ways. The most influential psephological analyses of Labour's predicament stressed its association with declining social forces, and industries and regions in decay. The influential 'New Times' thesis made the case for an 'epochal shift' in society founded on fundamental changes in social and occupational structures. While this thesis foresaw, inter alia, 'a profound ecological crisis' developing in the 1990s, it stressed that the old left was unlikely to respond creatively because it rested 'upon a world . . . fast disintegrating beneath its feet' (CPGB, 1989). The perception that social democracy was facing some sort of general crisis in Britain gathered strength in the 1980s, and several versions of this argument pointed to the evidence of divisions and contradictions within the left, as well as ideological assaults from the right, in support of this thesis.

Kitschelt's wide-ranging analyses of West European social democratic parties painted a similar picture for the whole of Western Europe. On one side of the equation he stressed the social and occupational transformations under-pinning the clash of new left values with those of old social democracy, which he reformulated as the challenge of a 'left-libertarian communitarian vision' set against traditional 'collectivist statist' values (Kitschelt, 1990, 1994a, 1994b). On the other side of the equation he stressed the challenge of neo-liberalism in a globalised international context – the heavy implication being that neo-liberalism was irresistible. Anthony Giddens also wrote of the need to move 'beyond left and right' if politicians were to keep in step with postmodernity, theorising that a statist, centralising, and controlling social democracy had been rendered obsolete by socio-economic and cultural change operating on an international as well as a national level. If equality was no longer a feasible objective in these globalised, neo-liberal, multicultural times, it might be reasoned that the best that the left could do would be to recognise these facts and seek to promote a different type of social justice based on 'communities' (Gray,

1997). This could provide encouragement to a conservative multicultural-ism in a country such as Britain, where – notwithstanding the alleged trans-ition to a new era – Kitschelt's left-libertarian communitarian axis failed to materialise as an alternative to collectivist statist values. Britain' selec-toral system, as mentioned, undoubtedly assisted the continuation of two-party dominance throughout the 1970s and 1980s, and worked against the emergence of challengers based on the new social forces and values. But a glance at Italy is enough to see that while electoral systems matter they are not sufficient explanations of national political forces; Italy's proportional representation system was used in general elections until the early 1990s and yet the Green challenge was very weak in Italian politics and there was very little greening of the left-wing parties.

Green politics and social democracy

When the vote for the Greens failed to translate into representation, even though it amounted to 14.8 per cent of the poll in the European elections of 1989, the voters seem to have concluded that it was a wasted vote. The Green vote subsequently declined, as the established parties – startled by the 1989 result – took up a Green rhetoric of their own, though none of them, including the self-styled modernisers of the Social Democratic Party (1981–88), had a history of taking environmental politics seriously. Radicals in British politics had long recognised the need to advance their policies within the established parties because of this electoral blockage. Similarly activists from the new social movements were forced to win influence in the Labour Party if they were to affect government policies. This is pre-sumably why elements of both new left and new social movement values could be found within the Labour party from the early 1970s, joining the coalition associated with Tony Benn's challenge to turn the organisation on a radical course. There were, however, special reasons why many of their concerns – including environmental politics – were not strongly represented in this movement. Britain's perennial economic crises ensured that the left as a whole was preoccupied by an Alternative Economic Strategy (AES) and this remained the case until the party's defeat at the general election of 1983. Environmentalist ideas had a very low priority in these circumstances and this continued throughout the 1980s as the AES was discarded and the party leadership turned to embrace 'the market' in an effort to modernise Labour and catch up with Thatcherism and the dynamic social forces it was supposed to represent.

Labour's relative lack of interest in environmental issues during the 1970s and 1980s has been explained as a function of 'the party's roots in the organised labour movement and its reliance on support from the urban working class [which] provided powerful constraints against the adoption of a comprehensive environmental programme'. It has been argued that

'Among Labour's traditional supporters and financiers the environment has been regarded, at best, as an irrelevance and, at worst, as inimical to growth and employment'. In this view the forces associated with the old social democracy stood in the way of progress on the environment. But with the transition to New Labour, or so the argument goes, the way was cleared for progressive change in this crucial area. The environment apparently supplied 'perfect credentials for inclusion as part of a so-called "third way" agenda' precisely because it 'is not easily located on a left/right ideological spectrum' (Garner, 1999: 26). Increasingly after 1983 Labour was led by its so-called modernisers and one might have expected that any 'modernisation' worth the name would have had to come up with some serious thinking on the range of big environmental issues facing the country. Certainly by 1997 and the formation of Tony Blair's first Labour Government the party leadership had been revising and rejecting old social democratic policies and values for over a decade. But while Labour's 1997 manifesto asserted that environmental policy was not to be regarded as 'an add-on extra, but informs the whole of government from housing and energy policy through to global warming and international agreements', there was little evidence of such a commitment. Instead there was much in government policy to discourage environmentalists. I will return to New Labour's basic policies later in the argument.

But first let us acknowledge that a very real clash of values occurred when environmental issues first became salient within social democratic parties all across Western Europe; similar obstructions were encountered by feminism, anti-racism, democratic participation and other concerns of the new social movements. Moreover, there is no doubt that if a pattern was to be observed it tended to involve the younger, university-educated, middle-class activists demanding priority for the environment while the older, working-class members – often represented by their unions or their parliamentary leaders – stressed jobs and economic growth. Such was the apparent fixity of this recurring collision that some commentators doubted Inglehart's view that the materialist and post-materialist left could co-exist in the same organisation, while others incautiously concluded that working-class parties were 'now in all likelihood on their way out' (Delwaide, 1993: 244; Galtung, 1986: 81).

The unfolding drama was by no means confined to West Germany, where the largest Green electoral challenge to social democracy emerged in 1983 when Die Grunen broke through the 5 per cent threshold for representation in the Bundestag. In Sweden the social democrats (SAP) lost governmental power for the first time in forty-four years in 1976 largely because their pro-nuclear energy policy split their traditional support, with sections defecting to the anti-nuclear energy parties of the right. The same issue divided the Austrian socialists when the country's first nuclear reactor was ready to go onstream at Zwentendorf in 1978. While the Austrian union federation

OGB supported the nuclear project and backed the lead given by Bruno Kreisky, the party leader, young leftists inside the SPO strongly opposed it. Kreisky subsequently lost a referendum on this issue. Green ideas made advances both within and outside the social democratic party organisations. The rift between trade unionists and environmentalists seemed to deepen. It surfaced again in 1984 when the SPO was divided over the construction of a hydro-electric power station on the Danube which threatened one of Europe's last remaining wetlands. Meanwhile in Sweden the SAP moved towards the abolition of nuclear power stations only after the Greens surmounted the 4 per cent threshold for elections to the Riksdag in 1988. In 1990 the SAP's conference agreed to enter negotiations with the other established parties on the decommissioning of the existing power stations. Once again, however, it was found that the party youth, together with the organisation's female and middle-class members, were keener environment- alists than the blue-collar unions in the main trade union confederation. The latter were more enthusiastic about jobs. The same pattern recurred in the controversies surrounding the proposed construction of a rail bridge linking Sweden and Denmark. It was also visible in West Germany where the SPD was divided over nuclear energy in the 1970s. The party leader, Helmut Schmidt, supported by the bulk of the parliamentary party and the DGB unions, backed the development of nuclear energy, stressing jobs and economic growth. But the youth section, the Jusos, together with a rather disparate left which straddled the party and the new social movements, was increasingly opposed to it on environmentalist grounds.

The SPD nevertheless quickly demonstrated that it could adapt to the new situation. Soon after the SPD government fell in 1982 the party began to adopt elements of the new environmental agenda which the Greens brought into national focus when they secured a parliamentary presence the following year. The party congress at Essen in 1984 voted to begin the development of a new basic programme, overseen by Willy Brandt, who was personally committed to winning back the SPD's 'lost children', as he called them, of the new social movements. The programme commission sought a new synthesis centred on the idea of 'qualitative economic growth' – an attempt to reconcile economic activity with environmentalism. The party became increasingly anti-nuclear. It also stressed the need to end the arms race, it promoted gender equality and began to discuss north–south issues: all prominent themes of the Greens' politics.

Some commentators claim in the light of all this that the SPD was trans- formed 'in the course of the 1980s into something fundamentally different than it was before' (Markovits and Gorski, 1993: 268). In my own view this is misleading, but there is no doubt that the SPD, in common with other social democratic parties in northern Europe, saw the necessity of assimilating Green ideas. In a similar way they absorbed much of what was taught by second-wave feminism, but I don't have the space to examine that here. What I want to draw attention to is that the greening of the SPD basic policy programme – a new one was adopted in December 1989 – took place alongside a reaffirmation of old social democratic values. These were actually given a more radical expression than had been the case thirty years earlier at Bad Godesberg. This green–red alignment was not confined to the SPD. A similar process was evident in the programmatic renewal of the Swedish SAP; and if we examine the recent programme of the Norwegian Labour Party (DNA), the same pattern is evident there too. The British Labour Party, by contrast, emerged from the 1970s and 1980s as preoccupied with conventional economic thinking as it had been twenty years earlier, though the journey had taken it from an 'alternative economic strategy' to recon- ciliation with 'the market' and even neo-liberalism. Throughout this pro- cess it displayed an anxiety about whether the voters believed that the economy would be safe in its hands. Confined to opposition in the 1980s Labour showed little interest in environmental issues until the Green Party shocked the established parties in the 1989 European elections. As we have see the Green threat was contained with the assistance of the first-past-the post electoral system, ensuring that the Labour party – unlike most of its continental counterparts – faced no effective electoral challenge to its left for either the parliament at Westminster or the one in the European Union. It did face, however, a seemingly hegemonic Conservative party wedded to neo-liberalism, and Labour's macro-economic policy was adapted accord- ingly, with 'Old Labour' values a casualty of the transition.

By contrast with Labour's policy review process after 1987 – which hastened the party's reconciliation to key aspects of the Thatcher settlement – early drafts of the SPD's contemporaneous basic programme were infused with both anti-capitalist and environmentalist values, and though th former were watered-down in the final version, the finished document suggested that the party was moving in a different direction from British Labour. (The first draft even talked of the need for 'a new social and economic order' that would break 'the power of capital over working people'). The final text was concerned with the power of 'international capital' exerting downward pressure on wages, working conditions, social and welfare pro- vision, and environmental standards. It wanted 'national and international control mechanisms [to] ensure that international capital does not with- draw from its social and ecological responsibilities and tax obligations' and demanded common standards of social and environmental policy across the EU (SPD, 1990: 33–5). Ecological restructuring, the programme declared, 'has become a matter of survival', and 'the preservation of nature must become a mission for all areas of politics'. The programme recognised that the affluent nations had done most to destroy 'the natural bases of exist- ence' and 'must bear the main responsibility . . . for [their] restoration'.

The marks of the 'New Politics' were as obvious in the new programme of the Swedish SAP (adopted in 1990) as they were in that of the SPD.

The Swedish party also argued that economic development since the industrial revolution had been achieved 'at the cost of plundering the environment and shortsightedly exploiting nature' with consequences that 'threaten to undermine the very foundations of human existence', not least because of the 'worldwide unrest' which grotesque global inequalities were said to portend. But the SAP programme was even more unambiguous than the SPD's in identifying the principal causes in the unregulated private profit motive and untrammelled market forces and these were named as the sources of both growing inequalities and environmental destruction. It restated the party's aim of achieving a classless society, and also identified the public sector as the principal instrument for this purpose. In similarly 'old labour' terms the party, having considered arguments stressing non-class cleavages in society, concluded that the new divisions, such as those based on knowledge and education, ran alongside and actually reinforced rather than displaced the materialist divisions of old. Yet the party also placed environmental progress on a par with the achievement of full employment; and, introducing the idea of a 'Green GDP', it insisted that ecological requirements would inform all areas of policy (SAP, 1992: 7–9).

The close links between the unions and the social democrats proved unable to prevent the 'greening' of the social democratic programme in Germany and Sweden – or, for that matter, in Denmark, Norway and Austria. Though the relationship between trade unions and social democratic parties in these countries is not identical to that pertaining in Britain its intimacy cannot be denied. Both the SPD and the SAP had close organisational ties with the trade unions in the 1970s and 1980s, and so had the social democrats of Denmark, Austria and Norway. Yet by the beginning of the 1990s all of these parties had adopted the language of 'environmentally sustainable growth'. In Norway and Sweden the unions of the LO confederation were collectively affiliated to the DNA and SAP at local level and enjoyed representation throughout the party organisations up to the level of their leaderships. Much the same was true in Denmark, where the unions acted as a significant faction of the party and played a notable role in determining its governmental policies in the 1970s and 1980s. The unions supplied the Scandinavian parties with leaders, finance, ideas and some of their most characteristic policies (such as the distinctive wage and active labour market policy in Sweden). Former trade union officials also formed a significant proportion of SPD parliamentarians and office-holders at local level. Though the biggest union confederation in Germany (the DGB) is not affiliated to the party, trade unionists exercised influence within it, for example through such media as the AfA (Arbeitsgemeinschaft fur Arbeitnehmerfragen) working circle founded in 1972. In the troubled decades of the 1970s and 1980s the unions normally supported the parliamentary leadership of the SPD against the left, as they had traditionally done in Britain.

Far from simply constituting an obstacle to the greening of social democratic parties – based on their materialistic and 'old social democratic' values – the unions have occupied a more complex relationship to the new ideas. There has been resistance to the green economy where this threatens employment and economic growth, as we have acknowledged. But one trade unionist's job could be another's blight, and the unions were capable of understanding and responding to this obvious truth. The DGB unions in Germany, for example, debated environmental issues over a two-year period in the 1970s before adopting a programme that reflected the new thinking as early as 1974. The major blue-collar federation in Denmark worked with the social democrats (SD) in developing environmental programmes in the early 1990s – while demanding that the adjustment costs should be met by the whole of society and not just by wage-earners. Though trade unions everywhere concern themselves with wages and jobs they also take a view of health and safety, working and living conditions, and the quality of life generally. Some policies that can be justified environmentally may even have a particular appeal to trade unions. This seems to have been the case, to take an example, with a number of policies contained in the British Labour party's 1992 manifesto, such as the restoration to public control of the National Grid and public ownership of water; opposition to the privatisation of the railways; ending the deregulation of bus transport; and reining back the growth of opencast mining. All these policies were subsequently dropped by New Labour, but not because the unions objected to them.

The evidence from the social democratic parties I have referred to is that close links with the unions have not prevented these parties from making 'sustainable development' their number one priority, as in the case of the DNA, or from proclaiming that the 'lack of equality and ecological balance challenges our social democratic values more than anything else' (DNA, 1996: 15). Unions with close links to social democratic parties have generally been influenced by the observation that an elected social democratic party is of more use to them than an unelected one. If evidence accumulates to the effect that programmatic modernisation is required to render the party electable, it is difficult and certainly self-defeating for trade union leaders to obstruct the process. From the earliest times of social democracy the trade unions have recognised the primacy of the electoral struggle and acknowledged the dominant role of party leaders in formulating policy. On the basis of the programmatic changes that have actually taken place in northern Europe, we might conclude from these generalisations that an adaptation to the Green agenda was perceived to be electorally expedient in these countries. Only around 5 per cent of voters support the green parties in Western Europe (which incidentally is not persuasive evidence that socio-economic change must engender electoral and party political upheaval); the biggest of these parties in electoral terms are to be found in

Germany, Sweden and Austria, while in Denmark and Norway (in common also with Germany and Sweden) the social democrats are faced with electoral rivals to their left espousing red–green policies.

It might be objected that the adaptations referred to are only verbal-rhetorical and programmatic and – as we implied about the British Labour Party's 1997 manifesto declaration – it is one thing to assert the centrality of environmentalism in a party programme, quite another to act upon this precept. Moreover, talk of sustainable development' is intrinsically unconvincing to those who believe that any economic development is environmentally destructive. One might expect the deeper green factions within the green parties to take this view. Though not of this persuasion, Anthony Giddens, the most prominent academic supporter of British Labour's 'Third Way', is himself sceptical about social democracy's 'ecological modernisation', arguing that 'it isn't really convincing to suppose that environmental protection and economic development fit together comfortably'. Giddens is also one of those who believe that the Greens 'pose ideological questions that are impossible to ignore, and that place in question some of the basic orientations of social democracy'. He is also of the view that 'most social democratic parties are split' on this issue, which he sees as 'a consequence of being in a halfway house where old left ideas remain prominent and no fully fledged alternative has been formed' (Giddens, 1998: 58, 52–3).

Green and left

But we have seen that the parties of social democracy that moved furthest to embrace the green agenda in the 1980s and 1990s include those which by the standards of New Labour were most decidedly old social democratic in their programmatic language of class, equality, state intervention and the critique of unfettered capitalism. It is unwise to dismiss either the red or the green passages in their programmes as mere rhetoric, for these are countries with the highest environmental standards in practice, as well as the most generous welfare provisions and the strongest societal commitments to equality. Though it would be naive to ascribe these characteristics to any one factor, they surely have something to do with the prevalence in these societies of the corresponding values and beliefs, as well as the fact of a green or red representation in parliament alongside the social democrats. Far from constituting a special obstacle to the new social movements and post-materialist values, social democracy and its affiliates such as the trade unions may lay claim to be among their best allies. The new left began to enter the social democratic parties after 1968. In West Germany the SPD was the first stop in the 'long march through the institutions' which radicals such as Rudi Dutschke recommended to young activists, many of whom joined the party and its youth section in the 1970s. Since the late

1980s, Germany also provides numerous examples of red–green pacts and coalitions at regional level; the inclusion of Die Grunen/Bundnis 90 – under the 'realist' leadership of Joschka Fischer – in Chancellor Schroder's governments of 1998–2005 is a particularly poignant example of their history of collaboration, bearing in mind the powerful connections which the Greens of West Germany had with the peace movement and the fact that Schroder's government supported NATO's bombing of Kosovo and Serbia in April 1999. That a party with its roots in the peace movement could come to such a pass is proof of its dependency on the social democrats in its quest for influence over policy, as well as evidence of internal changes in the party's composition and culture which the debate over its political orientation contributed to. In the process of adopting this orientation, Green fundamentalists had to be defeated within Die Grunen, many subsequently resigning from the party.

The German Greens remain essentially a party of the left, and the same is true of the Greens in Sweden. Like those red–green parties with electoral clout which exist in Denmark, Norway and the Netherlands, all of these parties are more likely to seek colllaboration with the social democrats than with the latter's conservative and liberal rivals. Though Kitschelt and Giddens question whether old social democratic values can be reconciled with those of the new social movements, it is a matter of fact that parties to the left of the social democrats with a tradition of militant espousal of socialist ideas, such as the former Communists in Sweden, transformed themselves under the impact of the new social movements ahead of the social democrats. The impact of the new social movements on the social democratic parties could be equally dramatic, as in the Netherlands, where the Labour Party, PvdA, was taken over by the new left in the early 1970s. But more typically it was usually a case of new left activists and ideas joining forces with, and helping to change, the existing social democratic left, as occurred in West Germany, Austria and Norway. This is hardly surprising given the elective affinities of the young, middle-class left in the late 1960s (feminist, pacifist, anti-racist, radical-democratic). In Sweden, for example, no political party did more for the cause of women's equality than the SAP, whether in the promotion of female employment, for example, the expansion of public childcare centres, the provision of parental leave and the growth of female participation in the leadership of both the party and its trade union partners. All this was something feminists were bound to take into account as the SAP and the blue-collar trade union federation (LO) gradually feminised their own ranks, as did their counterparts in Germany, Norway, Denmark and the Netherlands. Today the female social democratic vote is the largest and most stable bloc of electoral support which the SAP obtains across social classes in Sweden.

British Labour was influenced by the 'new politics' at around the same time as its sister parties – during the 1970s – and, as in the other cases, it was primarily young, university-educated activists drawn into the left of the party who first took up the new agenda. Moreover, it was not only the constituency activists who were attracted to recognisably new left themes. We saw earlier that an established Labour parliamentarian, Tony Benn, the leader for much of the 1970s and 1980s of the Labour left, announced his own conversion to the new politics in 1970 when he identified it with alienation from existing power relationships and the call for more participatory forms of democracy (Benn, 1970). Trade union 'barons' such as Hugh Scanlon and Jack Jones actively supported the campaign for industrial democracy. Benn himself championed the cause and became associated with industrial cooperatives, constitutional reform of the Labour party, democratisation of the media, curbs on prime ministerial patronage and greater transparency in central government – just the sort of 'expressive values' which Inglehart associated with the post-materialist left. The trade union block votes were also increasingly mobilised to support unilateral nuclear disarmament in the 1970s. Few issues were closer to the pulse of the new social movements than this, especially when NATO took the decision to site cruise missiles in Western Europe and a 'Second Cold War' got under way in 1980, following the Soviet invasion of Afghanistan.

But the Bennite left also favoured an Alternative Economic Strategy, as we have seen, and this contained numerous centralising features that could not easily be reconciled with the call for greater democracy. Environmental progress, moreover, was never central to the preoccupations of the Labour left. When, however, the AES was discredited in the course of 1983–87, a Labour left concerned with the issues of the new social movements continued to prosper for a while, particularly at local government level. Then, after its electoral defeat in 1987, the Labour party distanced itself from such councils, which the popular press anathematised as evidence of the 'loony left' – or what might be termed an unrepresentative assembly of cranks and extremists. Modernisation of the party, through the mechanism of the policy review, was increasingly linked to an appeal to 'middle England', a euphemism for Conservative voters. To press forward a 'new social movement' agenda now was apparently to link the party with the sort of 'bizarre' minority issues whose avoidance was recommended by influential advisers to the leadership, such as Philip Gould (Gould, 1998: 258). Activists concerned with such issues were accordingly demobilised and many resigned from the party – the steep decline in membership figures between 1987 and 1994 certainly suggests so, as does the considerable turnover of membership thereafter.

Conclusion

My argument, then, is that the Labour left of the 1970s and 1980s contained both advocates of the old social democratic values – class, equality, economic growth, state intervention, public expenditure and planning – as well as proponents of 'post-materialist' values and champions of the new social movement agenda. Interest in environmental issues was never uppermost among this Labour left, though whether it could have become so must remain moot. However, the dominance in British politics throughout the 1980s and 1990s of conventional economic ideology – and even the crudest of vulgar materialisms – can hardly be doubted. Labour's prolonged rapprochement with Thatcherite political economy actually led to the marginalisation of both old social democratic values and those of the new social movements, along with the neutralisation of their progressively demobilised advocates. These developments robbed Labour of the activist drive and push that was required to champion environmental issues within the party. New Labour emerged from this process in 1994 as a proponent of market forces and adaptation to an irresistible globalisation, while fixed upon the necessity of winning the marginal voters. In numerous speeches to decision-makers at home and abroad, Tony Blair and his Shadow Chancellor Gordon Brown emphasised their support for 'the entrepreneurial and flexible labour markets of the American economy' and for 'education not regulation, skills and technology, not costs on business, and open competition, not protectionism'. They made clear their opposition to 'Eurosclerosis' and their perception that the 'European social model' stood in need of urgent reform. Welfare systems, in this view, generally 'need[ed] reform to curb spiralling costs', while 'old-style tax and spend' was no longer an option. There was 'no right or left politics in economic management', Blair told the French Assembly in March 1998, just 'good and bad'.

New Labour's acceptance of the essentials of the post-Thatcher political economy – essentially the notion that Britain's comparative economic advantage lay in relatively cheap and flexible labour – was repeated in leadership speeches from Japan to Singapore, from Rupert Murdoch's Newscorp Leadership Conference to the City of London and the New York Chamber of Commerce; before the French Assembly and on the occasion of British assumption of the Presidency of the European Council in 1998. Labour had not only cleared out that sprawling, incoherent 'Bennite' left which stood in the way of 'modernisation' in 1983, it had modernised in such a way after 1983 as to marginalise the 'post-materialist' left. It talked of 'enhancing the dynamism of the market' in 1997 rather than of curbing it and in the process repudiated or played down just those instruments of policy which will be increasingly necessary if progress on environmental matters is to take place. Such policies appeal to continental social democrats and red–green parties alike: tougher regulations, taxes on polluters, curbs on corporate tax evaders, progressive taxation, stricter health and safety standards, integrated transport systems, bigger employer contributions, and other state interventions at regional, national and transnational levels. There may be a variety of ways of securing environmental progress but it seems that only New Labour expected to find one compatible with 'enhancing the dynamism of the market', to quote the aim of one its economic policy documents. As recently as June 2005 the former Chief Scientific Adviser to the Government (1995–2000), Lord May, described Labour's environmental policies as 'gutless'. Old social democratic values were not among the list of reasons given to explain this performance; the failure to rein-in market forces was (*Independent*, 2005). The only measure of environmental progress that New Labour could trumpet after eight years in office, after fighting three general elections in which such issues were never mentioned, was Britain's support for the Kyoto Protocol – the commitment to reduce carbon dioxide emissions. There is irony in the fact that this commitment was made to seem possible in Britain's case by Thatcher's prior elimination of the coal industry and the accompanying 'dash for gas' in the 1980s.

References

Benn Wedgwood, T. (1970), *The New Politics: A Socialist Reconnaissance* (London: Fabian Society).

Callaghan, J. (2000), *The Retreat of Social Democracy* (Manchester: Manchester University Press).

CPGB (1989), 'Manifesto for New Times', *Marxism Today*, June.

Delwaide, J. (1993), 'Postmaterialism and Politics: The "Schmidt SPD" and the Greening of Germany', *German Politics*.

DNA (1996), Norwegian Labour Party *Statement of Principles and Action Programme* (Oslo, DNA).

Galtung, J. (1986), 'The Green Movement: A Socio-historical Exploration', *International Sociology*.

Garner, R. (1999), 'How Green is Labour?', *Politics Review*.

Giddens, A. (1998), *The Third Way: The Renewal of Social Democracy* (Cambridge: Polity).

Gould, P. (1998), *The Unfinished Revolution: How the Modernisers Saved the Labour Party* (London: Little Brown).

Gray, J. (1997), *After Social Democracy* (London: Demos).

Independent (2005), 'UK's Top Scientist Delivers Stinging Attack on Government's Environmental Record', Michael McCarthy, 10 June.

Inglehart, R. (1977), *The Silent Revolution: Changing Values and Styles Among Western Publics* (Princeton, NJ: Princeton University Press).

Inglehart, R. (1987), 'Value Change in Industrial Societies', *American Political Science Review*, pp. 1289–303.

Kitschelt, H. (1994a), *The Transformation of Social Democracy* (London: Cambridge University Press).

Kitschelt, H. (1994b), 'Austrian and Swedish Social Democrats in Crisis: Party Strategy and Organisation in Corporatist Regimes', *Comparative Political Studies*.

Kitschelt, H. and Hellmans, S. (1990), *Beyond the European Left: Ideology and Political Action in the Belgian Ecology Parties* (London: Duke University Press).

Markovits, A. S. and Gorski, P. S. (1993), *The German Left: Red, Green and Beyond* (Cambridge: Polity).

Sainsbury, D. (1993), 'The Swedish Social Democrats and the Legacy of Continuous Reform: Asset or Dilemma?', *West European Politics*.

SAP (1992), *The Swedish Social Democratic Party Programme*, trans. Roger Tanner, adopted 1990 (Stockholm: Tryckeri AB).

SPD (1989), *Basic Policy Programme of the Social Democratic Party of Germany* (Bonn: SPD).

Touraine, A. (1991), *The Workers' Movement* (Cambridge University Press).

13

The meanings of 'social democracy': the British and West German protests against nuclear weapons, 1957–64

Holger Nehring

Introduction

Over the course of the 1950s, people all over the world came to believe that 'Hiroshima was everywhere' (Anders, 1982). Protest movements against nuclear weapons first emerged on a mass scale in the late 1950s and early 1960s. Although these protests appear, at first sight, as similar responses to a global danger, they remained in fact intimately connected with national political traditions. This chapter focuses on the two most important protest movements at the time, the British and the West German campaigns against nuclear weapons. It singles out social democratic traditions as crucial for their organisational culture, their language and their forms of protest. The term 'social democratic' is used here rather broadly to denote assumptions which are connected to different strands of the non-communist left. This shared social democratic heritage did not lead to smooth co-operation between the two movements. Rather, against the backdrop of the Cold War, the different cultural assumptions of the British and the West German protesters led to substantial problems for communication and co-operation between the two movements. The conflictual history of the relations between the British and West German anti-nuclear-weapons protests was, therefore, a corollary of the often problematic relations between the labour movements in both countries. It also reflected the very different ways in which they defined the 'democratic' part of the social democratic traditions.

Historians and political scientists have not yet fully established the role of social-democratic traditions for the British and West German movements (Otto, 1977; Parkin, 1968; Taylor, 1988). Combining a comparative and a connective historical approach, this chapter re-examines the movements by paying attention to the language of dissent in the social-structural context in which it was used. This is primarily an attempt at uncovering social trends rather than a study of social movements in all their aspects. The important question of how the movements staged their protests as events has therefore been left out. The argument proceeds in three steps. The first section provides a short organisational history of the British and West German movement. The second section uncovers the various social democratic traditions within the two movements, while the third section examines the cumbersome communication between the movements. The conclusion highlights some more general points for assessing social democratic traditions in 1960s' protest movements.

The British and West German protests

The British and the West German protests against nuclear weapons were nationally specific responses to the dangers posed by the arms race between the superpowers. They faced different political challenges. While the British movement's aim was unilateral nuclear disarmament, the West German protesters campaigned at once for a much smaller and broader cause. Their goal was smaller as it initially aimed only to prevent the equipment of the West German army with nuclear-capable *materiel*; it became broader, however, as it was increasingly concerned with global disarmament efforts. Both campaigns were functionally similar, however: they responded to an international situation which was characterised by the emergence of the arms race as a 'functional substitute for war' (Wenger, 1997: 248) and the ever increasing destructive powers of nuclear weapons.

Although there were precursors on a smaller scale, the emergence of the British movement for unilateral nuclear disarmament was directly linked to debates within the Labour Party. It was only after the Labour Party had declined to endorse a motion for unilateral disarmament at its annual conference in autumn 1957 (Priestley, 1957: 555) that a group of left-wing intellectuals – among them the historian A. J. P. Taylor, the New Statesman editor Kingsley Martin and the Canon of St Paul's Cathedral, John Collins – started to plan a campaign to reverse this decision. (Taylor, 1988: 19–112). On 17 February 1958, the new campaign went public in Central Hall, Westminster. Several thousand people attended the meeting. From March 1958 onwards, local CND branches spread all over the country. On Easter Day 1958, the first march took place from London to Aldermaston. CND had only adopted the idea after much internal discussion: the executive had originally intended the campaign to be a pressure group rather than an extra-parliamentary campaign. From 1959, the Easter marches became a fixed point of reference in the yearly calendar of political events. The route now went in the opposite direction from Aldermaston to London in order to attract more marchers than in their first year. It also showed the emphasis on the centres of mainstream politics: Westminster and Whitehall.

In 1960, a group around the octogenarian philosopher Bertrand Russell split off from CND and founded a parallel, much more radical campaign, the Committee of 100 (C100) (Taylor, 1988: 190–272). In addition to demanding that Britain disarm unilaterally, C100 campaigned for disarmament by other nations and the adoption of social reforms in Britain. Most notably, the group made systematic use of non-violent civil disobedience in its protests. The foundation of C100 forced CND to sharpen its message as well. After the Cuban missile crisis in autumn 1962 and with the beginning of detente between the superpowers, culminating in the Limited Test Ban Treaty in 1963, support for nuclear disarmament dwindled (Phythian, 2001).

As in Britain, the West German movement emerged as a result of developments within the labour movement. In the Federal Republic, however, the Labour Party was not one of the campaign's main opponents, but one of its main organisers. In April 1957, eighteen nuclear physicists, most of them former Nobel Prize winners, protested against Chancellor Konrad Adenauer's use of language: he had compared atomic artillery to conventional weapons (Cioc, 1988; Rupp, 1970). This sparked off a wide range of protests, from the local to the national level. In March 1958, the SPD launched the extra-parliamentary 'Campaign against Atomic Death' (*Kampagne Kampf dem Atomtod*). It aimed at bringing the various strands of protests together in order to mobilise public opinion against the purchase of nuclear-capable equipment for the federal army. The Christian Democratic majority in the federal parliament had just passed the necessary legislation as part of Chancellor Adenauer's 'Policy of Strength' towards the eastern bloc.

Regional and local campaign offices, all co-ordinated by the Bonn head office of the campaign, opened. There were exhibitions and film shows to alert the public to the dangers of radioactive fall-out and of nuclear-capable equipment on German soil. The campaign also tried to launch plebiscites in the German *Länder* (states) to repeal the federal government's legislation. Yet these plebiscites were ruled unconstitutional by the federal constitutional court in summer 1958. In the wake of their programmatic reform in the Godesberg programme of 1959, the SPD lost interest in the campaign. Starved of funds and personnel, it died a slow death.

In late 1959, however, a small group of Hamburg pacifists and Quakers, dissatisfied with the current campaigns, had already started to plan protest marches in Germany which were modelled upon the British Aldermaston Marches. At Easter 1960, the first German Easter march set off from Hamburg to the British rocket site Bergen-Hohne in northern Germany, near the site of the former National Socialist concentration camp at Bergen-Belsen. They protested against nuclear weapons on German soil and advocated a nuclear-free zone in Europe. They also condemned nuclear tests. From 1961, Easter marches took place all over Germany, to and from all major cities. From 1963 onwards, the Easter marches increasingly turned into protests against the Vietnam War, the planned Emergency Laws and for students' rights.

The importance of social-democratic traditions

In very specific ways, both movements responded to the growth of reformist trends in the British Labour Party and in the West German SPD (Nicholls, 1994). But while CND never reached beyond social democratic traditions, the West German Easter marches succeeded in forging a new approach to politics by fusing labour movement traditions with radical pacifism. A pluralisation of what 'social democracy' and 'democracy' meant had taken place. Thus, by and large, CND remained wedded to social-democratic notions of democracy through party political organisation, whereas the West German Easter marches championed what their supporters called 'democracy from below'. This direct political involvement in all kinds of activities from the local to the national level was advocated by the British New Left and by British pacifists as well, but it could not assert itself in the mainstream movement and remained limited to separate groups and movements such as the New Left or organisations such as the Committee of 100.

This development is rather surprising, given that it was initially the West German movement that was more closely wedded to organised social democracy. But it was precisely this close connection which – against the backdrop of the Cold War – prompted the West German activists to transcend the social-democratic heritage. In the Federal Republic of Germany, the Social Democratic Party and the trade unions, particularly the Federation of German Trade Unions (Deutscher Gewerkschaftsbund, DGB) and the Metal Workers' Union (IG Metall, IGM) played a major role in organising, running and financing the protests.

Yet there was growing dissatisfaction within the ranks about the limitations of the labour movement's approach, especially its heavy-handed organisational crack-down on anything which looked communist. Hence, once the SPD and the trade unions had abandoned the campaign in the wake of the reformist turn at the Bad Godesberg Conference (1959), the new Easter marches became the gathering ground for all those who were unhappy with the state of the SPD, such as the members of the Socialist German Student Federation (Sozialistischer Deutscher Studentenbund, SDS) which had been a party organisation, but was proscribed by the SPD executive in 1960 (Lönnendonker *et al.*, 2002). The marches thus became a laboratory for testing out new forms of democratic activism outside mainstream politics. It was here that activists who, because of their young age, had not been acquainted with the social-democratic traditions, recovered pacifist and social democratic ideas from the 1920s in order to challenge the importance of Cold War assumptions on German politics and to criticise what they regarded as the continued importance of National Socialist ideas in German politics and society (Krohn, 2000).

While in Britain these debates remained restricted to the Committee of 100 and to some individuals in CND, radical pacifism assumed a key importance in West Germany in adapting social-democratic traditions to the context of the 1960s. After the SDS had been expelled from the SPD, radical pacifism, as embodied by the War Resisters' International, offered this 'homeless left' a model for activism. Its emphasis on non-violent civil disobedience, which went beyond the social-democratic tradition of mass rallies and parliamentary representation, thus became the predominant form of protest during the 1960s.

The contest between social-democratic and communist traditions framed the debates within the West German protest movements much more than in the British ones. West German politics cannot be understood without reference to the German Democratic Republic, the other German state. The SPD's position was particularly awkward since it shared common traditions with the East German Socialist Unity Party (SED). And it was precisely the lack of open discussion of models of democracy which the Easter march activists found so aggravating. Communist influence on the West German protests cannot be denied and was particularly pronounced in the traditional Communist strongholds. Communist involvement was, however, far less the result of subversion, but rather the outcome of a complex interplay of shared Social Democratic, Socialist and Communist political traditions with the situation within the Communist groups in the Federal Republic after the KPD had been banned by the Federal Constitutional Court in 1956 (Kössler, 2004).

Communist involvement in the Campaign against Atomic Death and the Easter marches, was, therefore, not a danger to the democratic fabric of the campaign and of the Federal Republic as a whole, but rather a sign of the stabilisation of the West German political system and an indication of the many meanings of 'democracy' in a Cold War context. Groups of Communists that had before operated outside the liberal democratic order of the West German state were now integrated into a movement that avowedly wanted to strengthen West German democracy by working outside the established political channels and emphasising grassroots activism. In Britain, by contrast, with the exception of few local areas in Scotland and in the North of England, the Communist Party did not play any significant role in CND (Callaghan, 2003: 141–51).

Social-democratic traditions framed the British protests as well. The key difference to the Federal Republic was, however, that CND never became the laboratory for ideas and practices about 'democracy' that the Easter marches were. In Britain, these laboratories remained quite distinct movements, such as the New Left and the Committee of 100. A consensus about leaving traditions behind which operated within the party framework did, despite many discussions, not emerge. CND was originally a revival of the extra-parliamentary progressive movements and groupings that had sprung up in Britain during the 1930s. These left-wing groupings had been swamped by Labour's election victory in 1945, and the Cold War had so far prevented them from re-appearing. Only when Cold War tensions appeared to subside in the wake of the Geneva Conference in 1955 and when the Soviet Union started to send out signals of 'peaceful co-existence' could these ideas regain some of their original appeal. Yet none of these groups (with the notable exception of the New Left) mounted a challenge to the ideas and practices of social-democratic practices advocated by the Labour Party; rather, they were concerned with highlighting specific and mostly isolated issues which they regarded as particularly important. Although they operated outside the Labour Party structures and although they debated the precise stance towards the Labour Party throughout, the most active majority of activists continued to think in terms of party politics rather than grassroots democracy.

We can detect three overlapping social roots of the British campaign for nuclear disarmament which were all connected with social-democratic traditions. The historical significance of CND in the 1950s and early 1960s is to have brought these groups together for the last time in post-Second World War Britain. The first of these groups, composed of radical critics like the publisher Victor Gollancz, Kingsley Martin and J. B. Priestley, formed a very varied and unstable assemblage, coming from many different social and political backgrounds. Perhaps the most important features they shared was a radical idealism and an impatience with, yet no rejection of, the conventional channels of politics and reform. Their aim was to galvanise the British left by creating a more effective 'popular front' than the Labour Party itself could provide. During the 1930s, the members of this group had operated in bodies outside the Labour Party and had advocated a 'united front' with the more left-wing Independent Labour Party (ILP) and the British Communist Party (CPGB). During the 1940s, many of the later CND executive came together in J. B. Priestley's 1941 Committee, Sir Richard Acland's Forward March Movement and his Common Wealth Party, as well as more obscure bodies, such as the Federation of Progressive Societies and Individuals (Duff, 1971). In 1945, with Labour's general election victory, many of these intellectuals had realised that the only effective way to foster their ideals was the Labour Party itself, particularly because section 12 of the Labour Party programme *Let Us Face the Future* appealed to 'all men and women of progressive outlook, and who believe in constructive change, to support the Labour Party' (Labour Party Conference Report, 1945: 144). They found their way into the Labour Party, but the differences over foreign policy drove them out again in the late 1950s.

Members of this group were are all linked by their belief in 'planning' of society and the economy and by their generally progressive outlook. They could tap different intellectual roots, mostly Christian, technocratic, or liberal (Blaazer, 1992). Often, they were influenced by the social concerns and radicalism of the Anglican Church, particularly William Temple and at least partially by the reforming traditions of Nonconformity (Norman,

1976: 280–370). The technocrats who supported such a 'popular front' felt that science and social planning, combined with socialist principles, however defined, would ultimately lead to greater efficiency, fairness and equality, and that an educated elite would be needed to lead such an advance. Liberal thinkers were drawn towards these circles because of their belief that problems could be solved better through co-operation, discussion, and the use of reason rather than by party politics. Soon, however, the members of this group realised that their own social-democratic ideals had not been realised by the Labour government and were negated by the Conservatives in the 1950s. They thus became fierce critics of the post-war settlement and of the Labour Party's reformist policies.

From an intellectual-history angle, the activities of some of the protagonists, in particular Bertrand Russell, Richard Acland, and J. B. Priestley, can be linked to a tradition of post-Victorian intellectuals (Waters, 1994). CND thus appears as one of the last attempts of these intellectuals to leave a mark on British society. Many of these intellectuals, in particular Priestley and Acland, were in the tradition of the late Victorian 'public moralists' (Stefan Collini) who assumed that they had to school the citizens in the necessary public and private virtues, thus pulling the nation along the road of moral progress. This general outlook, whose emphasis on individual moral commitment sat awkwardly with the emerging affluent society, was very much in tune with the mood in sections of the Labour Party (Black, 2003; Fielding, 2001: 258). In the intellectuals' opinion, the Conservative government had negated this programme of social and moral renewal, and, as the *Tribune* wrote on 16 October 1959, the people needed to be reminded of the 'ideals they prized fourteen years ago'. For them, CND was one way of achieving that aim.

Those on the Labour left who had become 'homeless' through Aneurin Bevan's departure from their camp formed the second social democratic group behind CND. Some of them, like Barbara Castle, had been active members in the Socialist League which had been founded as an organisational focus for those on the Labour left who wanted to stay loyal to the Labour Party after the ILP had ended its historic connection with Labour in July 1932. Between 1939 and 1945, they had been united in their expectation that the war would lead to social change and bring about a 'new order' in society. In a rather idealistic fashion, they all stressed that Labour, together with other left-wing forces, had to have more than a purely economic agenda and had to offer a moral alternative to the conservatives. They tended to support ideas for Britain as a 'third force' between the superpowers to avert the division of the world into two massive blocs, which had the socialist, but non-communist left as one of its roots. With the MPs Ian Mikardo, Konni Zilliacus and Michael Foot, it also included some of the most vocal supporters of CND from within the Labour movement. But some of its members came together again in the late 1950s when the international situation and Krushchev's policy of 'peaceful co-existence' seemed to allow for such a policy again.

These two groups were joined by the New Left, which became the predominant supporter of the campaign from about 1961 onwards. It was the only group which advocated grassroots political activism outside the organisational framework of a party. Its members were, however, not able to promote this goal further through its involvement in the campaign: CND itself, with its executive committee and its various subcommittees, had an organisational structure resembled that of the Labour Party. The New Left was a loose and very complex movement around the journals *New Reasoner* and the *Universities and Left Review*, later the *New Left Review* and the New Left clubs which were established in late 1950s and early 1960s. Two main groups can be distinguished. The underlying intellectual consensus was one of a less dogmatic socialism which operated outside party organisation and which advocated an extended definition of labour movement politics to embrace cultural issues as well as economics.

One group emerged around the historians Edward P. Thompson and John Saville, based primarily in the north of England and consisting mainly of former Communist Party members. The most famous of them had been members of the CPGB before and had been involved in the CPGB's historians' group. After the violent suppression of the Hungarian uprising by Soviet forces and after Khrushchev's revelations about Stalin's atrocities in his 'Secret Speech' on the 20th CPSU Party Congress, they left the party. Most of them now gathered around the journal *New Reasoner*. The second strand of the New Left emerged around a group of members of a discussion circle within the Oxford University Labour Club out of dissatisfaction with revisionism and the lack of grassroots involvement in party politics. Through their journal *Universities and Left Review* they reached an audience across British universities. Both movements pooled their efforts by founding a common journal, the *New Left Review*, in 1959–60, thus tapping the tradition of the *Left Review*, a radical journal of the 1930s (Kenny, 1995).

Curiously, the protagonists of the British New Left had hardly any contacts with their West German counterparts. Their international connections were primarily with France. There were no reports on developments in the Federal Republic in the British *New Left Review*, the leading New Left journal. Prominent members of the British New Left complained about the 'confusion' in international affairs and about the fact that 'too many of our people regard these as personal contacts only', with the result that 'we learn about what they say only in chance remarks and gossip' (E. P. Thompson quoted in Nehring, 2005).

Yet even when students started to become more important in both campaigns from about 1961 onwards, the character of the movements continued to be dominated by labour movement traditions. The forms of protest and the music which accompanied the marches had more to do with the traditions of the radical and social-democratic life-reform movements of the 1920s and earlier than with a direct import of new forms of protest from the American civil rights movement (Osgerby, 1998: 82–104). In Britain, the marchers sang Spanish Civil War songs; often, new lyrics were sung with old tunes (such as H-bomb's thunder to the music of 'Miner's Lifeguard'). In West Germany, the protesting milieu was originally less clearly defined. In the industrial Ruhr area and in the south west where traditions of the labour movement and its front organisations such as the Friends of Nature (*Naturfreunde*) or the Falcons (*Die Falken*) were more important, the element of lively marches with jazz and skiffle groups dominated. This led to some contention within the German Easter March movement as some feared that it would make the whole protests appear as a joke (Otto 1977: 92). The songs were, however, not quite in tune with the most popular music of the time – the Beatles and the like – but rather represented old youth and labour movement traditions.

Problems with transnational co-operation

These different social-democratic traditions also had an impact on the relations between the two movements. Their problems in communication reflect the problems the two labour movements have had with each other since the early twentieth century (Joll, 1955). Both movements employed the classical radical language of dissent. It was the language of a common resistance by the people against their war-mongering governments which threatened the survival not only of their nations but of the world as a whole. It stressed the strong mutual interests of collaboration and called for the establishment of a world community of anti-nuclear-weapons protesters which would ultimately overcome Cold War tensions and re-establish peace.

Yet the different social-democratic traditions hampered proper transnational communication and co-operation. The traditionally strong bonds between German and British Labour and the organisational structure of the Socialist International could not be used to support the protests: although the British and West German parties' executives agreed on the importance of multilateral efforts for disarmament, this meant different things in each national context. This, in turn, led to different attitudes towards the protests. In Britain, the Labour executive's emphasis on *multi*lateral disarmament was diametrically opposed to CND's agenda of *uni*lateral nuclear disarmament. In the Federal Republic, the SPD, even while involved in the protests, campaigned for multi-lateral disarmament in the United Nations framework; and even West German Easter marchers thought that demands for unilateral disarmament would play into the hands of the Communists. Moreover, anti-Germanism was especially strong in those sections of the Labour Party which supported unilateralism. Thus, the connections between the British and West

German movement – apart from exchanging a few speakers and marchers – were rather loose. This caused several misunderstanding between the SPD and the Labour Party and between CND and the SPD-run Campaign against Atomic Death (Nehring, 2005).

The first contacts between CND and parts of the West German movements were thus not established between the SPD-run campaign and CND, but by the Munich Committee against Nuclear Armaments which was run by the German writer and intellectual Hans Werner Richter, the founder of the *Gruppe 47*, the most important literary circle in post-Second World War Germany. The Munich group was, as far as its social structure and organisation were concerned, very similar to CND. It consisted mainly of intellectuals with a social-democratic leaning, was governed by a committee structure and was, like the CND executive, initially not very keen on street protests, but emphasised the 'education of the public'. Also, it was, like the majority within the CND executive, firmly opposed to linking itself to a particular political party, but subscribed to ideas of a third force (Gallus, 2001: 94–108).

Yet even these contacts between two organisations with a very similar outlook – except for unilateralism which was not regarded as problematic by the Munich Committee – did not lead to the establishment of a transnational community of protesters. Richter, together with Canon Collins, initiated the European Federation against Nuclear Weapons which was founded in London and Frankfurt in early 1959. The Federation aimed to prevent nuclear proliferation, to achieve general nuclear disarmament and to campaign for the civilian use of atomic energy. The London headquarters of the Federation was supposed to co-ordinate joint campaigns in the future. But not much came of it. In particularly striking contrast to its rhetoric of a world community, all the participants at its meetings insisted that the Federation should not undermine the national position of the individual movements and be sensitive of different national issues (Nehring, 2005). Different interpretations of the Cold War within the British and the West German movement obstructed co-operation further. Particularly the co-operation with the Communist World Peace Council was highly contested both in the transnational movements and on a national level. And the speakers of co-operation had to tread very carefully, highlighting the different circumstances in different countries. This mirrored similar debates between the British Labour Party and the West German Social Democrats about contacts with the GDR (Berger and Lilleker, 2002).

The main channel of transnational co-operation between the British and the West German movement was thus the pacifist War Resisters' International, rather than one of the bodies linked to social-democratic traditions. But their ideals of political involvement differed greatly from those of most of the social-democratic groups. As its advocacy of non-violent civil disobedience transcended CND's politics of respectability, this strand of political activism could not significantly assert itself within the mainstream campaign. In West Germany, by contrast, the WRI's socially conscious pacifism provided the essential glue for the emerging New Left which helped it to reinvigorate social-democratic traditions (Nehring, 2005). These discussions of non-violent civil disobedience harked back to the reception of Gandhi's fight for Indian independence amongst European pacifists and radicals in the interwar years and to anarchist intellectual traditions since the end of the nineteenth century. These were now revived as the dissenters within European social democracy looked for new inspirations. Due to the different Cold War contexts, however, this revival took very different forms in Britain and West Germany. Both countries saw debates about whether this revival, in general, and about non-violent disobedience, in particular, could be maintained within the traditional social democratic discourses of respectability. In Britain, this debate was conducted within the social democratic milieu. This made a re-integration of the protesters into the Labour Party possible. Thinking outside the parameters of the Labour Party was therefore rare. In West Germany, by contrast, the Social Democratic Party cut the ties with those who advocated a return to the social-democratic traditions of the 1920s for fear of communist subversion. As the Federal Republic was a frontline state in the Cold War, this exclusion of groups left of the SPD meant that the protests became actions outside the accepted realm of politics. While the British protests were thus the last flickering of a progressive coalition in post-Second World War Britain, the West German ones already pointed towards the grassroots protests of the later 1960s and the 'new' social movements of the 1970s.

Conclusion

This article sought to establish the role of social-democratic traditions for the shape of the British and West German protests against nuclear weapons in the late 1950s and early 1960s. Rather than facilitating the co-operation between the two movements and rather than making the movements more international, these traditions hampered or even blocked contacts between the British and West German protests. The protests against nuclear weapons thus replicated the problems which the social-democratic parties and trade unions had with each other. Although the movements in both countries were directly concerned with a Cold War issue – that is: nuclear weapons – this did not even out the different national protest traditions and enhance transnational co-operation in an alliance against the Cold War. Rather, the Cold War served as a catalyst which made the movements' supporters look back for inspiration to the national protest traditions of earlier times.

This has important repercussions for our understanding of the contribution of West European social-democratic traditions for democracy in Western Europe in general. Geoff Eley has argued that social-democratic ideas were central for promoting democracy in Europe and around the world. Eley singles out extra-parliamentary movements in particular as harbingers of fairer and more participatory forms of government in the western world during the twentieth century (Eley, 2002). The findings of this chapter suggest a more differentiated interpretation.

Although Eley does not tell the teleological story of a victory of social-democratic ideas, he does not take account of the fact that historical actors have defined 'social democracy' and 'democracy' quite differently at different times and at different places. Like other scholars of social change (e.g. Schönhoven, 1999), he departs from an *a priori* definition of 'democracy'. Despite many common concerns, it was the different social-democratic traditions and the different concepts of democracy which made the relationship between the British and West German protests against nuclear weapons so cumbersome. Definitions of democratic involvement even varied within both movements, depending on which social-democratic traditions were tapped. Moreover, the different repercussions of the Cold War for West European societies made a common definition of 'democracy' even harder. Finally, both movements were in constant battle with the mainstream social-democratic parties about different interpretations of 'social democracy'. In this context, the fact that the West German movement had to compete with the peace propaganda of the other and allegedly also democratic German state should be noted in particular. As Tom Buchanan and Martin Conway have recently argued, the meanings of 'democracy' itself should become the object of historical investigations (Buchanan and Conway, 2002; Conway, 2004). Such analyses of the different meanings of 'social democracy' and their political and social context would not only contribute to a better understanding of protest movements, but also open up new perspectives on the history of post-Second World War Western Europe.

References

Anders, Günther (1982). *Hiroshima ist überall*. Munich: C. H. Beck.

Berger, Stefan and Darren Lilleker (2002). 'The British Labour Party and the German Democratic Republic during the Era of Non-Recognition, 1949–1973'. *Historical Journal*, vol. 45: 433–58.

Blaazer, David (1992). *The Popular Front & the Progressive Tradition: Socialists, Liberals, and the Quest for Unity, 1884–1939*. Cambridge: Cambridge University Press.

Black, Lawrence (2003). *The Political Culture of the Left in Affluent Britain, 1951–1964: Old Labour, New Britain?* Basingstoke: Palgrave Macmillan.

Buchanan, Tom and Martin Conway (2002). 'The Politics of Democracy in Twentieth-century Europe: Introduction'. *European History Quarterly*, vol. 32, no. 1: 7–12.

Callaghan, John (2003). *Cold War, Crisis and Conflict: The CPGB 1951–1968*. London: Lawrence & Wishart.

Cioc, Mark (1988). *Pax Atomica: The Nuclear Defense Debate in West Germany during the Adenauer Era.* New York: Columbia University Press.

Collins, Canon John (1966). *Faith under Fire.* London: Leslie Frewin.

Conway, Martin (2004). 'The Rise and Fall of Western Europe's Democratic Age, 1945–1973'. *Contemporary European History*, vol. 13, no. 1: 67–88.

Duff, Peggy (1971). *Left, Left, Left: A Personal Account of Six Protest Campaigns, 1945–65.* London: Alison & Busby.

Eley, Geoff (2002). *Forging Democracy: The History of the Left in Europe, 1850–2000.* Oxford: Oxford University Press.

Fielding, Steven (2001). 'Activists against "Affluence": Labour Party Culture during the "Golden Age", c. 1950–1970'. *Journal of British Studies*, vol. 40, no. 2: 241–67.

Gallus, Alexander (2001). *Die Neutralisten Verfechter eines vereinten Deutschlands zwischen Ost und West 1945–1990.* Düsseldorf: Droste Verlag.

Joll, James (1955). *The Second International, 1889–1914.* London: Weidenfeld & Nicolson.

Kenny, Michael (1995). *The First New Left: British Intellectuals after Stalin.* London: Lawrence & Wishart.

Krohn, Claus-Dieter (2000). 'Die westdeutsche Studentenbewegung und das "andere Deutschland"'. In: Axel Schildt *et al.*, eds., *Dynamische Zeiten: Die 60er Jahre in beiden deutschen Gesellschaften.* Hamburg: Christians.

Kössler, Till (2004). *Abschied von der Revolution: Kommunisten und Gesellschaft in Westdeutschland, 1945–1968.* Düsseldorf: Droste Verlag.

Labour Party (1945). *Labour Party Annual Conference Report.* London: Labour Party.

Lönnendonker, Siegfried, *et al.* (2002). *Die antiautoritäre Revolte: Der Sozialistische Deutsche Studentenbund nach der Trennung von der SPD. Vol. I: 1960–1967.* Wiesbaden: Westdeutscher Verlag.

Nehring, Holger (2005). 'National Internationalists: British and West German Protests against Nuclear Weapons, the Politics of Transnational Communications and the Social History of the Cold War, 1957–1964'. *Contemporary European History*, vol. 14, no. 4: 559–82.

Nicholls, Anthony J. (1994). 'Zwei Wege in den Revisionismus: die Labour Partei und die SPD in der Ära des Godesberger Programms'. In Jürgen Kocka *et al.*, eds., *Von der Arbeiterbewegung zum modernen Sozialstaat: Festschrift für Gerhard A. Ritter.* Munich: K. G. Saur: 190–204.

Norman, E. R. (1976). *Church and Society in England, 1770–1970.* Oxford: Oxford University Press.

Osgerby, Bill (1998). *Youth in Britain since 1945.* Oxford: Blackwell.

Otto, Karl A. (1977). *Vom Ostermarsch zur APO. Geschichte der ausserparlamentarischen Opposition in der Bundesrepublik 1960–1970.* Frankfurt/Main: Campus.

Parkin, Frank (1968). *Middle Class Radicalism: The Social Bases of the British Campaign for Nuclear Disarmament.* Manchester: Manchester University Press.

Phythian, Mark (2001). 'CND's Cold War'. *Contemporary British History*, vol. 15, no. 1: 133–56.

Priestley, J. B. (1957). 'Britain and the Nuclear Bombs'. *New Statesman* 54 (2 November): 554–6.

Rupp, Hans Karl (1970). *Außerparlamentarische Opposition in der Ära Adenauer: Der Kampf gegen die Atombewaffnung in den fünfziger Jahren. Eine Studie zur innenpolitischen Entwicklung der Bundesrepublik.* Cologne: Pahl Rugenstein.

Schönhoven, Klaus (1999). 'Aufbruch in die sozialliberale Ära: Zur Bedeutung der sechziger Jahre in der Geschichte der Bundesrepublik'. *Geschichte und Gesellschaft,* vol. 25: 123–45.

Taylor, Richard (1988). *Against the Bomb: The British Peace Movement 1958–1965.* Oxford: Clarendon Press.

Taylor, Richard and Colin Pritchard (1980). *The Protest Makers: The British Nuclear Disarmament Movement of 1958–1965, Twenty Years On.* Oxford: Pergamon Press.

Waters, Chris (1994). 'J. B. Priestley 1894–1984. Englishness and the Politics of Nostalgia'. In Susan Pedersen and Peter Mandler, eds., *After the Victorians: Private Conscience and Public Duty in Modern Britain. Essays in Memory of John Clive.* London and New York: Routledge: 209–26.

Wenger, Andreas (1997). *Living with Peril: Eisenhower, Kennedy and Nuclear Weapons.* Lanham, MD and Oxford: Rowman & Littlefield.

Conclusion

John Callaghan and Ilaria Favretto

Particularly when coming out of long periods of crisis and electoral decline, political parties need to over-stress the novelty of their renovated policies and identity. Electorates need to receive a clear message that something completely new is now out in the political market. The deeper the crisis, the fiercer is the iconoclasm shown by parties towards their past history; a sense of 'new beginning' has to be created. In this regard, the history of the European Socialist and Social Democratic parties has been quite exemplary. The end of what Nina Fishman describes in her essay as the 'post-1945 social democratic settlement' opened up in the late 1970s and 1980s a period of electoral and political crisis for European social democracy. Following the 1990s neo-revisionist ideological overhaul and recovery, socialist parties have now adopted an ambivalent attitude towards their past, regarded by many as a source of embarrassment if not a lengthy story of 'missed opportunities' to carry out the long-awaited 'Third Way' revolution.

However, as the chapters included in this volume illustrate, the picture of post-1945 European social democracy is far more complex and multi-faceted than the one commonly portrayed by neo-revisionist modernisers. The overview of more than one hundred years of Socialism provided by Donald Sassoon in his chapter does indeed present a narrative of a long-folding and uninterrupted process of transformations and changes, both in terms of policy agenda and ideology. Not only is there a far greater continuity between today's left and its past, but many of the 'caricatures' of post-1945 Social democracy that have now become conventional wisdom are simply inaccurate and untrue. For instance, as Sassoon points out, the often contended indissoluble link between socialism and *étatisme* – an electoral burden, which has led to symbolical gestures such as the ditching of Clause IV from the British Labour constitution in 1995 or the SPD's replacement of the 1959 Bad Godesberg declaration with the Berlin programme in 1989– made its way into socialist parties' agenda quite late, i.e. at the beginning of the twenteith century. That was when the growing and expanding role of the state into economy since the beginning of the First

World War prompted a reconsideration of socialists' earlier anti-state position and Marxists' dismissal of the 'bourgeois state' as an instrument of coercion, law and order. As a result, along the lines of Kautsky's Second International Marxism, socialists accepted that, while waiting for the right time for the revolution to come, they could in the meantime enter government and, thanks to the largely expanded role of the state, start contaminating capitalism with some socialist elements by means of gradual reforms. Nevertheless, as Sassoon puts it, 'the endorsement of the state was not part of the ideology of Socialism' but was rather 'instrumental to the achievement of their medium and short-term aims'.

As is always the case with the late converted, socialists were then to become staunch believers in state intervention, particularly as the deep economic recession of the 1930s produced a long list of necessary reforms while depriving most socialist parties of the means to do anything about them. True, as a result of the 1950s and 1960s revisionist wave, these parties introduced in their ideological and programmatic repertoire instruments other than outright nationalisation such as competitive public enterprise and state shareholding. However, state ownership, whether reconsidered and reinvented, was never discarded. And why should it be? Against the context of the 1960s' 'second scientific revolution' and the so-called 'Soviet challenge' – that is the fear that, as the Cold War had been moving from the military to the economic sphere, the capitalist world might capitulate under the supremacy of the Soviet Union's centrally planned and thriving economy – all political parties, whatever their colour, put state intervention at the centre of their political agenda. Far from remaining distinctive socialist items, the public sector and the welfare state met, in fact, throughout the post-war period universal consensus and legitimacy. The hegemonical influence of the mixed economy welfarist model and the attempt by anti-socialist forces to incorporate socialist demands were, no doubt, one of the most striking results ever achieved by the left.

The state's control of strategic economic sectors, by means of either ownership or planning, came to be regarded by the mid-1960s as a key instrument of redistribution but, above all, rationalisation and modernisation. This was the time when Western Europe started looking at French planning as the way forward: for 'booming' countries, like Italy and Germany, planning and a large public sector were meant to secure a continued and more balanced growth; for countries like Britain that had been suffering years of sluggish economy the adoption of the French 'recipe' of indicative planning was to end the country's relative decline. This was also the time when, in contrast to the emphasis often placed by commentators on past redistributive orientation contrasted with today's neo-revisionist growth-oriented agenda, socialist parties did, in fact, display a growing concern with economic growth and productivity (Tomlinson, 2003). Since their acceptance of parliamentary gradualist means, socialist parties have been caught

in the paradox that their success is strictly related to the prosperity of
capitalism, a system which, in theory, many of them were committed to
replace. In order to pay for social welfare, it was imperative that the market
be made as efficient as possible (Sassoon, 1996: 150). Wilson's well known
leitmotiv of the 'white heat of technological revolution' and British Labour's
new centre-left technocratic agenda (set out in contrast to centre-revisionists'
earlier emphasis on redistribution) acted as a model of inspiration for lots
of other European socialist parties, many of which were also about to return
to government after a long period of opposition (Favretto, 2003: 50).

There is no doubt that on taking office, whilst growing resources continued to be directed to the welfare state and social spending, very little
was done about planning or in relation to the long-term growth-oriented
reforms and modernisation schemes which socialists talked about. However, these strictures apply to socialist and non-socialist governments alike.
With just a few exceptions, most Western European governments – faced
with the end of the great post-war capitalist boom and caught in the vicious
circle of the 1970s 'stagflation' – experienced balance of payments and
exchange problems, together with spiralling public deficits, while leaving
their public sector unmodernised and heavily subsidised.

Another neo-revisionist element whose appearance can be traced further
back than the 1990s ideological overhaul, is socialist parties' effort to build
a supra-class consensus. The left always had to adapt to a social structure
that did not reflect the proletarianisation foreseen by vulgar Marxism. And
it did it successfully: Socialists' post-war exceptional electoral performances
could not be explained but by their ability to attract the middle class vote.

The 'Old' Left's allegedly unique interest in collective rights is also a
historical inaccuracy. As noted by more than one contributor in this volume,
if one looks at the early political struggle for universal suffrage, one should
not, in fact, forget that, in contrast to conservatives' and liberals' class-
conscious and restrictive idea of democracy, socialists put forward a
'staunchly individualist' case for the extension of political rights that was
not based on class principles but on the principle of individual rights.

When it comes to political and civil rights, today left-wing parties' political discourse has been characterised by a relatively apologetic and defensive tone. The crisis of the Keynesian model, the collapse of communism,
and the overall hegemony of neo-liberalism which followed have created since
the 1980s a new imbalance of power between left and right: while for most
of the post-war years the right was regarded with negative connotations,
particularly in those countries such as Italy which had experienced authoritarian regimes during the interwar years, the opposite is true today. Today
it is the left that is tainted with evils such as infringement of basic liberties,
bureaucracy, inefficiency and defeat. It is against this background that left-
wing European parties, after breaking with their Marxist past, have recently
made great efforts to add to their cultural heritage theoretical references that

reinforce their 'liberal' credentials, such as liberal socialism, New Liberalism or US liberal thought – particularly in its recent 'Third Way' variant.

However, as Geoff Eley argued in his *Forging Democracy*, a book which focuses on the central role played by left parties in the construction and consolidation of democracy throughout the nineteenth and twentieth century across Europe, for all the left's defeats and limitations, the history of socialism and democracy is that of two intermingled processes, in which the political and electoral advance of the former massively contributed to the progress of the latter. As he aptly reminds us, democracy in Europe was not a 'given' or something to be 'taken for granted'. Far from being the by-product of natural evolution or economic prosperity, it developed because masses of the people organised collectively to demand it. In particular after the 1860s when the constitutional conditions were created for popular democratic parties to emerge and socialist parties were formed, it was the latter, he argues, that most consistently advocated the enlargement of political and civil rights (Eley, 2002: 5). After constructing the foundations of democracy, they performed a crucial role in defending it from the interwar fascist threat and in increasingly expanding its boundaries for ever greater inclusiveness: after 1945, they were the main driving forces behind the construction of the post-war settlement that saw political rights being complemented with fundamental social rights.

True, the history of western Socialism and democracy is hardly a spotless success story. Later in the 1960s and 1970s, class-centred politics made it difficult for socialist parties to integrate into their policies and programmes identity politics, for example, a gender or an antiracist agenda. At the same time, socialism's state-centralist attitudes, militated against the endorsement of questions of local self-government, participatory democracy and decentralisation. It was against this context that, as authors such as Eley argue, by the late 1960s socialist parties lost their leading role as the 'main agency of democracy's advance' and were bypassed by new social movements such as feminism, gay–lesbian associations, antiracist movements, environmental activism, regionalist movements and others in expanding the boundaries of politics and the possible meanings of democracy' (Eley, 2002: 482).

The 'patriarchal productivism' (Sassoon, 1996: 699) of the Alternative Economic Strategy does indeed reflect a disregard for new social movement issues, such as feminism and ecological issues. However, as Stephen Fielding and John Callaghan argue in their essays, the view held by most contemporaries (a view that was to influence later historical perspectives) according to which the British Labour Party failed to respond to the calls for 'participation' that emerged in the 1960s and 1970s does conceal a far more mixed picture. In line with Tony Benn's Fabian Pamphlet *The New Politics*, the agenda of the Labour left throughout the 1970s came to endorse industrial democracy and democratic reform of the British state, as well as of the party itself. One should also remember the democratic, feminist, antiracist pacifist and community politics that marked municipal leftism of the late 1980s in Britain. Moreover, in contrast to British Labour's mixed response, other socialist parties, e.g. the German SPD or the Swedish social democrats, proved far more adept in integrating post-material issues into the new 'red–green' policy agenda that both formulated in the 1980s. This, if anything, disproves the allegedly fundamental ideological impermeability of the socialist tradition in regard to 'superstructural' issues and individual politics. As Callaghan notes, 'parties of social democracy that have moved furthest to embrace the green agenda include those which by the standards of New Labour are most decidedly old social democratic in their programmatic language of class, equality, state intervention and the critique of unfettered capitalism'.

In fact, other factors other than ideology – such as electoral considerations – proved far more influential in shaping the readiness displayed by individual socialist parties in 'gendering' and 'greening' their socialist agendas.

Since early in the late nineteenth century when the first women's organisations were formed, socialists' class-political programme combined with working-class cultures of workplace discrimination, relegated women's issues to low priority. Even when faced with a second wave of feminism in the 1960s, left parties long remained indifferent to the non-class specific interests of women. However, what critics seem to disregard is that, with the exception of a radical minority, women themselves long tended to be rather conservative in their political inclinations and traditionally voted disproportionately for the right. The so-called gender gap in voting behaviour has been on the decline only since the 1970s. Whilst today taking on board the 'needs of women' is now an electoral must for any progressive party, it was, in fact, an electoral hazard for socialists for the greatest part of the twentieth century.

A similar disregard for electoral constraints applies to the criticism of the left's attitude towards the 1968 movements. The left's delay in catching up with the 'post-materialist' revolution as described by Ronald Inglehart has certainly much to do with the class-centred bias of the 'Old Left' political programme and the incapability of an older generation of socialists and communists to tune in to New Left politics. However, mutual incomprehension and the generational gap were combined with the obvious electoral concern of too close an association with advanced and scarcely popular causes. Issues that pressure groups, mainly composed of highly educated middle class activists, propose hardly match ordinary people's common sense. Furthermore, it should not be forgotten that the alliance with Catholic inspired political parties which underlay the electoral strategy of parties such as the Italian socialists and communists, also acted as a further restraint to the endorsement of radical policies on family matters and civil rights issues.

As mentioned above, one further factor that should not be ignored to explain variations in socialist parties' opening to post-material issues is the political and cultural context in which they operate. For instance, the electoral threat posed by green parties is a crucial dimension to understand variations in Socialists' endorsement of green issues. As Callaghan puts it, the first-past-the-post electoral system ensured that there was no 'new left political formation challenging the British Labour party for votes, a force that might have given the parliamentary leadership the incentive to take new left ideas seriously in a period when programmatic renewal was a matter of political survival'. The protection from the left for British Labour was evident in 1989 when the Green Party secured 14.8% of the votes in the European elections – the highest anywhere in the European Community – but failed to elect a single candidate. Similarly in Italy, another country where green issues have been marginal to the left agenda, a weak green culture has meant that the Green party has never posed a real threat to the existing parties of the left. Founded in 1985, it never took off. Deeply divided and fragmented, it failed to capitalise on the breakdown of traditional political parties after 1992 and has remained a small party with a tiny electoral constituency (representing approximately 3 per cent of the electorate). Even under exceptional circumstances – such as during the mad cow crisis during the 2001 elections – the party proved unable to expand its constituency. The Green presence in the programme of the 1996 Olive Tree centre-left coalition should be understood more as the need to keep a useful ally on board rather than as a result of the influence of green thinking on national political debate (Favretto, 2003: 127).

If libertarian policies might be electorally damaging, the same applies to ecological questions and green politics. 'Sustainable development', a slogan that can be easily sold to vast electoral constituencies (particularly in the wake of ecological disasters), when turned into concrete legislation (for example carbon and petrol taxation or measures to facilitate traffic restraints), might also prove very unpopular. It is only where ecological issues took on a hegemonic role within national political debate that socialist parties turned into champions of the Green cause. The SPD's 'greening' in the 1980s is quite exemplary in this respect. Challenged by one of the most powerful green movements in Europe, German socialists developed a programme of eco-social democracy that was one of the most ambitious attempts to integrate the environment into left-wing politics. Faced with a similar 'green' threat, other socialist parties like the Swedish, the Norwegian and the Austrian carried out a significant greening of their programme and this in spite of the close link which they all enjoyed with the trade unions – though the latter is another factor that, together with ideology, has been often erroneously invoked by proponents of the 'incompatibility thesis' between the socialist tradition and a post-material agenda.

Today's neo-revisionist parties, at least in terms of rhetoric, all display an unprecedented concern with individual politics and post-material issues. In the light of the ideological impact of the 'me first' culture, reinforced by the growing success of neo-liberal experiments in the 1980s in all its national variations, it is now believed that individualism cannot remain an exclusive property of the right; the time has come to catch up with the people's newly emerging aspirations for self-fulfilment. However, for all the attempts made by parties like New Labour to disown the legacy of their past, one should not forget that the European Left's rapprochement with individualist politics was immensely facilitated by the exposure of today's most prominent European socialist leaders (all belonging to the boom generation) to the individualist ethos of the 1960s and 1970s and of the left-wing groups and formations which sprang up in those decades; it was this experience which made them far more at ease than the previous generation in dealing with post-traditional society.

There is no doubt that globalisation, the collapse of Communism, the crisis of Keynesianism and the socio-economic transformations underpinning the rise of post-industrial society have prompted a thorough re-appraisal of Social democracy. However, whilst acknowledging the profound changes undergone by the left since the 1980s, one should not forget that Socialist parties, as indeed all other political parties, have always confronted the need to adapt their policies and theories to altered socio-economic circumstances. The implementation of universal suffrage in the late nineteenth century challenged their belief in revolution as the unique way to socialism. Long waves of capitalist expansion, such as the one that occurred at the turn of the century, called for some reconsideration, like the one Bernstein attempted in 1899 in his *Evolutionary Socialism*, of the idea of the inevitable collapse of the system. The response of capitalism to the great slump of the late 1920s and the transformed role of the state that followed, laid the foundations for further reinterpretations of Marxism in the 1930s, such as Austro-Marxism and neo-socialism. Last but not least, post-war booming economies posed a serious blow to deep-rooted Marxist dogmas such as the 'pauperisation' theory, or the catastrophist creed that professed the imminent and inevitable collapse of capitalism. Neo-revisionist politics, while no doubt signalling an important and far reaching break in the socialist tradition challenging long cherished and consolidated 'totems', is in fact very much in continuity with the adjustments already made in the past by socialist and social-democratic European parties.

One fundamental difference that sets today's 'third way' apart from any earlier revisionism is the renunciation of the long-term aspiration of replacing capitalism with socialism. The latter is the distinctive feature of contemporary neo-revisionism. For all their pragmatism and moderation, no socialist parties had previously questioned that in the end – how distant this might have been being irrelevant – a better and more equal society would take the place of what was regarded as an inherently unjust model (namely, the free market economy). By contrast, capitalism is regarded today as something to be tamed, reformed and regulated but not replaced. Some scholars have described all this as a process of 'de-socialdemocratization', which as Gerassimos Moschonas puts it, risks depriving the concept of social democracy of any real meaning and cutting it off from its own history (Moschonas, 2002: 329). On the other side, Third Way intellectuals have portrayed the neo-revisionist turn as a healthy modernisation of the social-democratic tradition and the beginning of a new era for progressive politics (Giddens, 1998). Whatever the end destination may be, it is important that historians carry on tracing back the multiple and often contradictory stops and turns that have characterised journeys of social democracy since its inception, a mapping which we hope this volume will contribute to.

References

Eley, G. (2002), *Forging Democracy: The History of the Left in Europe, 1850–2000* (New York: Oxford University Press).

Favretto, I. (2003), *The Long Search for a Third Way: The British Labour Party and the Italian Left since 1945* (Basingstoke: Palgrave Macmillan).

Giddens, A. (1998), *The Third Way: The Renewal of Social Democracy* (Cambridge: Cambridge University Press).

Sassoon, D. (1996), *One Hundred Years of Socialism* (London: I. B. Tauris).

Moschonas, G. (2002), *In the Name of Social Democracy: The Great Transformation: 1945 to the Present* (London: Verso).

Tomlinson, J. (2003), *The Labour Governments 1964–70*, Vol. III: *Economic Policy* (Manchester: Manchester University Press).

Select bibliography

Anders, Günther (1982). *Hiroshima ist überall*. Munich: C. H. Beck.

Berger, Stefan and Darren Lilleker (2002). 'The British Labour Party and the German Democratic Republic during the Era of Non-recognition, 1949–1973'. *Historical Journal*, vol. 45: 433–58.

Blaazer, David (1992). *The Popular Front and the Progressive Tradition: Socialists, Liberals, and the Quest for Unity, 1884–1939*. Cambridge: Cambridge University Press.

Black, Lawrence (2003). *The Political Culture of the Left in Affluent Britain, 1951–1964: Old Labour, New Britain?* Basingstoke: Palgrave Macmillan.

Buchanan, Tom and Martin Conway (2002). 'The Politics of Democracy in Twentieth-century Europe: Introduction'. *European History Quarterly*, vol. 32, no. 1: 7–12.

Callaghan, John (2003). *Cold War, Crisis and Conflict: The CPGB 1951–1968*. London: Lawrence & Wishart.

Cioc, Mark (1988). *Pax Atomica: The Nuclear Defense Debate in West Germany during the Adenauer Era*. New York: Columbia University Press.

Collins, Canon John (1966). *Faith under Fire*. London: Leslie Frewin.

Conway, Martin (2004). 'The Rise And Fall Of Western Europe's Democratic Age, 1945–1973'. *Contemporary European History*, vol. 13, no. 1: 67–88.

Duff, Peggy (1971). *Left, Left, Left: A Personal Account of Six Protest Campaigns 1945–65*. London: Alison & Busby.

Eley, Geoff (2002). *Forging Democracy: The History of the Left in Europe, 1850–2000*. Oxford: Oxford University Press.

Favretto, Ilaria (2003). *The Long Search for a Third Way: the British Labour Party and the Italian Left since 1945*. Basingstoke: Macmillan.

Fielding, Steven (2001). 'Activists against "Affluence": Labour Party Culture during the "Golden Age", c. 1950–1970'. *Journal of British Studies*, vol. 40, no. 2: 241–67.

Gallus, Alexander (2001). *Die Neutralisten Verfechter eines vereinten Deutschlands zwischen Ost und West 1945–1990*. Düsseldorf: Droste Verlag.

Joll, James (1955). *The Second International, 1889–1914*. London: Weidenfeld & Nicolson.

Kenny, Michael (1995). *The First New Left: British Intellectuals after Stalin*. London: Lawrence & Wishart.

Kössler, Till (2004). *Abschied von der Revolution. Kommunisten und Gesellschaft in Westdeutschland, 1945–1968*. Düsseldorf: Droste Verlag.

Krohn, Claus-Dieter (2000). 'Die westdeutsche Studentenbewegung und das "andere Deutschland"'. In: Axel Schildt *et al.*, eds, *Dynamische Zeiten. Die 60er Jahre in beiden deutschen Gesellschaften*. Hamburg: Christians.

Lönnendonker, Siegfried *et al.* (2002). *Die antiautoritäre Revolte. Der Sozialistische Deutsche Studentenbund nach der Trennung von der SPD, Vol. I: 1960–1967*. Wiesbaden: Westdeutscher Verlag.

Nehring, Holger (2006). 'The Cultures of the Cold War and Transnational Relations: The British and West German Protests against Nuclear Weapons and the Pacifist Roots of the West German New Left, 1957–1964'. In Jessica Gienow-Hecht, ed., *Decentering American History*. New York and Oxford: Berghahn.

Nicholls, Anthony J. (1994). 'Zwei Wege in den Revisionismus: die Labour Partei und die SPD in der Ära des Godesberger Programms'. In Jürgen Kocka *et al.*, eds, *Von der Arbeiterbewegung zum modernen Sozialstaat. Festschrift für Gerhard A. Ritter*. Munich: K. G. Saur: 190–204.

Norman, E. R. (1976). *Church and Society in England, 1770–1970*. Oxford: Oxford University Press.

Osgerby, Bill (1998). *Youth in Britain since 1945*. Oxford: Blackwell.

Otto, Karl A. (1977). *Vom Ostermarsch zur APO: Geschichte der ausserparlamentarischen Opposition in der Bundesrepublik 1960–1970*. Frankfurt/Main: Campus.

Parkin, Frank (1968). *Middle Class Radicalism: The Social Bases of the British Campaign for Nuclear Disarmament*. Manchester: Manchester University Press.

Phythian, Mark (2001). 'CND's Cold War'. *Contemporary British History*, vol. 15, no. 1: 133–56.

Priestley, J. B. (1957). 'Britain and the Nuclear Bombs'. *New Statesman* 54 (2 November): 554–6.

Rupp, Hans Karl (1970). *Außerparlamentarische Opposition in der Ära Adenauer: Der Kampf gegen die Atombewaffnung in den fünfziger Jahren. Eine Studie zur innenpolitischen Entwicklung der Bundesrepublik*. Cologne: Pahl Rugenstein.

Sassoon, Donald (1996). *One Hundred Years of Socialism*. London: I. B. Tauris.

Schönhoven, Klaus (1999). 'Aufbruch in die sozialliberale Ära. Zur Bedeutung der sechziger Jahre in der Geschichte der Bundesrepublik'. *Geschichte und Gesellschaft*, vol. 25: 123–45.

Taylor, Richard (1988). *Against the Bomb: The British Peace Movement 1958–1965*. Oxford: Clarendon Press.

Taylor, Richard, and Colin Pritchard (1980). *The Protest Makers: The British Nuclear Disarmament Movement of 1958–1965, Twenty Years On*. Oxford. Pergamon Press.

Waters, Chris (1994). 'J. B. Priestley 1894–1984. Englishness and the politics of nostalgia'. In Susan Pedersen and Peter Mandler, eds, *After the Victorians: Private Conscience and Public Duty in Modern Britain. Essays in Memory of John Clive*. London and New York: Routledge: 209–26.

Wenger, Andreas (1997). *Living with Peril: Eisenhower, Kennedy and Nuclear Weapons*. Lanham/MD and Oxford: Rowman & Littlefield.

Index